BEYOND PARADISE AND POWER

Europe, America and the Future of a Troubled Partnership

edited by
Tod Lindberg

Routledge
New York • London

Published in 2005 by
Routledge
Taylor & Francis Group
270 Madison Avenue
New York, NY 10016
www.routledge-ny.com

Published in Great Britain by
Routledge
Taylor & Francis Group
2 Park Square
Milton Park, Abingdon
Oxon OX14 4RN
www.routledge.co.uk

10 9 8 7 6 5 4 3 2 1

Library of Congress Cataloging-in-Publication Data

Beyond paradise and power : Europe, America and the future of a troubled partnership
/ Tod Lindberg, editor.
    p. cm.
  Includes bibliographical references and index.
    ISBN 0-415-95050-3 (hb : alk. paper) -- ISBN 0-415-95051-1 (pb : alk. paper) 1.
Europe--Foreign relations--United States. 2. United States--Foreign relations--Europe.
3. United States--Foreign relations--2001– 4. Europe--Foreign relations--1989– 5.
Europe--Politics and government--1989– 6. European Union. 7. Iraq War, 2003. I.
Lindberg, Tod.
    D1065.U5B47 2004
    327.7304′09′0511--dc22

                                                              2004008432

BEYOND PARADISE AND POWER

CONTENTS

INTRODUCTION: THE LIMITS OF TRANSATLANTIC SOLIDARITY

by Tod Lindberg

THE FIRST FEW MONTHS OF 2003 saw the gravest crisis in transatlantic relations since—well, you could pick: perhaps since the debate over the deployment of Pershing intermediate-range nuclear missiles and nuclear-tipped cruise missiles in Europe in 1982–83, when hundreds of thousands took to the streets in protest. Or 1967, when Charles de Gaulle abruptly withdrew France from NATO and forced all U.S. and allied forces off French soil. Or the Suez crisis of 1956, when the United States sided with Egypt's Gamal Abdel Nasser rather than its erstwhile allies Britain and France after Nasser nationalized the Suez Canal, which the French had built.

The transatlantic breakdown over Iraq, by most accounts, was a disaster between the United States and her European allies. What are we to make of the spectacle of the American secretary of state frantically dialing the foreign ministers of members of the UN Security Council in quest of support on Iraq as the French foreign minister sped off to each capital to lobby against it? Or an Atlantic alliance strained to the breaking point over the defense of Turkey, a frontline state in the war against Iraq? Or the snarling caricatures of George W. Bush throughout Europe as a holy-rolling, trigger-happy cowboy—as flagrant and rampant as America's rechristenings of everything French? Or of the charge, after the war, that because Saddam Hussein did not have weapons of mass destruction after all, the supposed security threat he posed was nothing but a pretext proffered by a "neoconservative" cabal for a war for oil, for the advancement of American empire, for imperial domination of the Middle East, and to promote the interests of Israel?

Nor, of course, were tensions alleviated by an easy occupation and reconstruction in postwar Iraq. International engagement in the rebuilding effort there seemed to come in fits and starts, thanks not only to ongoing violent resistance to the occupation but also to ongoing concerns about the legitimacy of the military action. Although policy makers in the United States and Europe began to converge on the need to promote democratic transformation in the Greater Middle East—a proposal first advanced by Ronald D. Asmus and Kenneth M. Pollack in the journal I edit, *Policy Review*[1]—precisely what actions should be taken to promote such a transformation remained hotly contested. And days after the March 2004 terrorist attack in Madrid, Spanish voters in national elections ousted a conservative government that had supported the United States in Iraq in favor of a socialist party pledging Spanish withdrawal. Web sites associated with al-Qaeda granted the attacks credit for toppling a Western government, with the promise of more to come. And some in Europe, though hardly all, wondered if conspicuous dissociation from the United States might spare them from what Spain suffered.

Well, at least we were warned. For many years now, notwithstanding such genuine headline achievements as the enlargement of NATO into Central and Eastern Europe and its Kosovo campaign against Serbian atrocities directed at ethnic Albanians, policy professionals have felt a sense of drift in American–European relations. In the case of a whole range of subjects—the death penalty; global environmental protection; regulation of all the economic, political, and cultural phenomena that go by the collective name of "globalization"—it's not drift but sometimes schism.

The 1990s was a decade of unprecedented peace and prosperity—and a mounting insularity in both the United States and Europe. Domestic squabbles preoccupied Americans. In Europe integration was an all-consuming chore. Euphoria over the collapse of communism quickly gave way to confusion about how to structure the post–Cold War new world order. What the new threats to international peace and security now were—and how this situation fit with the existing alliance structure—was unclear. Drift was perfectly understandable, especially because ignoring the question seemed to everyone not to matter much.

In the summer of 2001, I decided to organize a Washington conference for the following winter on the subject of American power and the position of the United States in the world. It seemed to me then that these topics were alarmingly neglected, especially in the United States. Hubert Védrine, then the French foreign minister, had offered a searching and brilliant assessment of American *hyperpuissance*. Nevertheless, it seemed to me that even in the capital of the hyperpower, the dimensions of American capability as well as of the American global commitment were poorly understood.

An alternative conference theme, I joked, might be "American Hegemony and How to Thwart It: A Practical Guide." Who might want to try, I surely did not know. American power seemed essentially uncontested—no real enemies and lots of friends. But I still thought it would be a good thought-experiment to try to figure out how someone might contest "hegemony," "preeminence," "dominance," "indispensability," "unipolarity," or whatever you might want to call it. I asked Robert Kagan of the Carnegie Endowment for International Peace to prepare a conference paper for publication in *Policy Review*, and we settled on the topic of transatlantic relations, about which he thought he had some new things to say. I concluded the preliminary planning for "Managing American Power in a Dangerous World" in a conference call with my Hoover Institution colleagues late in the afternoon of Monday, September 10, 2001.

Nous sommes tous Americaines. So said the famous headline in *Le Monde* two days later. Within days, NATO members had voted unanimously to invoke Article 5 of the Washington Treaty, declaring the September 11 attack (if of foreign origin) an attack on all member-nations of the alliance. The expressions of solidarity were intensely moving. Tens of thousands gathered in candlelight vigil around the Brandenburg Gate in Berlin, a scene repeated on a smaller scale throughout Europe. I traveled to Sophia, Bulgaria, early in October for a summit of the Vilnius 10—the nations then aspiring to membership in the Atlantic Alliance. Seven of these would be invited to join at a NATO summit in Prague a year later. The mood in Sophia was appropriately somber and tense, and security was tight. All ten aspirants issued a joint communiqué declaring the attack on the United States to be an attack on them. Though they were not yet allies by treaty, they would be allies in fact. Tears stung my eyes as I listened to this.

Solidarity—for the moment. Soon, we discovered that the Taliban regime in Afghanistan was Osama bin Laden's safe haven and that it had to be taken down. It did not take long for the administration to decide to do so, not through NATO but by itself. The inevitable signal was that allies were optional for the United States. President Bush's October speeches were well received not only in the United States but also in Europe. Not so his state of the union address in January 2002. The phrase "axis of evil" jarred European sensibilities on grounds that it was simplistic, crude, and moralizing. What really seemed to chafe was his us-or-them characterization of the struggle ahead. The United States would do what it was going to do. The rest of the world would fall in line—or face the consequences. This was not the sort of solidarity that Europeans thought they had signed up for, even after September 11.

Thus the paradox—before September 11, American–European relations had drifted uncertainly. Then al-Qaeda attacked and the ennui vanished, replaced by fellow-feeling (leaving aside the few who thought the United States had it coming). In grave crisis the United States and Europe did come together, as they have so many times before. But the solidarity did not last, as the events of September 11 also resulted in the emergence of a new global agenda for the United States, one that will likely dominate American foreign policy for a generation, that many in Europe simply do not agree with.

The Bush administration intended to respond to September 11 not "just" by toppling the Taliban and conducting a worldwide manhunt for al-Qaeda operatives. Bush began to spell out a far broader agenda in a series of speeches in 2002, culminating in the September 2002 *National Security Strategy of the United States*—potentially including preemptive or preventive military action, and regime change, in what looked to some like a U.S. policy of remaking the world by force of arms.

The administration's rhetoric was clear to the point of stark: you were either with the United States or you were with the terrorists. In the

United States many praised Bush for his "moral clarity." In Europe many worried about his lack of moral nuance. The conclusion of many in Europe and elsewhere was that they must reject this characterization. Solidarity has to be freely offered. It cannot be commanded, even by the strongest.

No particular policy follows immediately from reaching the conclusion that the American "us or them" must not stand. One may reject the Bush characterization and then decide nevertheless to support the United States on a particular matter at hand. This was the position of, for example, Britain's Tony Blair on Iraq (notwithstanding the insults he suffered: "America's poodle"). Germany's Gerhard Schröder and France's Jacques Chirac opposed not only any doctrine of automatic solidarity but also the particular policy for Iraq. In the future it is quite possible that France and Germany will agree with Washington, whereas Britain will disagree—or that the European Union, speaking for all its members, will lay out a position in agreement or disagreement with the United States. Whatever the division at any given moment, however, the visceral sense of solidarity with the United States is gone. One wonders if we will ever see its like again.

As the divergence spectacularly emerged, however, so did a guidebook. In the spring of 2002, shortly after my Washington conference, *Policy Review* published Robert Kagan's article "Power and Weakness."[2] It at once created a global intellectual sensation, evoking comparisons to Francis Fukuyama's "The End of History?" and Samuel Huntington's "The Clash of Civilizations."[3] Some went so far as to compare the Kagan article with George Kennan's famous postwar "Mr. X" article in *Foreign Affairs*,[4] in which he laid out the strategy of containment vis-à-vis the Soviet Union.

"On major strategic and international questions today," Kagan wrote, "Americans are from Mars and Europeans are from Venus." He offered an ingenious dual argument to account for this phenomenon. First, powerful states and weak states see the world differently because of their very power or weakness. When the United States was weak in the nineteenth century, it favored a multilateral, rules-based approach to international affairs, much as Europeans do now. Now that the United States is strong, it prefers to decide for itself whether and when and how to act—just as European great powers did in the heyday of their own global reach.

But it is not just that power or weakness determines attitudes toward the use of force or a preference for rules. It is also, Kagan argued, that ideas about power and its use determine how much power one pursues. For Kagan, Europeans have adopted a Kantian, postmodern, perhaps posthistorical view that force is an unnecessary and counterproductive element in the settlement of disputes. Americans, by contrast, see themselves as residents in a Hobbesian world still very much characterized by danger of a kind that from time to time can only be met by force.

For Kagan, the European view poses no danger to the American position. It is, he said, a great blessing for the United States and Europe alike that Europe is no longer "strategically relevant." The only real danger would come if Americans adopted the European view as their own—something they seem disinclined to do, in Kagan's view, pleased as they are with their country's position in the world.

By the fall of 2002, "Power and Weakness" had been reprinted and translated in whole or in part (often both) in all major European capitals, as well as in many capitals in other parts of the world. An expanded version of the article appeared in book form in 2003 as *Of Paradise and Power* [5] and became, in defiance of conventional expectations about how well books on the transatlantic relationship fare in the marketplace, a *New York Times* best seller. It has become almost literally impossible to attend any event in the United States or Europe on the subject of the transatlantic relationship without hearing reference to Kagan's thesis.

Unsurprisingly, perhaps, such references often precede expressions of partial or full disagreement with Kagan. What is decisive, however, is that "Power and Weakness" marked a turning point in the debate over U.S.–European relations. It simultaneously cleared away a vast underbrush of misunderstanding and began a serious effort to rethink the essential character of the transatlantic relationship. If it is not the last word, it is surely now the point of departure for future assessments of the subject.

It was in this spirit that I approached the authors of this volume, asking them not so much for essays in response to Kagan but for their own distinct assessments of the state of the transatlantic relationship, the structural and other considerations underlying the relationship, and the direction the relationship is likely to be going. It will come as no great surprise that a substantial amount of disagreement comes to the fore in the pages that follow. Nevertheless, the ongoing importance of Kagan's dual theses is unmistakable here as well.

The book begins with the assessment by Steven Erlanger of the *New York Times* on the extent of the breakdown between the United States and Europe over Iraq (but, of course, not only over Iraq). In assessing the current rift, Anne Applebaum of the *Washington Post* distinguishes between attitudes in the "old Europe" of France and Germany and the "new Europe" to the east. Ivo Daalder of the Brookings Institution then explores the question of whether the rift now apparent, or at any rate the worst of it, is after all not a product of the particular personalities of the current leaders on both sides of the Atlantic.

From here we move to some European reactions. Gilles Andréani, the head of policy planning in the French Foreign Ministry, rejects the misleading and potentially dangerous loose talk about a new American imperialism. Wolfgang Ischinger, the German ambassador to the United States, argues that a course of action based on the premise that the United States can readily act unilaterally is doomed to fail. Kalypso Nicolaidis of Oxford University argues that the heart of the matter is the failure of the United States to understand "Europe," specifically, European integration. Timothy Garton Ash of Oxford University and the Hoover Institution stands the subject of anti-Americanism in Europe on its head and inquires into the new anti-Europeanism in America.

At a broader conceptual level, Francis Fukuyama of the Johns Hopkins School of Advanced International Studies asks the question of whether, given emerging differences, it is still meaningful to speak of "the West" as a locus of common values and perspectives. Walter Russell Mead of the Council on Foreign Relations argues that current conditions, in which the United States assumes by itself the principal burdens of providing security around the world, are likely to persist, especially given demographic and other trends indicating a diminishing role for Europe. And Simon Serfaty of the Center for Strategic and International Studies states the claim that neither the United States nor

Europe alone can accomplish what the world needs to see done, but that together they can.

Finally come some reflections that are largely philosophical in character. Peter Berkowitz of the George Mason law school and the Hoover Institution offers an assessment of the problem of power and the use of force in relation to democratic governance and liberalism more broadly. And I offer an attempt to take a giant step back from the current disputes to show that they take place in the context of a more elemental agreement between the United States and Europe, one that is likely in my view to persist despite superficial differences, no matter how painful.

Whether or not these essays contain the right answers, I am fairly confident that they are at least asking the right questions. This is in no small measure because Robert Kagan framed the issues so well from the start, though of course many disagreements with him emerge in the twelve essays that follow.

I should add that I have not invited those who would like to blow up the transatlantic relationship to join the discussion here. I find such positions, no matter what the grounds on which they are articulated, to be almost willfully perverse. If there is nothing whatsoever in common between Americans and Europeans, nothing abiding that binds, then I suppose we will one day find out. It will not require encouragement. The more plausible case, it seems to me, is that the relationship is what we make of it, and I think the authors here share the view that we should make more of it rather than less.

Notes

1. Ronald D. Asmus and Kenneth M. Pollack, "The New Transatlantic Project," *Policy Review* 115 (October–November 2002).
2. Robert Kagan, "Power and Weakness," *Policy Review* 113 (June–July 2002)
3. Francis Fukuyama, "The End of History?" *National Interest* 14 (Summer 1989). Samuel P. Huntington, "The Clash of Civilizations," *Foreign Affairs* 72, no. 3 (1993).
4. George Kennan (writing as "X"), "The Sources of Soviet Conduct," *Foreign Affairs* 25, no. 4 (1947).
5. Robert Kagan, *Of Paradise and Power: America and Europe in the New World Order* (New York: Knopf, 2003).

PART ONE

THE EMERGING CRISIS

1

ANATOMY OF A BREAKDOWN

by Steven Erlanger

THE ANGLO-AMERICAN ROMP through Iraq and its wearying after-math have clarified transatlantic relations considerably. But it is not a happy picture, and it does not promise any radiant future.

The administration of George W. Bush, swollen with hubris, acted as if it disdains all allies, even the loyal Tony Blair, whose government has been badly weakened by all this martial success. With gratuitous uni-lateralism, on issues both serious and utterly inconsequential, Bush threw away his chance to have his war and the backing of the Security Council, too. In the aftermath, with the grinding process of pacifying and rebuilding Iraq, Bush behaved grudgingly, with clear divisions in his own administration over the wisdom of seeking friendly help and advice. Now that Bush found himself in need of allies to share the pain of postwar Iraq he seemed astonished that so few were willing to help— and that some barely bothered to hide their hope that he lose his bid for reelection.

But the European Union, with ten new members whose loyalties were already considered suspect by many founding members, seemed more feckless and self-absorbed than ever, even in the face of Washington's patronizing disdain. Its constitution and dragging economy are preoccupations, while even the Balkans, taken on by the Europeans as a prime responsibility, again began to smolder. NATO, traditionally the strongest barrier to real transatlantic division, looks increasingly irrelevant to anything but a political effort, however valuable, to preoccupy the Russians and civilize the Central Asians. Will NATO take on a seriously larger role in Afghanistan? Agree with nose averted to help in a concerted and effective way in Iraq? Confront the considerable danger of an Iran with nuclear ambitions? Doubtful. The sudden resignation of Lord Robertson as secretary general is an extraordinary admission of failure, another case of a true friend of Washington being repaid with incomprehension and scorn.

To be sure, not all of this collateral damage from such a famous victory is the fault of the Bush administration. Nor does much of it stem inevitably from the overwhelming military might of the United States compared with Europe, let alone with Iraq. European armed forces could have defeated Saddam Hussein's Iraq without American help, if they had had a mind to do so. The United States and Britain simply failed to convince enough friends and allies that this war was necessary, urgent, or even legal, an outcome that the Bush administration preferred to blame on anyone other than itself.

Yet by its own manifold incompetence, the European Union, even unenlarged, confirmed all the suspicions of those in Washington who belittle its importance and hold its military and policy ambitions in contempt. After all, it was Tony Blair who wanted a second resolution at the United Nations in the face of French warnings; it was Gerhard Schröder, the German chancellor, who grabbed at a slim chance for reelection by endorsing a pacifist unilateralism that humiliated his foreign minister, Joschka Fischer, just as much as Bush humiliated his own secretary of state, Colin Powell.

And it was Jacques Chirac, the French president, who reacted with such callous arrogance to the prospective new members of the European Union who dared to speak up at the adults' table and express their own sovereign views. After years of trying to intimidate the Poles, in particular, by warning that Warsaw had to choose between membership in the European Union and its close relationship to the United States, Chirac lost hugely as Poland decided not only to support Bush's war in Iraq but also to participate in the fighting. Polish discomfort with Iraq will not soon dilute its mistrust for Paris.

Even the conservative Spanish leader José María Aznar, who supported Bush's decision to go to war and then paid the political price for it after the Madrid bombings, refused to send any Spaniards to fight in Iraq. In this brave stance Aznar found a colleague in the noisy and operatic Italian prime minister, Silvio Berlusconi.

For a supporter of the idea of a strong and independent European Union, with the muscle to defend itself and to support its policy decisions on important global issues, the opéra bouffe quality of European policymaking during the entirely predictable crisis over Iraq has been discouraging, even dispiriting. The United States, under any administration, not only needs friends and allies but also honest critics who have differently shaded understandings of the world—and who are able to support those understandings with effective policymaking and force projection.

But the confusion in Europe over Iraq has made the idea of a common European defense and security policy look farther away than ever. Even as an aspiration, a unified policy now seems more than faintly ridiculous on any issue that actually matters to member nations, or that requires rapid decision-making. Javier Solana, the elegant and empathetic embodiment of what passes for a common European defense and security policy, was humiliated, through little fault of his own, by Chirac, who presumably favors that aspiration so long as it falls short of giving up France's Security Council seat at the United Nations. As for the Germans, it is hard to describe the precise shape of the loneliness this largest nation of Europe now feels, outside its customary bed of alliances with both Washington and the United Nations, groveling again to France. Is there any European leader who admires the tactics of Schröder or who retains the slightest respect for him?

Part of the entire concept of embedding Germany into NATO and the European Union was not just to prevent a future war with France but also to protect Germany from too many French demands. Yet the price of Chirac's friendly hand to a reelected but isolated Schröder was immediately paid in euros and in Europe—the Germans abandoned serious reform of the absurd and absurdly expensive Common Agricultural Policy and moved closer to the French on a constitution for an enlarged Europe that is more presidential and less federal than Berlin wanted.

The debt also has included an ill-judged triple entente with Russia that cannot long outlast the rancor over Iraq and the perpetuation of ill-feeling with Washington, which regards Schröder with disgust and Germany as having reverted to its pre-Kosovo paralysis on security.

Even after the expected and rapid victory in Iraq, Bush continued to act with pettiness, personalizing foreign policy to the embarrassment of numerous top aides. An effort by Blair at a recent summit meeting to get Bush simply to accept a telephone call from Schröder was met with a simple "No," senior British officials say. Meetings since have been formal and awkward, and Schröder could barely disguise his glee when Aznar's party lost in Spain and the new Socialist prime minister Jose Luis Rodriguez Zapatero announced that Spanish troops would pull out of Iraq.

As for Chirac, Bush said publicly, the French president cannot count on an invitation to the Bush ranch in Crawford, Texas, "any time soon." Amazingly, that did not get Chirac into line.

So what follows this disgraceful collective failure on both sides of the Atlantic? Nothing wonderful; certainly nothing graceful, if the boycott of French goods, restaurants, and even French's mustard (named after a New Yorker, Robert French) was any indication. The emptiest clichés continue to be thrown back and forth across the ocean, about European cowardice and anti-Semitism and American stupidity and crassness.

A postwar Iraq always has looked to be more complicated than Washington could handle, but there are no allies especially eager to help. And why should they be? Who enjoys being humiliated and scorned and then asked for assistance? And what price would they exact, both at the United Nations and elsewhere?

Given a successful war and a complicated peace, given the unchallenged hyperpower, given the need to restrain Gulliver even by flattery, given the desire to prop up Powell and not diminish him further, given the need for European nations to continue to play a role in the Middle

East, given the stakes for European companies and multinationals in a calm relationship with the United States, and especially given the sense that Bush may be reelected; what are the Europeans to do?

The answer is already obvious: embarrassing efforts to make up to Washington, despite private fury and disdain, further acid on the already weakening foundations of transatlantic ties. NATO is still trying to find some role in peacekeeping in Iraq, with some vague UN mandate, precisely the kind of "washing up" after a Washington-cooked meal that Europeans keep insisting they are too powerful and important to do. The French in particular are trying to use the United Nations, the only place they play a role of global import, to influence the postwar Iraqi regime.

There is new emphasis on the "road map" for the Middle East, despite every European's expectations that Bush could not, would not confront Ariel Sharon in any meaningful way before the next American presidential election.

And Solana, a patient soul with a longer view, whose job is already being shopped around, has now been charged by European foreign ministers with preparing yet another report on the "European Security Concept," a postwar effort to restore coherence, let alone credibility, to the European project, even before it enlarges to twenty-five members. Solana drafted a common threat assessment on issues ranging from weapons of mass destruction and terrorism to refugee flows. But the use of force will always be controversial in a European Union that has no clear identity, no single citizenship or army, and no larger European patriotism for which, so far, any young European man or woman is likely to want to die in battle.

As Robert Kagan reminded us in his vivid essay "Power and Weakness,"[1] later expanded into a book, Europe imagines a region without conflict, where threats are social and developmental and the cures are aid, education, and moralistic hand-wringing, not military power or military spending. Kagan made a serious case that the European model of shared sovereignty has brought a lasting peace to the bloody center of Western history, a remarkable achievement, and has led to a weakening of the nation-state in the name of a larger collective. He suggested that the multilateral model—multilateralism as the weapon of the weak against the strong—has become the European model for global relationships.

But even granting Kagan's self-admittedly simplified views, Europe's greatest weaknesses stem from the continuing power of the nation-states and the continuing jealousies among them. It is not only France or Britain, martial powers with global interests and Security Council seats, who resist a European consensus. Belgium, Greece, Italy, and even Luxembourg have their own amour propre, their own politics, their own navies, and their own scale of victories and defeats.

Every European summit I have ever covered, and there have been too many to remember, has been perceived by national officials and national journalists as a competition for national politics and policies. European decisions are judged in terms of national wins and losses; there is no sense of any common good, nor is there much praise for those politicians who make any sacrifice for it, however perceived.

Solana has already put together an effective if tiny foreign-policy team in Brussels with the help of Robert Cooper, the former director of the British Foreign Office and the coiner of the concept of "failed states." There is a small but vital intelligence unit that has access to military and civilian intelligence reports from Britiain and a few other key states. And Solana, unlike any other European official, has a direct, scrambled hotline to Washington, on which he could participate, during the Kosovo war, for example, in meetings of the National Security Council.

But all this preparation, however serious, cannot minimize the impact of the senior European foreign-policy official traveling on commercial airlines or tiny corporate jets—or begging member governments for transport. Contrast and compare with the American secretaries of state and defense, with their purpose-built Boeing 757s, equipped with scrambled satellite communications, missile defenses, bedrooms, offices, and a captive press corps.

Why should Europe be taken seriously, after all, if it does not take itself seriously? An even unenlarged Europe has a larger population than the United States and as large an economy—it simply chooses to spend its higher taxes on other, more social goals, and then it feels understandably smug about its quality of life.

Despite the efforts of Solana and Lord Robertson, there is simply no evidence that Europe will ever spend enough on its military, whether inside NATO or outside it, to be taken seriously as a competitor to the United States. The problem, again, is not so much the few percentage points of its taxes, because Europe as a whole already spends quite a lot on its armed forces, as the reluctance to tear down the trappings and prerogatives of the nation-state enough to agree on a common policy on any issue that might make Europeans targets, let alone to rationalize its military spending.

After all, must every European nation have a navy and an air force? Must the Germans continue to absorb their unemployment problem in a highly wasteful and inefficient policy of universal conscription that is now so limited in time that inductees finish their service barely able to shoot a rifle?

Germany, of course, has always been the European exception around which European policy revolves. And having most recently been a correspondent there, I feel I should here take a more serious look at its problems and perceptions. This is because Europe will never be more than it is unless the Germans are willing to come along; more than that, unless the Germans are willing to take their indispensable place as the vital center of an enlarged Europe—its largest nation, its largest economy, its engine, not its caboose.

Yet Germany now seems even more exceptional than during the long reign of Helmut Kohl, more wounded, more alone, more ambivalent, more schizophrenic, more conflicted, more torn between its ambitions and its past. The Germans are, if anything, more smug than ever about the ideology of peace, environmental protection, and aid to the Third World that we, their conquerors, helped to instill. They are deeply mistrustful of any national role that would require them to lead anyone, anywhere, in anything that looks like a battle. And they are almost psychotically blind to the need for a serious restructuring of their postwar model of economic development in the face of reunification, let alone the rise of China or even the Internet.

During the German election campaign of September 2002—and how long ago that already seems!—I spent quite a lot of time chatting to people who would have been ordinary, except that they had actually come to listen to the candidates who sought their vote. They stood politely, mostly, sometimes with children, sometimes on a break from work, sometimes festooned with facial jewelry and sometimes with furs, and heard out their politicians: Schröder, Stoiber, Fischer, Schily, et al. It was the kind of "retail politics" we do not see very much anymore in the United States, where the enormous size of constituencies means campaigning by radio and television, with the unhappy proliferation of attack advertisements that suggest that the other party, if it wins, has a secret plan to murder children and eat them.

But I found these conversations disconcerting and even troubling in a different way. Intelligent, cosmopolitan people, from Cologne to Cottbus, Munich to Rostock, seemed puzzled by my efforts to discuss Iraq. Do Germans currently see a threat from anyone, I would ask. People looked almost embarrassed—for me. From Iraq? Only if we attack them, a smart young businessman said.

But is there a German responsibility to its allies, in NATO and the United States? Is there a special responsibility to Israel that comes into play? Again, most people shrugged, annoyed by the question or what they perceived to be the American bias within it.

What would Germany do if a terrorist seized a Lufthansa plane and crashed it into the Kanzleramt, I asked. Apologize? Go to war? Again, there was a deep, tense silence. I know what Germany would do, I would say, and people would look up, interested. You'd go to NATO, I'd say, and people would nod, quite relieved.

And, by the way, I would ask, who is your European member of parliament? Perhaps one person in fifty actually knew.

Germany is a country that should make the United States proud. It is a strong and vibrant democracy, a prosperous land of goodwill and decency, with antibodies to fascism and anti-Semitism, and a younger generation of great sophistication and generous instincts about the environment and the underdeveloped world outside Europe.

But Germans seem to live in a postwar, postconflict geopolitical fantasyland, where the greatest threat to existence, it seems, is the mixing of green glass with brown. Germany is the best example of Kagan's thesis, which may also be its greatest weakness. But the exception may in this case prove the rule.

There is in Germany a kind of secularized evangelicism: that the world can be bettered only by German instruction and aid, that a duty to the poor and the oppressed is transcendent above any other obligation, and that this attitude is the only modern, appropriate, or even decent position to take. And it leads to a kind of sanctimoniousness, just as grating coming from a German mouth as from an American one. And it can lead to absurdity.

The following analogy has flaws, I grant. But I have sometimes asked Germans who are angry with the United States for its policies on genetically modified grain why they still smoke cigarettes. It is right to be worried and motivated by potential dangers, but surely it is schizophrenic to ignore the proven danger of the cigarette in your own mouth.

The past, bad enough, serves as an object lesson for the present. But it also serves as a kind of rationalization, a "pass" from responsibility, a constant excuse for immaturity for a nation that has a deep reluctance still to getting involved with its allies in the world.

Sometimes I think that German teachers must spend so much time on the horrors of the German past that Germans think the crimes of Nazism were unique. As someone who has reported from Cambodia and Chechnya, let alone large stretches of the Middle East and the Balkans, I find it quite bizarre that Germans, and Europeans generally, given the history of this blood-spattered continent, consider the world such a benign and harmless place.

Faced with the simplistic and sometimes inane comments of Bush, it can be easy to feel superior. And the sheer power of an American president, at the head of the hyperpower that prompts so many contradictory feelings anyway, is infuriating to Europeans who feel that the cowboy is their president, too, unelected and unwanted.

But this is not the first right-wing Republican to claim to know the difference between good and evil: Ronald Reagan was despised and feared far more in Europe than George Bush is today. And we all survived, even if the Soviet Union and all its satellites did not.

My point here is not supercilious. It is simply to say that the free world is more resilient than it seems, and that the cycle of power, from one administration to the next, one party to the next, one politician to the next, is a crucial brake on enduring stupidity—and Germans, too, must take the longer view: of the United States, of their continent, of their own economy and well-being.

Germany is to me a nation of sleepwalkers, like the title of Hermann Broch's famous novel. People are asleep not to the dangers of fascism but to the dangers of economic stagnation, which also has moral consequences. It is easy for the prosperous to ignore the poor and to say that high taxes are punishment enough. Even in Berlin, though, one can see one shuttered shop after another, businesses dropping like rotten teeth in a brave smile.

To travel in eastern Germany is to experience the analogy of a neutron bomb. The buildings, city centers, sidewalks, and public structures show every evidence of the $1 trillion in investment since reunification. But the young people are gone. It is shocking, really, and not enough discussed. There is no work for the relatively old and little for the young, who are fleeing to the west as fast as possible for the jobs that remain.

What Walter Ulbricht feared when he built the Berlin Wall is actually taking place today—the depopulation of the best, most ambitious, and most capable citizens of the east. But among Germans there is not nearly enough outrage about this issue or self-examination about its causes—and its implications.

The famous Rhine model of managed worker–employer relations is outdated, creaking, and becoming self-defeating, when even a Social Democratic chancellor cannot challenge the ability of the unions to set wages over whole sectors of the economy—including enterprises with which the union has no contract at all.

The situation makes a realistic labor market difficult if not impossible because it overprices labor in the east, given comparative productivity. It makes outside investment in the east too expensive, it makes freelance employment too complicated, it encourages a wide black market that pays no tax to the state, and it undermines the very basis of the generous social benefits the state is proud of providing. What's even worse, perhaps, is that this continuing tax on the productive part of the economy has drained growth away, pulling the whole country into stagnation and even recession. The election campaign was deeply unsatisfying for these reasons. Edmund Stoiber lectured on some of these problems, but he shied away from promoting serious solutions. If Schröder played politics with peace, Stoiber played dangerously with immigration, working to undermine a necessary reform that would give needed life and energy to an aging population desperately in need of computer engineers and other skilled workers.

Nor did Stoiber risk announcing a specific program of structural change that might have rallied people behind him. Although it is true that the floods showed Schröder at his best, it is also true that Stoiber fumbled an enormous opportunity to capitalize on widespread unhappiness with the state of the economy.

If Schröder is being criticized now for lack of bravery, it is precisely Stoiber's cowardice that undermined his credibility and cost him the election. He was no Margaret Thatcher. His hesitation showed itself again on foreign policy, where he was less experienced. Still, his unwillingness—or inability—to attack Schröder effectively on the question of Germany's responsibilities abroad, as a member of NATO, the European Union, and the United Nations, was astounding.

The cost has been severe both inside Europe and with Washington, and yet it was perfectly predictable. Stoiber simply showed that the Christian Democrats and their Bavarian partners were not ready for prime time. As for the Free Democrats, Guido Westerwelle, by his misplaced notion of fun and his own fumbling inability to deal with Jürgen Möllemann, a senior party official who played with anti-Semitism to try to attract Muslim votes, should have resigned.

The German economic condition is worse than it seems, hidden by the beautiful buildings, the excellent infrastructure, and the fine trains, subways, and busses. If matters go on as they are, even with an eventual global upturn, Germany could face serious comparative economic decline, a gutting of its generous social welfare system and social disorder that goes beyond union demonstrations.

These fundamental issues of economic weakness, stagnation, and pessimism are at the heart of the European problem and, pace Kagan, have as much to do with the European self-image and reluctance to face challenges as any other factor.

But societies do react when circumstances become bad enough. Britain did in the 1980s, and Germany will, too. And, as in Britain, the outcome will be uneven and less than revolutionary. Angela Merkel, the Christian Democrat who is likely to be the conservative candidate for chancellor next time, is already being referred to as Maggie Merkel.

But Germany still must confront the real meaning of reunification, both economically and in human terms. It is admirable to be generous to the Third World, but Germans must also be both understanding and generous to the easterners and to the Turks and other immigrants who have worked so hard in Germany and made it their home.

The people in the east are hampered by the past, but they are not shirkers and parasites, as some western Germans find it comforting to think. Germany must find a broader and more generous sense of identity to encompass all those who chose to live and work there. Citizenship and belonging must be about commitment and behavior, not just about blood; a task that Schröder has begun, juridically at least.

There also has been serious nervousness in the West about the new German obsession with its own victims during World War II, as exemplified by Günther Grass's new novel *Crabwalk* and by historian Jörg Friedrich's *The Fire*, an examination of the massive bombing of German cities.

Personally, I think it is healthy for the Germans to examine what the Allies did to them during the Second World War or what angry Czechs and Poles did to the Germans of the east. And it is healthy for Germans to examine their own actions and reactions. At some point, every person and every people—Germans, Japanese, Serbs, Britons, French, and Americans—must be accountable for what they do and what is done in their name. But what matters, however, is not to find any moral equivalency between Nazi crimes and the crimes of others, as if the Nazi horrors can somehow be excused, explained, or justified through relativism.

There is such a thing as "victor's justice," but there is also such a thing as incontrovertible guilt and responsibility, no matter the injustices or crimes of others. But it is certainly fair to ask the following questions: If this was genocide, was Dresden not mass murder? What are the differences, and what can or cannot be excused or justified by either the rules or the fog of war?

And it is fair to ask similarly searching questions about the policies of allies, whether they be American or Israeli, and to criticize those policies vehemently. Such criticism is part of what it means to be a mature country, aware always of its past but able to act responsibly in the world—the kind of Germany I would like to see.

But what is not permissible, as the Möllemann affair finally showed, is to blame the actions or manners or opinions of individual Jews, or even the Israeli state, for anti-Semitism.

In an odd way I have found Germany almost uncomfortably philo-Semitic, overly anxious to treat its Jews as precious, like fragile exhibits in a museum. So when Germans ask me if is it permissible for Germans to criticize Jews, I must answer, of course it is permissible. But it would be better if Germans could see their Jewish compatriots—like their Turkish ones—as Germans. Can there be a new conception of what it is to be truly German?

As for Europe writ large, a Europe in which this unfinished Germany uneasily sits at the lynchpin, what is it really to be a European? What is a European policy that is not defined in contradistinction to American policy? What kind of European identity can there be to which a Romanian peasant or a Muslim immigrant can happily aspire? What kind of European state can there be for which a new European would willingly lay down his or her life?

These questions are not about Mars and Venus, or Hobbes and Kant. They are, as ever, about identity and loyalty, the first principles of patriotism, as central to Europe's future as to America's.

Note

1. Robert Kagan, "Power and Weakness," *Policy Review* 113 (June–July 2002).

2

"OLD EUROPE" VERSUS "NEW EUROPE"

by Anne Applebaum

SOMETIME IN THE AUTUMN OF 2001, a few months after the Italian parliamentary elections, I found myself on a highway, stuck in traffic, about halfway between Milan and Florence. The Italian friend traveling with me groaned as we ground to a halt behind what seemed to be a never-ending line of cars. After we had inched along, a few yards at a time, for a good two hours, he turned to me. "Now," he said, "you know why we voted for Berlusconi."

My friend—who did not vote for Berlusconi—went on to explain that plans to expand and upgrade this particular highway had been in existence for decades. Nothing had come of them, as nothing had come of so many Italian government ventures. Italians knew it, and they felt deeply frustrated—right now in particular. After enduring nearly a half-century's worth of weak, corrupt, inefficient postwar governments, the Italians in the 1990s went through the wrenching drama of the "Mani Pulite" (clean hands) campaign, a series of corruption investigations that ultimately led to the downfall of the entire Italian political class. But although the constitution changed, as a result of the trials and arrests, although politicians were jailed and whole political parties vanished overnight, the heavy state bureaucracy and confusing tax system had remained in place.

Berlusconi, a media mogul and businessman whose political career began at the end of the decade, promised (without offering much detail) to do away with both. Across Europe everyone from *Le Monde* and *Suddeutsche Zeitung* to *El Mundo* and the *Economist* denounced Berlusconi and his multiple television stations as a dangerous, financially dubious, possibly neofascist threat to Italian democracy. But although they knew about his shady past, although they have accepted that he was probably as much a part of the old elite as the politicians they kicked out, although they knew he controlled a good chunk of the Italian media, the Italians, by a surprisingly large majority, voted for him anyway. They had hopes, however slight, that he might at least be different. He might, for example, fix the roads.

Far-fetched though it may sound, Italian frustrations with the manifest failures of their ruling class are not irrelevant to Prime Minister Berlusconi's decision, in the spring of 2003, to join the American "coalition of the willing" in Iraq. Whatever else they might think of him, Italians believed Berlusconi might represent a break with the status quo; whatever else he might be, Berlusconi himself believed he represented a break with the status quo. And part of that status quo, over the past twenty years, included a more or less open assumption, in Italy as well as in most other west European countries, that European and American paths were slowly parting. However gradually, European social organization and European cultural life were heading in a distinctly different direction from American social organization and American cultural life. However subtly, European politics were adopting a different style from American politics. Most of all, European politicians—left-wing, right-wing, and centrist—overwhelmingly agreed that European capitalism had diverged from American capitalism, and would continue to do so.

Berlusconi, by contrast, was an open admirer of the United States. And in his admiration for American-style capitalism and American-style politics he was not alone, either. Over the past few years, a new breed of west European politicians—in southern Europe, Scandinavia, and Britain—have begun to sound similarly discontent with the European status quo. At the same time, east European politicians, who are wary of a European status quo that has largely excluded them, have begun to play a bigger role in European institutions. Yet Americans, accustomed to speaking of "Europe" as if it were a single country, have been slow to notice this change. One of the few who saw it coming was the American Defense Secretary Donald Rumsfeld, who put his finger on this new development in an off-the-cuff comment in January 2003. Asked, at that time, about the tepid European support for the U.S. military buildup in the Persian Gulf, he dismissed the comment. "You're thinking of Europe as Germany and France," he replied. "I don't. I think that's old Europe."

Old Europe. If Rumsfeld had been deliberately searching for a way to simultaneously irritate the leadership of Europe's two largest countries, expose their deepest national insecurities, and undermine the entire European Union political project, which has long revolved around a "Franco-German axis," he could not have found a better way to put it. The German foreign minister, Joschka Fischer, called on Rumsfeld to "cool down." When asked, the French environment minister said, "If you knew what I felt like telling Mr. Rumsfeld …" but refused to go on, saying that the words she wished to use were too offensive. "Old Europe Kicks Back" is how the headline in the French newspaper *Liberation* summed up the general reaction to Rumsfeld's comments.

And yet he was, as it happens, correct, possibly more correct than he knew at the time. Although all concerned vociferously deny it, Europe is indeed beginning to divide—slowly, unevenly but perceptibly—into two very distinct camps. One camp, led, at the moment, by France and Germany, retains the traditional skepticism of American power and remains committed to the idea of a "different" European form of social organization and a European foreign policy. The other camp, led, at the moment, by Britain, Italy, and Poland, welcomes the growth of American power and is even interested, at least some of the time, in following a more American economic and foreign-policy model. New lines are being drawn, tentatively, and new alliances are being created on both halves of what once was a differently divided continent. What follows is first the Western, and then the Eastern, side of that story.

Since its conception at the end of the World War II, the European Union has—sometimes openly, sometimes quietly—seen itself as a potential rival to the United States. Behind the drive to create a European single market lay the European desire to match American economic efficiency. Behind the European drive to create a single currency lay the European desire to produce a currency as powerful as the dollar.

Those sentiments have continued into the present. Behind France and Germany's willful opposition to American foreign policy, before and after the Iraq war, lay their desire to produce a European foreign policy distinctly different from that of the United States. "This is not about Iraq," said French president Jacques Chirac at the height of the battle over UN Security Council resolutions. "This is about the United States." Clearly the French president saw defiance of the United States as an opportunity to create a different international identity, for Europe at best, and for France at the very least—and not just a different international identity but an oppositional one.

Not every European politician shares that vision, however, nor have they all shared it in the past. Indeed, the first to reject it in a dramatic manner was Britain's former prime minister, Margaret Thatcher. In her domestic policy she openly identified her economic reforms—privatization, the weakening of the all-powerful trade unions, the beginnings of the reforms of the welfare state—with the tax-cutting, antistate rhetoric of the Reagan administration. In her foreign policy she enthusiastically supported what was then perceived in the rest of Europe as a hawkish American policy toward the Soviet Union.

Thatcher did not win many European friends by doing so. On the contrary, she shattered the collegiality of the meetings of the European Union leadership. Her constant demands for a fairer division of the European community budget, her suspicion of European military projects, and her skepticism about European monetary integration won her the cordial loathing of her colleagues. But she did transform the politics of her own country. The current prime minister, Tony Blair, is a self-described admirer of Lady Thatcher, who has never challenged either her pro-American legacy or her rejection of Continental socialism. To win election, he dragged his Labour Party reluctantly to the right, where it reluctantly remains.

Outside of her own country, it did seem, at first, as if Lady Thatcher would have few imitators. Throughout the 1990s Europe's Socialist and Christian Democratic parties actually seemed to grow more similar and more hostile to the worldview of Lady Thatcher. During that decade most of the European leadership espoused the same social-democratic economic policies, and repeated, as I say, the same criticisms of American-style capitalism, American culture, and American foreign policy, regardless of their political leanings. The views of French President Chirac, an old-fashioned right-wing politician, differed little, in this sense, from the views of German Chancellor Gerhard Schröder, an old-fashioned left-wing politician. Partly as a result, the very first meetings between European leaders and President George W. Bush went badly. According to some accounts, Bush's otherwise inexplicable fondness for the Russian President Vladimir Putin dates from his first trip to Europe, when Putin was the only politician he met, other than the Polish president, Alexander Kwasnewski, who did not want to harangue him about the Kyoto Protocol on global warming.

More recently, however, Europe does not look so homogeneous. Unexpectedly, in the first decade of the new millennium, a series of surprise elections created unexpected openings for a new generation of unorthodox European conservatives, many of whom describe themselves as "Thatcherites." The Italian general election of May 2001 brought Silvio Berlusconi to power. In November of that same year, Danish elections brought economic liberals to power in Denmark for the first time in eighty years. After elections in March 2002, Jose Manuel Durao Barroso, another economic liberal and admirer of Margaret Thatcher, became Portugal's prime minister. In January 2003, a shaken center-right government took over the Netherlands, too, after a strange election marked by the assassination of the popular, maverick conservative leader, Pym Fortuyn. With Blair still running Britain, and José Maríe Aznar, another center-right politician, running Spain, Europe in 2003, on the eve of the war with Iraq, suddenly looked much different than it had a few years earlier.

In part, these elections were about the economic status quo. Without a doubt, many Europeans want to emulate what they perceive to be America's economic success—which means, among other things, privatizing, liberalizing, and cutting taxes. Yet the changes were also, in part, a reaction to the events of September 11, 2001: the fact that a number of the 9/11 hijackers had lived for many years in Europe, collecting European welfare benefits, was not lost on anybody. Along with economic change, many of Europe's newer conservative politicians favored greater controls on immigration than had been in place in recent years. This was certainly true of the Danes and the Italians, as well as of Fortuyn, and his legacy lived on, at least in that narrow sense, in the Netherlands.

This is not, of course, to imply that all of these new ruling parties are identical or that they have the same goals. In their origins, traditions, and culture, the new Euro-right parties do not necessarily have much in common, either with one another or with the Republican Party in the United States. The conservatives now running Portugal are actually called Social Democrats (the losers were Socialists). Denmark's new rulers belong to the Venstre party, venstre being Danish for "left." Berlusconi's Forza Italia harbors a wide variety of people under its umbrella. And, of course, Tony Blair's Labour Party is not right wing in any sense at all.

Yet to their constituents, all of these politicians do sound different from their predecessors. And that different sound, that different tone, goes a long way toward explaining why, in January 2003, the leaders of Britain, Spain, Italy, Portugal, and Denmark, as well as Poland, Hungary, and the Czech Republic, all signed an open letter, published in the *Wall Street Journal,* calling for "unwavering determination and firm international cohesion on the part of all countries for whom freedom is precious"—as well as for the full application of UN Security Council Resolution 1441 and the complete disarmament of Saddam Hussein. The letter openly backed the American position on the conflict and openly chided the leaders of France and Germany, who were resisting the war. "We must remain united in insisting that his regime is disarmed," they wrote. "The solidarity, cohesion and determination of the international community are our best hope of achieving this peacefully. Our strength lies in unity." Soon afterward, another group of ten countries, all east European, signed a similar letter, too.

These letters hit the French and German political establishments like a cannonball. Both countries were furious that they had not been consulted, furious that they had not even been told the letter was going to appear. The leadership of the European Union in Brussels was even more distressed: the absence of a European consensus on the war in Iraq could not have been made more painfully obvious. Yet President Chirac did not, in reaction to the letter, openly criticize his west European colleagues. Instead, he reserved the full force of his scorn for the three east European nations who had also signed the letter: Poland, Hungary, and the Czech Republic. He informed the three that their opposition to France's wishes was "dangerous," that their proposed membership in the European Union was now at risk. Worse, he chided them like children: "It is not really responsible behavior. It is not well-brought-up behavior. They missed a good opportunity to keep quiet. ... If they wanted to diminish their chances of joining Europe, they could not have found a better way."

Which brings us, quite naturally, to the "new east Europeans." If the story in the West begins in 1979 with the ascent of Margaret Thatcher, the story in the East begins in 1989, with the fall of the Berlin Wall. Strange though it now sounds to say so, the collapse of communism in eastern Europe actually came at an awkward moment for the leaders of western Europe. They had just embarked on a project to strengthen and deepen the European Union. They had hoped to establish a European free market and a European currency, to create common passports, common borders, and ultimately a common foreign and defense policy. They had not planned to spend the 1990s integrating the East.

As a result, the liberation of the Eastern block presented the European Union leadership with a quandary: should they continue deepening the union—or stop, slow down, and work out how to make room for the east Europeans? Without even thinking much about it, they took the first path. Although not all aspects of the "closer union" are yet completed—there is still no European constitution—the European Union did complete the single market, as well as the single currency. Only in the fall of 2002 was a deal finally done to allow ten new members into the European Union, among them Poland, Hungary, the Czech Republic, Slovakia, Slovenia, Lithuania, Latvia, and Estonia, as well as Malta and Cyprus.

Nevertheless, thirteen years is a long time in politics, and it was certainly long enough for many east Europeans to become disillusioned with the European Union and its leadership. Accession negotiations were long, drawn out, and rife with bad feeling. Arguments broke out over whether east Europeans would have the right to work freely in western Europe and how soon west Europeans would be able to buy east European land. The bitterest arguments, without a doubt, were over the European Union's agricultural policy. Eastern farmers wanted the same lucrative arrangements as their western counterparts. Western politicians worried that eastern subsidies would cost far too much.

The result of these long negotiations was a set of compromises that left nobody satisfied, and left many east Europeans more suspicious of the intentions of their western neighbors than they had been in 1989. Many still suspect they will be treated as second-class Europeans. Many are still worried by the strength, within the European Union, of France and Germany, and fear being bullied by their leaders. The attachment that many feel to NATO, and the energy they have put in to joining NATO, reflected, above all, a desire to see the United States remain in Europe, as at least a partial counterweight to the power of France, Germany, and the European Union leadership in Brussels.

Fears of being dominated by the central continental powers might well have been enough to propel some east Europeans, at least, to seek to shift the balance of power in Europe toward Britain, Italy, and Spain, and away from Germany and France. But behind the decision of the east European countries to sign letters supporting U.S. policy in Iraq, there were other factors at play as well. One is continued anxiety about what a rejuvenated Russian state might be like a few years down the road. Generally speaking, east Europeans like the idea of NATO and want the United States to remain firmly committed to its military presence on the European continent. To encourage America to remain in Europe, many argued, it made sense to support America's war in Iraq.

East Europeans also, it must be said, had fewer qualms about America's disproportionate military capabilities than their western cousins. At least part of the explanation for the French opposition to the war lay in French opposition to growing American power. But east Europeans generally have fewer objections to America's "hyperpower" status: better a single hyperpower, after all, than the bipolar system that left them under Soviet occupation. Whereas many west Europeans remember the Cold War era as a time of economic growth and political strength, east Europeans remember it as a time of national catastrophe. There is little nostalgia for the days when American power was checked by the Soviet Union.

There is also, in some parts of eastern Europe, a particularly strong affinity to the United States. This is particularly true of Poland, the country the state department reckons to be possibly the most pro-American country in the world. The combination of the large Polish immigration to the United States at the turn of the nineteenth century, President Woodrow Wilson's support at the end of World War I for an independent Polish state, and President Ronald Reagan's support during the 1980s for the dissident Solidarity movement has left Poles with great faith in the positive power of the United States—a faith that actually transcends left-wing–right-wing divisions and party politics. This admiration for America has persisted even though it has sometimes been unrequited: Poland's early attempts to enter NATO were rebuffed, for example, and most Poles still find it extremely difficult to get visas even to visit the United States. The American decision, made in the immediate wake of the war, to grant Poland a "sector" of Iraq and full status in the occupation coalition will go a long way toward making Poles feel, at last, as if not only do they have a stake in the west but also that the West has a stake in them. Early suggestions, in the spring of 2003, that the United States might be willing to move some of its European military bases to Poland encouraged Polish mayors to rush to the Polish media, all claiming that their city or town would make the best new home for American troops. Later, when U.S. military spokesmen made the offer of east European bases official, enthusiasm only increased.

In the specific case of Iraq, there is also an additional factor. Although it was possible to drum up a good deal of sympathy for Saddam Hussein's regime in the west, it was harder to find much enthusiasm for a tyrannical regime among east Europeans who have more recently lived under tyrannical regimes themselves. On a visit to Washington in the fall of 2002, Adam Michnik, a former Polish dissident with close ties to the European Left, told a group of *Washington Post* journalists that he felt out of line with his French and German friends on the question of whether America should invade Iraq. If political freedom was at stake, then he was in favor of it.

Few westerners were prepared to take seriously such high-minded motives. On the contrary, eastern European participation in the Iraq coalition seemed, to many—particularly those who had other reasons to dislike the war—an occasion for satire, not to mention snobbery and ignorance. In the *New York Times,* columnist Maureen Dowd sneered at Bulgaria, one of the few members of the UN Security Council to support the United States, as a "pipsqueak power." In the *New York Review of Books,* Tony Judt dismissed east European support out of hand. "Yes, they like America and will do its bidding if they can," he wrote. "The US will always be able to bully a vulnerable country like Romania into backing America," a comment that does not fully explain why the United States was unable to bully a vulnerable country like Guinea, a Security Council member that did not side with the United States, or what might be different about Romania, or why that might matter a great deal in the future. One Polish politician who appeared on a talk show to discuss the American decision to grant a "sector" to the Poles to control in Iraq told me that he was dismissed, on air, by a Canadian professor who thought Poland a "country of 8 million people." Actually, my Polish acquaintance pointed out, Poland has thirty-eight million people, significantly more than Canada's twenty-four million. Poland also has some thirty years of extensive peacekeeping experience, from North Korea to Haiti, Lebanon, and Bosnia, not to mention an army three times the size of Canada's. It is hard to see what Canadians, from their position of global near-irrelevance, have to look down on.

But Canadians are not the only western members of the old NATO alliance to have this problem. In the first half of the twenty-first century, no country—not China, not Russia, and certainly not Canada—will even come close to matching American military prowess. In the year 2002 American military spending was not only the highest in the world, it was higher than that of the next fifteen countries—combined. If it is true that Poland or Bulgaria might have little to offer the United States in the way of military hardware or technological capability, it is equally true that Belgium has little more. Outside of Britain and France, no army in Europe has any significant heft or experience by comparison with the U.S. military—and even the British and French forces are comparatively tiny. What will matter to the United States, in the foreseeable future, are allies who can help provide bases, flyover rights, peacekeeping troops, and possibly the odd specialized chemical weapons or special operations troops, not to mention moral, political, and intelligence support. These are things the Poles, Spaniards, and Italians can do as well as the Belgians, Luxemburgers, or even the Germans.

There is, of course, one legitimate criticism of the whole notion of "new Europe" in general, and eastern Europe in particular. As many have noticed, a distinct gap emerged between the leaders of some of the members of the pro-war coalition in Europe and their constituents. Other than Britain and Poland (and Australia), where opinion polls did show significant support for the war, the citizens of many countries whose leaders backed the United States remained, if not opposed, at least unenthusiastic about it. This is a complicated issue, one that reflects a number of trends: the general left-wing tilt of the media in most European countries, a half-century-long tradition of pacifism on the European continent, a series of American diplomatic mistakes, the peculiarities of the war on Iraq, and the appalling, and continuing, American failure to communicate with the outside world. Although military planning for the war in Iraq began in the summer of 2002, there was no attempt to explain or promote the war in Europe until much later. Even after the war, President Bush rarely bothered to address himself to anyone other than his domestic constituents, although the entire world could see him and hear him every time he made a speech.

Clearly, new Europe is not a stable structure, and the British–Italian–Spanish–east-European axis is hardly a permanent part of the diplomatic system. The stunning downfall of Spain's Conservatives following the March 2003 terrorist attacks on Madrid demonstrated as much. A handful of elections could bring new Europe to an end: if a left-wing Labour leader were to come to power in Britain, if Berlusconi were replaced by anti-American opponents, if rural populists take over in Poland, the mood could shift, and the European status quo of the 1990s could be quickly reestablished. On the other hand, a Christian Democrat victory in Germany could change the mix, too. Many Germans have felt uneasy about their troubled relationship with the United States, and a different German government might well take a different approach. For that matter, in the post-Iraq period, some French commentators also began questioning the wisdom of their president's challenge to the United States.

Leaving domestic politics aside, other more permanent forces will always act to pull all Europeans closer to whatever is considered the European mainstream, and away from the United States. A wave of west European money is about to hit Eastern Europe, coming from the

European Union—and threats to halt it will prove very powerful. Elites on both halves of the continent can be individually seduced with the stipends, scholarships, and jobs that the European Union has to offer. German political parties are intimately involved with their western and eastern counterparts, and millions of eastern Europeans study on the western half of the continent.

By contrast, the United States is far away, and few American politicians take any particular interest in Europe, east or west. Issues of scant importance in the United States, such as visa policy, have enormous repercussions abroad. New restrictions on students and visitors mean that many people who might have come to study in this country now go elsewhere. America's failure to follow up on promised military funding for the easterners, failure to engage in diplomacy with the westerners— all of this contributes to a sense that Americans are not really interested in Europeans, except as mercenaries. A great deal of bitterness is felt in Eastern Europe over decisions that do not even register on anyone's political radar in Washington, such as the failure to give any post-war contracts to Eastern European companies that did business in Iraq for many years.

And yet—the fact that so many politicians chose to override their opinion polls and continue to support the United States in the conduct of an unpopular and poorly explained war is not insignificant either. If only one or two politicians had chosen to support the United States despite public opinion, their decision might have been dismissed as an aberration. In the event, many politicians of many ideological backgrounds made this choice, which means that it must be seen as a part of a pattern. In the western half of the continent, it does seem as if politicians who are committed to a vision of a different kind of Europe count close diplomatic relations with the United States as a part of that vision, even if their voters disagree. In the east, it seems that much of the political class believes that ensuring the continued American presence in Europe is more important than lack of public enthusiasm for one particular war.

In the end, the survival of the pro-American "bloc," if that is even the right word for it, depends a great deal on how Americans treat Europeans in the next few years. Americans must keep their attention focused on their European friends, both old and new, rewarding those who take the political risk of supporting American foreign policy but also remembering that those who do not always support us still share many of our political values. No European countries can ever be counted "in" or "out" completely: domestic politics change, opinion polls shift, moods will turn.

If Americans make the effort, it will pay off. Even if the new Europe turns out to be nothing more than a temporary, shifting alliance of countries that only occasionally vote together, this is a bloc with the potential to create a revolution in the politics of the European Union. Back in 1952, when the precursor to the European Union was founded, the organization contained six countries. Germany and France dominated them. With the latest round of enlargement in May 2004, the European Union contains twenty-five countries. The eastern European members will jointly have more delegates to the European Parliament than Germany. Britain, Spain, Italy, and Poland will easily outvote Germany and France in the weighted voting system of the European Council.

Operating together within European Union institutions, new Europe could bring an end to the Brussels bureaucracy in its current form, if not halting trends toward a common European army and foreign policy, then at least making sure that these new institutions do not become anti-American. As long as a handful of countries are willing to ally themselves with the United States, Europe cannot become a powerful American opponent. As long as a handful of countries are willing to work together with the United States, the west will continue to exist. And the United States needs western allies, if not necessarily to fight wars then to help catch terrorists, to help manage the global economy, and to help keep the peace.

Careful American diplomacy can help push at least a part of the continent toward a closer, deeper alliance with the United States. Arrogance and neglect, on the other hand, will unify Europeans against us. Europeans and Americans remain part of a single community, with elements of shared history and a long tradition of cooperation. It is worth putting in the effort to ensure that we stay that way.

3

THE END OF ATLANTICISM

by Ivo H. Daalder

THE IRAQ WAR EXPOSED DEEP fissures in transatlantic relations. On the eve of the war, Secretary of State Colin Powell warned of the Atlantic Alliance "breaking up," while Henry Kissinger, a close and long observer of U.S.–European relations, concluded that differences over Iraq had "produced the gravest crisis in the Atlantic Alliance since its creation five decades ago."[1] Since the war, tempers have cooled, but serious differences remain.

Are the current difficulties among the transatlantic allies different from the many crises that occurred in the past? Some, like Robert Kagan, argue that the changing structure of U.S.–European relations— and especially the great and growing imbalance of power—makes this crisis different. Others have a more optimistic view. For all their differences, noted Philip Gordon, "basic American and European values and interests have not diverged—and the European democracies are certainly closer allies of the United States than the inhabitants of any other region." The differences that do exist, Gordon argued, are the result largely of a sharp policy shift in Washington under President George W. Bush. But only "if policymakers on both sides of the Atlantic act on the assumption that fundamentally different worldviews now make useful cooperation impossible" is a transatlantic divorce conceivable.[2]

Rather than conflicting, both contentions are in fact on the mark. There has been a profound change in the structure of U.S.–European relations, though the differentiation of power is only one, and not the most important, factor accounting for this change. One crucial consequence of this transformation is the effective end of Atlanticism—American and European foreign policies no longer center on the Atlantic Alliance to the same overriding extent as in the past. Other concerns—both global and local—and different means for addressing them have now come to the fore. As a result, it is no longer simply a question of adapting transatlantic institutions to new realities—to give NATO a new mission or purpose. The changing structure of relations between the United States and Europe means that a new basis for the relationship must be found, lest the continued drift end in separation and, ultimately, divorce.

Nothing in the new structure preordains an end to transatlantic cooperation and partnership. But the gratuitous unilateralism that marked the Bush administration's years in office—the embrace of American power as means to all ends and the deliberate neglect of international institutions and other structures of cooperation—has had a profoundly negative impact on European elite and public opinion. Bush's personal style has only made matters worse. The swagger, pugnacious language, and deep religiosity of his main message strike Europeans as profoundly foreign. Many no longer see a common basis for action—and not a few now fear the United States more than what, objectively, constitute the principal threats to their security.

American policy toward Europe and the Atlantic Alliance represents the tipping point determining the future of a drifting relationship between the United States and Europe. Wise policy can help forge a new, more enduring strategic partnership through which the two sides of the Atlantic cooperate in meeting the many major challenges and opportunities of our evolving world. But a policy that takes Europe for granted—that routinely ignores or even belittles European concerns—may drive Europe away. For under circumstances like these, Europeans may come to resent being dragged into problems that are not of their own creation. There may come a point, perhaps sooner than many think, when Europe says: *Basta! Fini! Genug!* even *Enough!*—when Europe refuses to continue sharing the risks of international engagement without having an equal share in decisions that create those risks.

There is nothing inevitable about this sober conclusion, but the U.S.–European relationship cannot sustain the kind of beating it has endured these past few years for much longer. The aftermath of the Iraq war, in fact, may turn out to be the test case for the sustainability and longevity of the relationship. An effort to forge complementary and mutually supportive policies to rebuild Iraq and stabilize and reform the Middle East may solidify the faltering relationship, whereas a determination by the United States to go it alone or fail to engage sufficiently may push it over the edge. Either way, U.S.–European relations will be profoundly different for it.

SHIFTING PRIORITIES

For more than half a century, American and European foreign policy has centered on the transatlantic axis. For America, Europe and the allies stood center stage—Europe was both the locus and the focus of America's confrontation with the Soviet Union. For Europe, America was its guardian and protector, enabling it to emerge from the ravages of war and providing it with the confidence necessary to overcome the stark differences that had produced two bloody world wars in three decades. The phenomenal success of American and European policy helped end the Cold War confrontation with a whimper rather than a bang. And once this victory was consolidated during the 1990s, the structurally determined need to mediate U.S. and European foreign policy through the transatlantic prism effectively came to an end. America's and Europe's immediate concerns have increasingly diverged—one focusing globally, the other locally. And the differences between them have been further accentuated by diverging perspectives of what drives the new age of global politics that replaced the familiar transatlantic world of the Cold War.

The fundamental purpose of American foreign policy for most of the past century was to ensure that no single power would dominate the Eurasian landmass. As the British geographer Sir Harold Mackinder theorized at the outset of the past century, power in international politics depends crucially on who controlled what he called this "Heartland," for he who ruled the Heartland ruled the world.[3] This reality was not lost on America's statesmen. Three times during the past century, they sent massive numbers of military forces overseas to defeat those who sought dominion of the Eurasian heartland—in World War I, World War II, and during the Cold War, which was to last the better part of half a century. Together, these interventions constituted what Philip Bobbitt aptly called the "Long War."[4] Once the Soviet empire was no more, the last serious challenge for territorial dominion over the Eurasian landmass had been removed. The primary purpose of American foreign policy had thus been achieved.

It took some years to realize how much Europe's strategic relevance to the United States had been reduced. The 1990s (a period now best remembered as the post–Cold War era) were given over to consolidating the victory of the Long War. Together with its European partners, Washington set out to create a peaceful, undivided, and democratic Europe.[5] NATO evolved from a collective defense organization into Europe's main security institution—helping to stabilize the Balkans, transforming military practices with no less than twenty-seven partnership countries, and forging new relationships with erstwhile opponents. By 2004 it had expanded its membership to twenty-six countries, ten more than were members at the end of the Cold War. A new relationship with Russia emerged after ten years of intensive effort. In 2001 Russia under President Vladimir Putin turned toward the West, engaging the United States as a partner in the war on terrorism and negotiating a fundamentally cooperative relationship with NATO a year later. Finally, although pockets of instability remain in the Balkans, the Caucasus, and beyond, Europe's main institutions—from the Organization for Security and Cooperation in Europe and the EU to a revitalized NATO—have proved more than capable of handling such problems. As a result of these efforts, Europe is today more peaceful, more democratic, and more united than at any time in history.

The terrorist attacks of September 11, 2001, reinforced America's strategic shift away from Europe. Rather than worrying about a single power's ability to dominate Eurasia, Washington focused on trying to defeat the terrifying trinity of terrorists, tyrants, and technologies of mass destruction. Seen from Washington, Europe can be a partner—even a crucial one—in U.S. efforts to defeat this new threat, but only to the extent that it supports the fundamental course that Washington has embarked on. As a strategic concern, Europe has moved from being the object of American policy to performing a supporting role.

Europe's shift in strategic priorities has been much less dramatic, at least through now. The principal focus of European foreign policy today is what it has been for more than fifty years—to eliminate the possibility of a return to internecine conflict through an ever greater commitment to shared sovereignty within a European union. The European Union (EU) is the focal point for European policy and activity over a vast range of areas—from trade and monetary policy to judicial, social, and (increasingly) foreign and security policy. For the immediate future, the EU has embarked on a fantastically ambitious phase, encompassing both deeper cooperation among existing members and enlargement of the overall Union to incorporate many of the neighboring countries in the east. An intergovernmental conference, following on the conclusions of the constitutional convention in 2003, will decide the parameters of Europe's union in future years—including whether Europe will emerge more and more as a single international actor in foreign and security policy, as it has been in the economic sphere. The enlargement project—through which ten countries joined in 2004, to be followed by Romania and Bulgaria a few years later—is equally ambitious. More than 100 million people will be added to the EU, increasing its overall population by nearly a quarter. Yet the combined gross domestic product of the countries joining is only 5 percent that of the current members. The costs and consequences of enlargement are likely therefore to be enormous. Think, by way of comparison, of the United States incorporating Mexico into a North American union.[6]

For at least the remainder of this decade, Europe is likely to remain focused on completing this ambitious project. So while America's focus has shifted away from Europe, Europe's focus has shifted ever more inward.

AMERICAN POWER AND GLOBALIZATION

The shifting foreign-policy priorities, and potential differences that arise from them, are accentuated by the diverging ways in which Americans and Europeans perceive the current international environment. We live in an age of global politics—an age characterized by two unprecedented phenomena.[7] One phenomenon is the sheer predominance of the United States. Today, as never before, what matters most in international politics is how—and whether—Washington acts on any given issue. The other is globalization, which has unleashed economic, political, and social forces that are beyond the ability of any one country, including the United States, to control.

Americans and Europeans differ about which of these two aspects of our new age is the most important. Americans, and especially the Bush administration and its supporters, believe that U.S. primacy is the defining feature of the contemporary world. "The collapse of the Soviet empire led to a fundamental reordering of the international system, and to the current situation in which American global hegemony is the leading factor that shapes the present and, almost certainly, the future," argued Robert Kagan.[8] "The unipolar moment has become the unipolar era," wrote Charles Krauthammer in an essay trumpeting America's primacy.[9] Or, as the opening sentence of the Bush administration's 2002 *National Security Strategy* put it, "The United States possesses unprecedented—unequaled—strength and influence in the world," which it should use "to promote a balance of power that favors freedom."[10]

Europeans, in contrast, tend to see globalization—including the constraints it places on any one nation's power—as the defining feature of the current era. "The new era," Christoph Bertram observed, "can be summed up in one word: globalization. Just as capital, commerce and communication operate around the globe unhindered by distance, so security and insecurity have become globalized—they can no longer be defined by reference to specific regions and territorial borders."[11]

The sheer speed and volume of cross-border contacts and the fact that globalization is occurring across multiple dimensions simultaneously mean that neither the positive nor the negative consequences of globalization can be managed by individual countries on their own. As a consequence, whether the issue is terrorism, organized crime, weapons proliferation, infectious diseases, democratization, or trade in goods and services, no single country—not even the most powerful— can secure its goals without the aid of others. "The lesson of the financial markets, climate change, international terrorism, nuclear proliferation [and] world trade" as British prime minister Tony Blair told a Labour Party conference on October 2, 2001, "is that our self-interest and our mutual interests are today inextricably woven together."[12]

The differing perspectives on what defines the age of global politics are reflected in very different foreign-policy preferences. The Bush administration and its supporters favor a hegemonist foreign policy, which is based on the belief that the preponderance of power enables the United States to achieve its goals without relying on others. As Krauthammer put it in 2001, "An unprecedentedly dominant United States ... is in the unique position of being able to fashion its own foreign policy. After a decade of Prometheus playing pygmy, the first task of the [Bush] administration is precisely to reassert American freedom of action."[13] The attacks on the World Trade Center and the Pentagon only underscored the vital importance of maintaining the freedom to act as Washington sees fit. As Bush argued, in rejecting advice that he take account of allied views in conducting the war on terrorism, "At some point we may be the only ones left. That's okay with me. We are America."[14]

The premium hegemonists place on freedom of action leads them to view international institutions, regimes, and treaties with considerable skepticism. Such formal arrangements inevitably constrain the ability of the United States to make the most of its primacy. Hegemonists similarly take an unsentimental view of U.S. friends and allies. The purpose of allied consultations is not so much to forge a common policy, let alone build goodwill, as to convince others of the rightness of the U.S. cause. Finally, hegemonists believe that the fundamental purpose of American foreign policy is to maintain and extend American power for the indefinite future. "America has, and intends to keep, military strength beyond challenge," Bush argued at West Point in June 2002, "thereby making the destabilizing arms races of other eras pointless, and limiting rivalries to trade and other pursuits of peace."[15]

In contrast, Europeans favor a globalist foreign policy, one that relies on international cooperation as a means to deal with the multiple challenges and opportunities globalization creates. None of these can be harnessed or blocked by individual states alone. International cooperation is necessary to defeat terrorists, preserve biodiversity, stop the spread of infectious diseases, halt weapons proliferation, promote democracy, ensure free trade, and deal with the host of other issues on every nation's foreign-policy agenda. In addition, although the United States is by far the most powerful state in the world today, one important consequence of globalization is the diffusion of power away from states. Nonstate entities, ranging from businesses to transnational citizens organizations, from crime cartels to terrorist groups, are often more nimble than states and frequently succeed in frustrating their policies. The changing policy agenda and rise of these nonstate actors mean that even the most powerful state is losing its ability to control what goes on in the world. "In an era of globalization that has dark aspects as well as bright," Chris Patten, the EU's external affairs commissioner, argued, "I would strongly argue that America's national interest is better served by multilateral engagement. It's the only way to deal with the dark side of globalization."[16]

CONSEQUENCES FOR TRANSATLANTIC RELATIONS

The main consequence of these changes in U.S. and European policy priorities is to make the transatlantic relationship less pivotal to the foreign policy of both actors. For America, Europe is a useful source of support for American actions—a place to seek complementary capabilities and to build ad hoc coalitions of the willing and somewhat able. But Washington views Europe as less central to its main interests and preoccupations than it did during the Cold War. For European countries, America's protective role has become essentially superfluous with the disappearance of the Soviet threat, while its pacifying presence is no longer warranted, given the advance of European integration. The task of integrating all of Europe into the zone of peace now falls squarely on Europe's shoulders, with the United States playing at most a supporting role. Even the stabilization of Europe's periphery—from the Balkans in the south to Turkey, the Caucuses, and Ukraine in the east—is a task where Europeans will increasingly have to take the lead.

These shifts are becoming apparent in all sorts of ways—from the mundane to the profound. Diplomatic contact across the Atlantic is dropping precipitously in terms of quantity and quality, whereas within Europe it continues to rise. Take meetings among foreign ministers. During the 1990s the U.S. secretary of state traveled to Europe on average nearly once a month. There were biannual NATO meetings, and frequent diplomatic forays interspersed among them—be it for U.S.-EU meetings, Organization for Security and Cooperation in Europe summits, or issue-specific discussions ranging from arms control to the Balkans. In contrast, Secretary of State Colin Powell traveled six times to Europe in 2001 and only three times in 2002. Even in the midst of one of the most bitter transatlantic debates in memory, Powell flew to the World Economic Forum in Davos, Switzerland, in January 2003 to deliver a tough speech on Iraq, but he did not stop in any other European capital to make the case in person. To be sure, Powell spends considerable time on the telephone with his European counterparts. But the quick phone call is more useful for delivering a démarche than gaining a true understanding of what it might take to arrive at a common position. Such diplomacy is best conducted in person. The unwillingness to engage in this kind of personal give-and-take underscores the declining importance of Europe to Washington policymakers and raises questions in Europe about whether the United States is more interested in stating firm American convictions than in forging common positions.

Contrast the paucity of recent transatlantic personal interactions with the European norm. European foreign ministers see each other as often as three times a month. There are monthly General Affairs Council meetings of the EU, the quarterly meetings of the European Council, biannual and annual meetings of international organizations ranging from NATO to the UN General Assembly, and frequent bilateral contacts. Each meeting provides an opportunity to resolve outstanding questions—and often enables countries to preempt disagreements that would otherwise occur. Of course, frequent contacts do not guarantee that conflict will be avoided, nor is infrequency of contact a guarantee of conflict. But contact helps create mutual understanding, making conflict less and agreement more likely.

Just as personal contact is apparently becoming less important across the Atlantic, so NATO, the embodiment of Atlanticism, is beginning to lose its central role. For five decades, the Atlantic Alliance has served the dual purpose of military deterrence and political reassurance. Deterrence operated against the threat from the east, a threat that no longer exists. Reassurance operated across the Atlantic as well as within Europe proper. In both purposes, the Alliance proved to be spectacularly successful during the Cold War. But as priorities and interests have shifted on both sides of the Atlantic, NATO's confidence-building role is being increasingly marginalized.

The Alliance's marginalization became especially apparent after September 11. Within twenty-four hours of the horrendous attacks, the nineteen NATO members did something they had never done before—they invoked Article 5 of the North Atlantic Treaty declaring the attack on the United States an attack against all. But aside from the symbolically important deployment of NATO AWACS surveillance planes to the United States to assist in providing air cover over the country, the Alliance was assigned no role in devising or carrying out a military response to the terrorist attacks. Plans for retaliating against al-Qaeda outposts in Afghanistan were drawn up by U.S. military commanders in secret. And offers of military assistance from allied countries were largely spurned. "I don't like this principle that the 'mission defines the coalition,'" complained Javier Solana, NATO's secretary general at the time of the Kosovo war and now the EU's foreign-policy chief, referring to Defense Secretary Donald Rumsfeld's oft-quoted dictum. "NATO invoked its most sacred covenant, that no one had dared touch in the past, and it was useless! Absolutely useless! At no point has General Tommy Franks even talked to anyone at NATO."[17]

Iraq, initially, was no different. When Rumsfeld traveled to an informal NATO defense ministerial meeting in Warsaw in September 2002 and was asked what role NATO might have in a possible war against Iraq, he answered, "It hasn't crossed my mind; we've not proposed it."[18] Two months later, Bush, while declaring in a speech at NATO's Prague summit that "never has our need for collective defense been more urgent," emphasized that if the peaceful disarmament of Iraq proved impossible "the United States will lead a coalition of the willing to dis- arm Iraq."[19] Bush thus rejected the advice of Czech President Vaclav Havel, offered during a joint press conference, that in case "the need to use force does arise, I believe NATO should give an honest and speedy consideration to its engagement *as an alliance* [emphasis added]."[20] Perhaps partly in response to these sentiments, the Bush administration in January formally asked NATO to support a possible war in Iraq in a number of indirect ways, including deploying AWACS radar planes and Patriot antimissile systems to enhance Turkey's defense, taking respon- sibility for protecting ships in the eastern Mediterranean, providing per- sonnel to defend U.S. bases in Europe and possibly the Persian Gulf, and filling other shortfalls arising from the redeployment of American troops to the Middle East. France, Germany, and Belgium's wrong- headed decision to oppose this request, of course, very much undercut European complaints that it was the Bush administration that was weakening NATO.

Nevertheless, it is clear that the central role NATO once played in U.S. foreign and defense policy has dissipated in recent years. Part of the reason, to be sure, is the growing capabilities gap separating U.S. and European military forces. Yet that gap provides only part of the ex- planation. Washington is also extremely wary of having its power tied down by coalition or alliance considerations. Now that it has the power to go it largely alone in the military field, few in the current adminis- tration believe there is much to gain from constraining the use of that power by subordinating the planning and execution of a military cam- paign to the dictates of alliance considerations. As Rumsfeld explained, "I said last year [2001] that the mission defines the coalition, and I think that was not only a correct statement, but it has been an enormously helpful concept in this war on terror. Every nation is different, with dif- ferent cultures and geographies, and the thought that they should all agree at the same moment how to contribute to this war is nonsense. That will never happen, and it never has. Countries ought to decide in- dividually what they can do. That's not a blow to NATO."[21]

From this perspective, the United States, not coincidentally, can do what it wants without regard for the views of others—be they Alliance partners or not. And what of NATO's role? Rather than providing a common front, the Alliance's military utility lies increasingly in providing the Pentagon a "useful joint-training-and-exercise organization from which the United States can cherry-pick 'coalitions of the willing' to participate in U.S.-led operations."[22]

As U.S. interest in the Atlantic Alliance wanes, Europeans are left with two alternatives. One is to try to reinforce the fraying bonds by emphasizing the importance of transatlantic unity and the continued centrality of NATO in U.S.–European relations. Often, this translates into expressing support for U.S. policy, even in otherwise objectionable cases, in order to demonstrate continued fealty to the transatlantic ties. This was at least one reason why a majority of NATO allies decided to support Washington when it went to war against Iraq, and why many of them subsequently made at least a small contribution to the military stabilization effort that followed Saddam Hussein's ouster. Moreover, being good allies, as Tony Blair has emphasized, is also the only way in which a weaker partner can effectively influence a powerful country like the United States.[23]

Another way to fill the void created by America's lessened interests would be to try to forge a stronger and closer EU. "If we don't speak with a single voice, our voice won't exist and nobody will hear us," warned Romano Prodi, president of the European Commission.[24] This impulse often fuels opposition to U.S. policy in an effort to rally a common European position on a particular issue. These efforts are most often successful when the goal is creating new rules, norms, or multilateral institutions to deal with global challenges—as European efforts with regard to global warming, antipersonnel land mines, and the creation of an international criminal tribunal have underscored. But on major security issues—as in the case of Iraq—both tendencies will be reinforced simultaneously. Thus, Britain led the effort to forge a coalition of European countries in support of Washington's policy, while France and Germany tried to develop a common EU position that would set a separate course. Neither has succeeded—leaving Europe divided and the United States with little reason to heed its concerns.

THE TIPPING POINT

Where does this leave the transatlantic relationship? In a major speech on the impact of Iraq on U.S.–European relations at the World Economic Forum in Davos, Switzerland, in January 2003, Powell noted that the transatlantic "marriage is intact, remains strong, will weather any differences that come along."[25] But some marriages are sturdier than others. Every marriage, moreover, requires a continued commitment by both partners to make it work. And sometimes even the best of marriages end in divorce. What, then, will be the future of the transatlantic marriage? Will it end in divorce, with the United States and Europe calling it quits after more than fifty years of happy, fruitful, and successful marriage, and each going its own way? Or will the United States and Europe renew their partnership, once more take their vows, and update the relationship in ways appropriate for the new era in which they now live?

Ever since the Cold War ended, the United States and Europe have slowly drifted apart, like the couple that has stayed married for all these years, continues to live together, but now communicates less and less as each partner goes his and her own way.[26] But the long drift has become unsustainable. Either relations will end in divorce or they will confront a crisis so severe that leaders on both sides of the Atlantic will have to take steps to update and renew the partnership. Which of these outcomes will come to pass will depend to a significant extent on the policy and preferences of the dominant player in the relationship.

Bush, and the policies his administration has pursued, represented the tipping point in U.S.–European relations. Nothing preordains the end of this alliance, but Bush's policies—and even more so, his personal style—aggravate the deep fissures that have emerged in transatlantic relations as a result of the structural shifts discussed earlier. There are major differences between the United States and Europe (and, to some extent, even within Europe) about what should be the foreign-policy priorities and how these should be pursued. At the same time, in casting many of his positions in black-and-white terms and employing a rhetoric with stark religious overtones, the American president has appeared more interested in demonstrating the righteousness of his positions than finding ways to accommodate other perspectives into U.S.

policies. Far from softening this approach, the terrorist attacks against the World Trade Center and Pentagon only reinforced it.

For all the shared sense of shock engendered by the television images beamed across the globe, Europeans and Americans reacted very differently to the September 11 attacks. Whereas little changed in Europe's policy, perspectives, and priorities, the impact of the attacks on the United States was truly profound. For the American people, the terrorists shattered a sense of physical security that their seeming invulnerability at home had long ensured. For the administration, the attacks came to define its policy, foreign and domestic, in every conceivable dimension. And for Bush, the devastating events provided the fundamental purpose of his presidency. He would destroy the terrorists before they could strike again. He would defeat tyrants who harbored terrorists or ruled rogue states. And he would make sure terrorists and tyrants could not get their hands on the technologies of mass destruction.

Because America and Europe experienced September 11 differently, their policy convergence on dealing with the threat represented by these attacks has been tactical rather than strategic. There is significant cooperation on counterterrorism between U.S. and European law enforcement agencies, intelligence communities, and financial regulators. And there is a joint commitment to weed out terrorist cells before they strike again. But there is no agreement on the broader strategic context of these efforts.

For much of Europe, this fight against terrorism at home must be complemented by a major new effort to tackle the root causes of terrorism abroad—the seething conflicts, poverty, and despair, and the constraints on liberty, that supply the terrorist army with its dedicated soldiers. As Tony Blair put it just weeks after the attacks, "I believe this a fight for freedom. And I want to make it a fight for justice too. Justice not only to punish the guilty. But justice to bring those same values of democracy and freedom around the world. ... The starving, the wretched, the dispossessed, the ignorant, those living in want and squalor from the deserts of Northern Africa, to the slums of Gaza, to the mountain ranges of Afghanistan: they too are our cause."[27] For Europe, therefore, diplomacy, peacekeeping, and nation-building efforts;

economic aid; and democracy-promoting assistance had to play as critical a role as brute force in the antiterrorist campaign.

In contrast, for the Bush administration, the strategic context of what it calls the global war on terrorism is the nexus between terrorism, rogue states, and weapons of mass destruction.[28] Regime change—by force if necessary—represents the strategic thrust of this global war. Once rogue states have been liberated, terrorists will have no place to hide and weapons of mass destruction will not fall into the wrong hands.

What makes these differences in perspective and approach starker still is Bush's personal style—the certainty with which he holds his views, the manner in which he defends them, and above all the religious overtones of his rhetoric. The 11th of September, in many ways, was an epiphany for George W. Bush—it defined the true purpose of his presidency. "I think, in his frame, this is what God has asked him to do," a close acquaintance told the *New York Times* days after the attacks.[29] More than a year later, a senior administration official confirmed that Bush "really believes he was placed here to do this as part of a divine plan."[30] The "this" is what Bush refers to as the fight between good and evil—a fight in which America, representing the good, will triumph over the "evildoers." Once the world is delivered from evil, the good people everywhere will be able to get on with their lives free of fear. America's mission—George W. Bush's mission—is to make this vision come true. "We understand our special calling," the president declared in his January 2004 State of the Union speech, "This great republic will lead the cause of freedom."[31]

The clearly defined mission provides the Bush administration with a great clarity of purpose and explains the complete conviction on Bush's part that his is not only the right way but the only way. Supreme self-confidence was a trademark of the Bush presidency even before September 11—Bush, for example, took great pride in staring down the EU heads of government during their first encounter in June 2001, which was dominated by the U.S.–European disagreement over global warming.[32] This self-confidence became complete after the terrorist attacks: there would be no more doubting America's purpose or preferred course of action. America's policy preferences were unquestionably right, and the sole purpose of talking to others would be to convince them of that fact. As Powell told European journalists in summer 2002, President Bush "makes sure people know what he believes in. And then he tries to persuade others that is the correct position. When it does not work, then we will take the position we believe is correct, and I hope the Europeans are left with a better understanding of the way in which we want to do business."[33]

Because there is only a single correct policy—because, as Bush put it shortly after September 11, "either you are with us, or you are with the terrorists"[34]—the value of other states, including those allied with the United States, is judged by their fealty to and support for American policy. Thus, when Rumsfeld drew a distinction between "old" and "new" Europe, he based the difference on the fact that new Europe supported U.S. policy toward Iraq whereas old Europe (France and Germany) did not.[35]

Rumsfeld may be blunter than most, but he very much reflects the president's view that loyalty to America's cause is a key requirement of allies. As the *New York Times* reported, Bush "has redrawn his mental map of America's alliances."[36] In the wake of the Iraq debate, Bush's ranking of allies started with Blair's Britain (the "center of his universe"), followed by Poland ("the most gung-ho member of NATO"). Next was Spain (whose leader Prime Minister José Maríe Aznar was a particular favorite of Bush prior to the defeat of his party following the 2004 terror attack in Madrid), followed by Australia, Italy, and Russia. Germany and France fell to the bottom of the list because, according to a senior Bush aide, both "failed the Bush loyal test."[37]

Although some European countries have been flattered by their elevation in Bush's rank ordering—and many, especially the newer allies, have sought to ingratiate themselves to Washington by astutely playing to the American president's predilections. Thus, most Europeans have experienced the Bush administration's certitude on policy matters with great unease. Even before U.S.–German differences over Iraq boiled over, German officials complained bitterly about Washington's supposed arrogance. "Alliance partners are not satellites," Foreign Minister Joschka Fisher noted pointedly in early 2002.[38]

But it is the White House's religiosity that is most striking—and disturbing—to many Europeans. The difference in perspective reflects in part a societal gap. Although American and European societies share similar perspectives on the importance of democracy, human rights, liberty, transparency, and other sociopolitical values, their attitudes diverge notably on religious and traditional values. The United States is a far more religious country than the countries of Europe, and traditional values find far greater adherence in the United States than in European countries (including Britain and other countries that aligned with Washington over Iraq).[39] Javier Solana has been struck and surprised by the degree religion has permeated White House thinking on core issues. For Washington, "it is all or nothing," Solana once observed. "The choice of language is revealing," he noted—with us or against us, axis of evil, rogue state, evildoers. "For us Europeans, it is difficult to deal with because we are secular. We do not see the world in such black and white terms."[40]

There is, of course, nothing new about policy differences between the United States and Europe. These have occurred for as long as the Alliance has existed. What is new, though, is the near-zero tolerance in Washington for those who might see the world differently. Today, terrorism, rogues, and weapons of mass destruction are Washington's all-consuming interests. Nothing else matters. "When people are trying to kill you and when they attack because they hate freedom," Condoleezza Rice observed, "other disputes from Frankenfood to bananas and even important issues like the environment suddenly look a bit different."[41] No doubt. But these other issues remain important—and to some countries at some moments perhaps more important than the war on terrorism. It should be possible to discuss different strategies for dealing with common threats without meeting the opprobrium of the White House or being relegated to a lower rank on the Bush loyalty list. Style matters, sometimes as much as substance. As Robert Kagan argued, in concluding his treatise on Europe's weakness and American's strength, the United States

> could begin to show more understanding for the sensibilities of others, a little more of the generosity of spirit that characterized American foreign policy during the Cold War. ... It could pay its

respects to multilateralism and the rule of law, and try to build some international political capital for those moments when multilateralism is impossible and unilateral action unavoidable. It could, in short, take more care to show what the founders called a "decent respect for the opinion of mankind."[42]

A EUROPEAN FAREWELL?

The single-mindedness of Bush's foreign policy may be both its greatest strength and its greatest weakness. There is little doubt where America stands these days, no confusion about its goal or purpose. Nor is there any question that this president does what he says and says what he does. Such clarity can be welcome in foreign policy. More problematic, especially for America's closest allies, is the narrowness of Washington's foreign-policy agenda and the inflexibility that characterizes its foreign-policy approach. This White House knows what it wants, and nothing or nobody is able to move it off course. To change direction is regarded as a sign of weakness, not wisdom. Anyone with a different policy perspective or prescription is either ignored or dismissed as clearly wrongheaded. There is little apparent concern about how America's actions may affect the interests of others.

So far, the immediate consequences of American single-mindedness have been manageable. Differences between the United States and its major European allies have continued to grow but have not yet reached a breaking point. But that point may be approaching faster than is generally realized. The current crisis in relations comes at a time when the centripetal forces keeping the Alliance together are probably weaker—and the centrifugal forces are at least as strong—than at any time since World War II. There is a growing anxiety among many Europeans that their inability to affect American foreign-policy behavior renders the costs of alignment with the United States increasingly great—perhaps even greater than the benefits.

Iraq may become the turning point for many Europeans. The way Bush went to war, the failure to find weapons of mass destruction, and the chaotic postwar effort created grave doubts about Washington's competence. The distrust left deep and lasting scars in Europe's psyche. With time—and astute American care and diplomacy—it is possible that the scars will heal, but there has been precious little of this care and diplomacy to date. As a result, it is becoming quite possible—perhaps even likely—that major European countries will conclude that an overt distancing from U.S. policy is not only desirable but also necessary. In a reverse of George Washington's Farewell Address, Europeans may come to conclude,

> The Great rule of conduct for us, in regard to foreign Nations is in extending our comercial [sic] relations to have with them as little political connection as possible. ... [The United States] has a set of primary interests, which to us have none, or a very remote relation. Hence she must be engaged in frequent controversies, the causes of which are essentially foreign to our concerns. Hence therefore it must be unwise in us to implicate ourselves, by artificial ties, in the ordinary vicissitudes of her politics, or the ordinary combinations & collisions of her friendships, or enmities. ... Why, by interweaving our destiny with that of any part of [the United States], entangle our peace and prosperity in the toils of [American] Ambition, Rivalship, Interest, Humor or Caprice?[43]

There is nothing inevitable about this scenario. There is a more hopeful, and equally plausible scenario by which the deterioration of U.S.-European relations will lead to a realization on both sides of the Atlantic that a major readjustment is necessary to renew and update the partnership. Europe would invest in the resources necessary to complement its soft-power capabilities with real, hard-power capabilities. The United States would once again come to realize that allies and alliances are assets to harbor and strengthen rather than abandon or take for granted. A partnership of relative equals could emerge from this readjustment to deal with common challenges ranging from terrorism and weapons of mass destruction to energy security, climate change, and infectious diseases—provided both sides decide this is what they want.[44] What is no longer possible is for the relationship to continue to drift. There is too much resentment, and too many are becoming alienated, for the drifting apart to continue indefinitely.

Relations between Europe and the United States have reached a turning point. Either their long marriage comes to an end, or it will be renewed. Which one of these futures comes true will depend especially

on the United States, which, as the senior partner, has the greatest
power to put the Alliance back on track or to derail it completely.

Notes

1. Quoted in Julia Preston and Steven Weisman,"France Offering Plan to Expand Iraq Arms
   Hunt," *New York Times*, February 12, 2003, p. A1. Henry Kissinger, "Role Reversal and
   Alliance Realities," *Washington Post*, February 10, 2003, p. A21.
2. Philip H. Gordon, "Bridging the Atlantic Divide," *Foreign Affairs*, vol. 82, no. 1
   (January/Feburary 2003), pp. 74, 83.
3. Harold Mackinder, *Democratic Ideals and Reality* (New York: Norton, 1962). See also
   Colin S. Gray, *The Geopolitics of Superpower* (Lexington: University of Kentucky Press,
   1988).
4. Philip C. Bobbitt, *The Shield of Achilles: War, Peace, and the Course of History* (New York:
   Alfred A. Knopf, 2002), pp. 21–61.
5. For details, see Ivo H. Daalder, "The United States and Europe: From Primacy to
   Partnership?" in Robert Lieber (ed.) *Eagle Rules? Foreign Policy and American Primacy in
   the Twenty-first Century*, (Upper Saddle River, NJ: Prentice Hall, 2001), pp. 70–96; and Ivo
   H. Daalder and James M. Goldgeier, "Putting Europe First," *Survival* vol. 43, no. 1 (Spring
   2001), pp. 71–92.
6. Charlemagne, "Europe's Mexico Option," *The Economist*, October 5, 2002, p. 50.
7. Parts of this section draw on a longer exposition of this argument in Ivo Daalder and James
   Lindsay, "Power *and* Cooperation: An American Foreign Policy for the Age of Global
   Politics," in Henry Aaron, James Lindsay, and Pietro Nivola (eds.), *Agenda for the Nation*,
   (Washington: The Brookings Institution Press, 2003).
8. Robert Kagan, "One Year After: A Grand Strategy for the West?" *Survival* 44, no. 4 (Winter
   2002–03), p. 135.
9. Charles Krauthammer, "The Unipolar Moment Revisited," *National Interest*, no. 70 (Winter
   2003), p. 17.
10. *The National Security Strategy of the United States* (Washington: The White House,
    September 2002), p. 1.
11. Christoph Bertram, "Shaping a Congenial Environment," *Survival* vol. 44, no. 4 (Winter
    2002–03), p. 141.
12. Tony Blair, "Building an International Community," Address to the Labor Party Conference
    October 2, 2001.
13. Charles Krauthammer, "The New Unilateralism," *Washington Post*, June 8, 2001.
14. Quoted in Bob Woodward, *Bush at War* (New York: Simon & Schuster, 2002), p. 81.
15. President George W. Bush, Remarks at 2002 Graduation Exercise of the U.S. Military
    Academy," West Point, NY, June 1, 2002, available at: http://www.whitehouse.gov/news/re-
    leases/2002/06/20020601-3.html (accessed August 2002).
16. Quoted in Jame Kitfield, "Pox Americana?," *National Journal*, April 6, 2002. p. 984.
17. Quote in Kitfield, "Pox Americana?," p. 986.
18. Quote in Bradley Graham and Robert Kaiser, "On Iraq Action, U.S. Is Keeping NATO
    Sidelined," *Washington Post*, September 24, 2002, p. A14.
19. George W. Bush, "Remarks to Prague Atlantic Student Summit," Prague, November 20,
    2002, available at http://www.whitehouse.gov/news/releases/2002/11/20021120-4 html
    (accessed January 2003); and "At News Conference: NATO Role vs. Iraq," *New York Times*,
    November 21, 2002, p. A19.
20. "At News Conference" (emphasis added).
21. Quoted in James Kitfield, "US to NATO: Change or Else," *National Journal*, October 12,
    2002, pp. 2978–79.
22. Kitfield, "US to NATO," p. 2978.

23. In a speech setting out Britain's foreign-policy principles, Blair listed as the first principle, "remain the closest ally of the U.S., and as allies influence them to continue broadening their agenda." Tony Blair, "Britain in the World," speech to the Foreign Office Conference, London, January 7, 2003, available at: http://www.number-10.ov.uk/output/page1353.asp.
24. Quote in Emma Daly, "Spain's Chief, on Bush's Side, Comes Under Attack at Home," *New York Times*, February 4, 2003, p. A12.
25. Colin Powell, "Remarks at the Davos Economic Forum," Davos, January 26, 2003, available at: http:// www.state.gov/secretary/xm/2003/16869.htm (accessed February 2003).
26. See Ivo H. Daalder, "Are the United States and Europe Headed for Divorce?" *International Affairs* vol. 77, no. 3 (July 2001).
27. Tony Blair, "Building an International Community."
28. For a representative statement, see *National Security Strategy of the United States* (Washington: The White House, September 2002).
29. Quote in Frank Bruni, "For President, A Mission and a Role in History," *New York Times*, September 22, 2001, p. A1.
30. Michael Hirsh, "America's Mission," *Newsweek: Special Edition* (December 2002–February 2003), p. 10.
31. George W. Bush, "The State of the Union," Washington, January 20, 2004, available at: http://www.whitehouse.gov/news/releases/2004/01/20040120-7.html (accessed March 2004).
32. As Bush recalled upon his return from the U.S.–EU summit, "I think Ronald Reagan would have been proud of how I conducted myself. I went to Europe a humble leader of a great country, and stood my ground. I wasn't going to yield. I listened, but I made my point. And I … patiently sat there as all 15 [European leaders] in one form or another told me how wrong I was" about the Kyoto accords. "And at the end I said, 'I appreciate your point of view, but this is the American position because it's right for America.' " Peggy Noonan, "A Chat in the Oval Office," *Wall Street Journal*, June 25, 2001, p. A18.
33. Quote in "Old Friends and New," *The Economist,* June 1, 2002, p. 28. See also Woodward, *Bush at War*, p. 281.
34. George W. Bush, "Address to a Joint Session of Congress and the American People," Washington, September 20, 2001, http://www.whitehouse.gov/news/releases/2001/09/20010920-8.html (accessed February 2003).
35. Donald Rumsfeld, "Press Briefing at the Foreign Press Center," Washington, January 22, 2003, available at: http://www.defenselink.mil/news/Jan2003/t01232003_t0122sdfpc.html (accessed February 2003).
36. David Sanger, "To Some in Europe, the Major Problem Is Bush the Cowboy," *New York Times*, January 24, 2003, p. A10.
37. Thus, in early Feburary no less than 18 European countries either signed a newspaper opinion article or open letter expressing their support for the United States over the issue of Iraq. See Aznar et al., "United We Stand," and "Statement of the Vilnius 1 Group," Feburary 5, 2003.
38. Quoted in Steven Erlanger, "German Joins Europe's Cry That the U.S. Won't Consult," *New York Times*, February 15, 2002, p. A18.
39. "Living with a Superpower," *The Economist*, January 4, 2003, pp. 18–20.
40. Quoted in Judy Dempsey, "Europe's Foreign Policy Chief Sees Widening Gulf with U.S.," *Financial Times*, January 8, 2003, p. 14.
41. Quoted in Judy Dempsey and Richard Wolffe, "Different View," *Financial Times*, May 2, 2002, p. 12.
42. Kagan, *Of Paradise and Power*, pp. 102–103.
43. George Washington, "The Farewell Address," February 19, 1796, available at: http://gwpapers.virginia.edu.farewell/transcript.html.(accessed February 2003).
44. The case for an "elective partnership" has been well made by James Steinberg, "The United States and Europe — An Elective Partnership," paper prepared for the Transatlantic Group meeting of the Bertelsmann Foundation, Florida, February 15–17, 2003.

PART TWO

THE VIEW FROM EUROPE

4

IMPERIAL LOOSE TALK

by Gilles Andréani

IN 1900 NO LESS THAN seven great states in the world called themselves empires. In Europe there were four: Russia, Germany, Austria-Hungary, and the Ottoman Empire. These were multinational political constructs, bringing a number of contiguous states or peoples under a unique rule, tempered by various degrees of local autonomy and a nascent parliamentary life. (Germany was more a multistate than a multinational construct, however, except for its Polish and Alsatian minorities; it was also a colonial power on the rise with possessions in Asia and Africa.) In addition two other powers combined the character of a democratic nation-state in Europe and a large colonial empire abroad: Great Britain and France (but only the British called their possessions abroad an empire). In Asia there were three empires: China, Persia, and Japan; the first two under foreign influence if not formal rule, the third a westernized nation-state that had itself embarked on an ambitious policy of colonial expansion.

Fewer than seventy years after, these empires disappeared, and with them, seemingly, the imperial idea and imperialist ideologies that had played such a dominant role in international relations from the late nineteenth century to the mid-twentieth century. The "central empires," along with the Ottoman Empire, fell apart as a result of military defeat in the first world war; Japanese imperialism, from defeat in World War II; west European empires, as a result of three waves of independence that freed their colonies from their rule: the American wave from 1776 to 1825, the emancipation of British dominions at the turn of the nineteenth century, and de-colonization proper following the second world war, a process more or less completed in the 1970s with the independence of the Portuguese possessions in Africa. The process of extinction of empires was concluded by the eventual downfall of the Soviet empire, remarkably the only one to pass without any meaningful violence.

THE DOWNFALL OF THE IMPERIAL IDEA: A SUMMARY

The reasons for the destruction of empires in the twentieth century are complex, if only because many different political constructs were subsumed under an "imperial" heading and each fell following specific causes and circumstances. But all in all, the two main forces responsible for the disappearance of empires were democracy and nationalism. These twin forces naturally manifested themselves at the periphery of empires. Those peoples subject to imperial rule naturally claimed greater autonomy, and then independence, as an educated elite borrowed these ideas from their rulers and turned them against them.

They also manifested themselves at the center, where imperial rule abroad soon came to be seen as contrary to democracy within. The co-existence of two different sets of norms, democracy at the core and authoritarian rule in one's imperial domain, was increasingly untenable and rightly seen as a cause of corruption for democracy within. Imperial ambitions, although they tended to blend with nationalism (sometimes in its most extreme, xenophobic, and racist form), were also often criticized by genuine nationalists as a distraction of moral and material resources from more pressing national objectives. (Clémenceau was the staunchest opponent of Jules Ferry's colonial policy on both grounds; as a democrat he objected to the very principle of colonization, and as a nationalist he claimed that France's vital interests were in Europe, not overseas.)

It is actually remarkable how successful these contradictions were in weakening the imperial idea sooner rather than later in the twentieth century. Following Wilson's fourteen points and the Versailles Treaty, not only did empires disappear from Europe's political map but also the legitimacy of colonial empires overseas was increasingly questioned. Under the League of Nations, the newly established mandates tended to turn colonies from what had heretofore been private property (literally so in the case of Congo) into a kind of tutelage to be exercised in the interest of junior peoples on a temporary basis and under public scrutiny. European colonial powers resisted this trend the best they could, but the prevalent international norms evolved to the detriment of the imperial idea. Italy's attack on Ethiopia in 1935—on the face of it not dissimilar to French or British expeditions in Africa fewer than forty years before—was condemned as an act of aggression by the League of Nations: this was not only a case of double standard, as the Italians saw it, but also a reflection of how fast the global mood had gone to weaken the imperial cause.

As the colonial empires of Western democracies rested on shakier legal and ideological foundations, the imperial designs of authoritarian regimes before and during World War II further delegitimized the concept of empire: Japanese expansionism was aimed at Western imperialism in Asia but was itself an imperialist design of the crudest kind. From both angles, it dealt a mortal blow to the imperial idea in Asia. Nazi Germany's brief imposition of "a new European order" was nominally the resurrection of a new German Reich. Although different in inspiration from the previous one, it also purported to be an empire. It showed the extremities to which the notions of hierarchy among races—a key justification of Western imperialism of the nineteenth century—could lead; that is, the physical destruction and enslavement of subjected peoples.

Altogether, by the end of World War II the idea of empire had been by and large discredited. The Cold War and Soviet communism somehow slowed its ultimate demise, however. The former forced the United States to moderate its traditional anti-imperial stance and to occasionally side by colonial powers as they fought wars they chose to characterize as wars against communism rather than as wars of independence (most notably France in Indochina). Soviet communism, having established its domination in Eastern Europe after World War II, in practice ran the last European empire in all but name. The Soviet Union thus was able to enjoy the support of the nonaligned movement against Western colonialism while remaining an imperial power, a twin privilege that ended in the early 1980s when the Afghan resistance and the Polish Solidarity movement turned the tide of global opinion against the Soviet Union, whose hegemonic character was exposed for all to see to an unprecedented degree.

From the 1940s onward, the name "empire" had thus assumed an essentially negative and polemical sense. It served both sides in the Cold War to denounce the true nature of each other's power, American imperialism versus the evil empire. It served thinkers like Raymond Aron in *République impériale,* or Paul Kennedy in *The Rise and Fall of Great Powers* to warn against the burdens and contradictions for American policy, which its leading role in the Cold War entailed, as well as to prophesy (more the latter than the former) its weaknesses and ultimate decline. But very few actually defended the notion of empire.[1] The downfall of the Soviet Union not only was the triumph of Western liberalism over communism but also could be construed as the ultimate defeat of the imperial idea by its twin perennial adversaries, democracy and nationalism.

A NEW IMPERIAL CREED

Under these circumstances, with empires and imperialism seemingly gone for good, the revival of the imperial idea in America following the end of the Cold War looks very strange. Actually, this revival has taken two distinct forms.

One form is a renewed interest in the historical roots of American foreign policy, and especially two of its forgotten traditions: one of them is a national populism going back to the origins of the Republic but most closely associated with the person and policies of Andrew Jackson in the early nineteenth century ("Jacksonianism," as described by Walter Russell Mead);[2] the second is the imperialist wave that struck America in the 1890s and that remains associated with Theodore Roosevelt and the Spanish-American war.[3] This scholarly and public interest was natural enough as America was wondering whether its Cold War policies and attitudes should go on or whether other traditions were not to be reexamined—a search through its past for examples to inspire its foreign policy in the future.

In addition, there was a second trend, associated with the neoconservative movement, that positively asserted that America should fully assume its dominant position in the international system, see itself as an empire or a hegemonic power, and stop pretending it wasn't. This latter trend drew on the former, which sometimes helped it take a positive view of the imperial episodes of American history. It further went on to revisit the role that cooperative and multilateral structures had played in the Cold War and that it deemed alien to the truest American tradition.

This latter stream of imperial revivalism, associated with the names of William Kristol, Max Boot, Robert Kagan, Tom Donnelly, and a few others, should normally be seen as an oddity in the history of ideas, one more chance to confirm Tocqueville's observation that America is a place where the strangest beliefs abound.[4] The events of September 11 decided otherwise and seem to have given these ideas a good measure of respectability and influence. The imperial role of America is now casually debated. The Pentagon is reported to have commissioned a study on great empires of the past.[5] As a result the notion that the time has come for an American global empire cannot just be put alongside black UN helicopters, millenarian and pagan cults, and other bizarre U.S. beliefs but now calls for serious analysis and discussion.

The new "imperial" school of thought rests on a number of key propositions whose starting point—America's role as the guarantor of last resort of the international system—is by and large uncontroversial, but from which it derives a number of highly controversial consequences. I sum them up below:

1. The disorder of the world can be addressed only if the United States assumes a global police role.
2. Willingly or unwillingly, this role will lead to (or will be best fulfilled through) the establishment of an American global hegemony.

3. This global hegemony should (or should not) be called an American empire, but the two notions are functionally broadly similar.[6]

4. This role will bring to the United States hatred and resentment from others, but this is a price empires have to pay (see: "the white man's burden"), and the events of September 11 showed these feelings to be there anyway.[7]

5. Indeed, these feelings (and the terrorist threat as a result) have been encouraged by past U.S. weakness, which now must give way to a policy of strength (and a positive and warrior-like relation to force).[8]

6. The U.S. imperial role has solid historical foundations: America inherited the liberal imperial role that Britain used to assume in the nineteenth century, and its own long record as a colonizer and an interventionist power is one of unparalleled success.[9]

7. The United States can fulfill its imperial role because its power is dominant in the world to a degree unseen since (or superior to) the Roman Empire.

8. The United States should maintain a military dominance such that its enemies (or any other state or group of states) would be deterred from even thinking of emulating it.

9. The United States does not really need allies and should stop pretending it does. Its European allies are enjoying the delights of Kantian peace and have turned their backs on the Hobbesian universe of world politics anyway. International law and organizations are respected in proportion of one's own weakness and are irrelevant (or positively harmful) to the success of America's imperial (or hegemonic) mission.[10]

10. The American empire (or hegemony) should be neither feared nor resisted by the world because of the unique benignity of U.S. policy.

To be sure, this is a slightly caricatured summing up of the views of the proponents of the American empire. They are different in style and include respected researchers like Robert Kagan, as well as political activists with less interest in academic ideas such as Tom Donnelly. They disagree on some issues, disagreements that the alternatives in the ten points above try to capture. For one, some of them gladly accept the term empire, but others reject it in favor of a terminology that avoids the E word (e.g., "benevolent global hegemony" or "liberal imperialism"). But these expressions evoke a dominance of America over the rest of the world whose limitations—liberal, benevolent—rest only with its inner goodwill, but whose scope—global—and degree—hegemony (synonym: domination)—can properly be labeled "imperial." Empires are political constructs that purport to exert power (empire and power are actually synonyms) on a large scale, including on other peoples, and by force if necessary. This triple component is by and large there in the authors I quoted previously.

As for the content of these points, lumping them together may make them appear more provocative or naive than they sound in the original, but each can be traced to the sources at the end of this chapter (e.g., for point 10: "It is because *American foreign policy is infused with an unusually high degree of morality* that foreign nations find they have less to fear from its otherwise daunting power [emphasis added]").[11]

FANTASTIC IDEAS FOR A FANTASTIC WORLD

Altogether, five main sets of criticisms can be directed at these propositions.

They are unspecific. What is so new about the threats America faces and the disorders plaguing the world that would warrant an American empire, as opposed to the existing structures (international cooperation, organizations and alliances, and American leadership), which have brought to the United States unprecedented success and to the world unparalleled progress in the form of the absence today of any conceivable prospect of a general war after centuries of conflicts and armed peace in succession? Empires brought peace and stability in exchange for subservience: with the risks to peace essentially local today, and the aspiration for democracy, that is, the rejection of subservience, at an all-time high, why should the imperial solution be tried again against all odds? More specifically, it is unclear in the previous quotes where the American empire stops and whom it includes. Is there a need for an American empire only to rule failed states (like Afghanistan) or hostile ones after defeat (like Iraq), in which case it would be a rather narrow and circumstantial empire? Alternatively, should an imperial rule substitute for the American leadership role, or has the latter become so compelling as to result in the former in practice, to include every country that is not an enemy of the United States? In fact, there is a little of both, which leaves ordinary foreigners like myself guessing the sense of the word *empire* as far as they are concerned: either hyperbole for the leadership the United States has enjoyed in the West for nearly sixty years or a much more ruthless kind of political influence where the difference between willing allies and countries subjected to forceful domination would be one of degree, not of nature (just like real empires used to resort to either direct or indirect rule).

They are ahistorical. What is so special about America that would make an American empire prevail against the forces of democracy and nationalism, a contest that no other imperial power has been able to sustain? The British precedent, to which Max Boot traced the current U.S. imperial role, is not an answer: Britain never was a hegemonic power in Europe but a force balancer that tried to tip the scales among roughly equal powers using a relatively limited amount of force (and failed to perform even this limited mission when it witnessed the rise of German power in the second half of the nineteenth century)—nor is America's own limited colonial experience: other colonizers were often well meaning and brought significant well-being and progress to their possessions. They had to give in all the same. Imperialism and empires as a usable political model are gone. Maybe the United States could be described as more powerful in relative terms today than the Roman Empire. Assuming this comparison had any interest, it would require some objective and timeless measure of power, one of the most protean and relative concepts of political science. But the Roman Empire rested in the end on two pillars: force (and more specifically cruelty and terror as casual tools of policy) and inclusiveness to the degree that all free men of the empire were granted the status of Roman citizens— two options incompatible with America's character, either as a sovereign nation-state or as a democracy, and that make any comparison between America and Rome an anachronistic fallacy.

They are misleading. The notion that it is weakness that breeds respect for international law and organizations is in direct contradiction with the fact that twice in the twentieth century, the United States, having emerged as the dominant power from both world wars, took the lead in asserting the rule of law and the role of global multilateral organizations at the center of the international system. In the aftermath of the Cold War, they reaffirmed that same choice by proclaiming the advent of a new world order resting on the UN and international law. This U.S. role did a lot to reassure others as to the "relatively" predictable and orderly character of U.S. power, much more than the benign character of America's inner self. (All countries see their own power as benign, and the force of that conviction is usually lost on foreigners.) Imagining that this benign character, however precarious in the eyes of others, would continue to make itself perceived to the world as the United States proclaimed an imperial policy unbound by any cooperative or legal framework would be a self-delusion of the worst kind. Moreover, every international system is a combination of relative strength, order, and norms. The militarily dominant power usually relies on force, but never on force alone. It also tries to shape the international order, to influence international norms, and to surround its own dominance with legitimacy. There is no such thing as countries that rely on force on one hand and those that rely on order and norms on the other hand: it is only a matter of different emphasis in the balance of those elements. The United States has used all three and will continue to do so. Some are fascinated by its dominance in the field of military force to the point where they advocate discarding the two other elements: such an option would have no precedent in history, could only lead to the estrangement of the United States from other nations, and, at the end of the day, is no option at all.

They are hierarchical. In the end empires are about ruling foreigners, more often than not without their consent. They are also about assuming toward the outside world a self-assertive and domineering attitude. The international legitimacy of empires was dependent on the acceptability of these hierarchical attitudes with regard to the prevalent norms of the day. Forcefully establishing and maintaining one's rule on other peoples by force was justifiable only in a world where societies themselves were hierarchical and where wars of conquest and the notion of hierarchy among peoples were acceptable as well. These two notions, however, have rightly become abhorrent to world opinion. The American military dominance may or may not be acceptable to other nations; it is a fact, and they have no choice but to adjust to it. They do so with various degrees of comfort, some of them with reluctance and resentment, especially when they see American military dominance used in a way they deem disproportionate, biased, or potentially detrimental to their interests. This is the dominant view in the Muslim world, and it is shared by major rising powers like India or China, whose interest in maintaining good relations with America is by no means incompatible with deep misgivings about its dominance. These misgivings, which are widespread, including in Europe, are not going to be eased by American statements to the effect that this dominance reflects the superior nature or morality of the United States, a view commonly expressed by the authors already mentioned. It is bad enough to be dominated, but seeing the dominant power proclaim its domination to be virtuous and just would be adding insult to injury. In the end it can only make matters worse.

They are un-American. America was founded by men of the Enlightenment, infused with a sense of decency, restraint in the conduct of political affairs, and faith in the limits that prudence and natural law should put to man's eagerness to transform the world. Along with these attitudes came a high degree of deference to the collective opinion of nations. Tom Donnelly and other contemporary American imperialists have come up with quotations of the founding fathers that describe America as an empire: Jefferson speaks of America as an "empire of liberty," Hamilton as Hercules in the cradle and as "one of the most interesting empires" of its time. But the meaning to be given to these quotes must take into account the fact that in the second half of the eighteenth century, empire (or its contrary, the nation-state) was not yet a defined concept. Modern "imperialism," and the world itself, had to wait another hundred years before they appeared. "Empire" usually meant "force" or "power" (as in "the empire of reason," or the above-quoted "empire of liberty") rather than any particular political organization, and, when it did, it was very vague: it simply meant a great state or a large reign. Although America's sense of being an exceptional people was very strong from the start, its sense of belonging to a plurality of nations of equal rights and dignity, a sense incompatible with an imperial creed, was equally strong. The *Federalist* praised "the attention to the judgment of other nations" and "the opinion of the impartial world" as "the best guide that can be followed" by America in case "the national councils [should be] warped by strong passion or momentary interest."[12] That is hardly an imperial attitude, but rather one typical of the cosmopolitan sense of moderation shared by the educated elite of the eighteenth century.

Altogether, the new American imperial creed rests on a set of beliefs that are extreme, and highly debatable, if only because of their anachronistic character and their incompatibility with the norms that dominate Western societies and the international system today. Rather than a series of refutable analyses, they form a cohesive worldview, which can properly be labeled an ideology. Despite this character they are now part of the American foreign-policy debate. They do not command much scholarly respect. Nor do they really seem to inspire U.S. foreign policy in any meaningful way. But, as an ideology, they matter, for two reasons: because they may influence U.S. foreign policy, even if it is more in style than in content, and because they have an audience in the United States and abroad, where they reinforce the worst stereotypes on American foreign policy in a world already deeply suspicious of its true motives.

WHAT IMPACT ON U.S. POLICY?

President Bush stated in his West Point speech in June 2002, "America has no empire to extend or utopia to establish." So much at least is clear. When it comes to actual policies, however, the notion of America as an empire is less easily dismissed, both in style and substance: first, because there are imperial undertones in the foreign-policy pronouncements of the Bush administration, and, second, because the nature of the American agenda in and around Iraq could well be labeled imperial, despite the fact that it is still unclear.

In style, one can detect, here and there, faint traces of an imperial language. President Bush sometimes refers to "the civilized world," an expression that belongs to the nineteenth century and was rarely heard in American foreign-policy speeches before his presidency. On various occasions he proclaimed the need for America to be feared by its adversaries, a pronouncement understandable in a post-9/11 world but that also echoes the Roman *oderint dum metuant* ("let them hate us as long as they fear us"). The neo-imperial creed indeed includes the notion that America was perceived as a weak power by its enemies and that the United States must now be shown as implacable. This administration has never hesitated to be intractable and confrontational when dealing not only with enemies and terrorists but also with those who merely oppose its views. These attitudes, however, are not exclusive to the neo-imperial group. One can only hope that in adopting them (sometimes at great costs to American diplomacy) the administration has not endorsed the proposed rationale, that is, that America was perceived as a weak power. Before 9/11 the world was by and large well aware, and often fearful, of U.S. power, especially in the Middle East. It may be even more so now, after the Iraq war, but victory over international terrorism will also entail winning the hearts and minds of the undecided. In particular, it will require winning those of the Muslim masses, who in the end will decide whether bin Laden and al-Qaeda were an isolated group or to some extent spoke for their grievances. This will be a decisive test in the fight against terrorism, one that America is less likely to win if it adopts imperial attitudes that further alienate world opinion.

Further to the vocabulary, America now claims for its military power a measure of superiority, as well as a qualitative difference, which may to some degree be a reflection of the neo-imperial ideology. The September 2002 *National Security Strategy* stated in this respect that America's forces should "be strong enough to dissuade potential adversaries from pursuing a military buildup in hopes of surpassing or equaling the power of the United States." (A previous statement in President Bush's West Point speech was even broader: "America has, and intends to keep, military strengths beyond challenge, thereby making the destabilizing arms races of other eras pointless, and limiting rivalries to trade and other pursuits of peace.")

This seems a pronouncement actually void of any prescriptive content, as America already spends as much on its defense budget as the next ten or twenty powers together, with none of them harboring any such hope or manifesting any intent of pursuing such a buildup. It is positively fascinating to compare these pronouncements with what the *National Security Strategy* has to say about others; China, for instance, which, "in pursuing advanced military capabilities that can threaten its neighbors in the Asia-Pacific region ... is following an outdated path that, in the end, will hamper its own pursuit of national greatness. In time, China will find that social and political freedom is the only source of that greatness." So much for China: military power is outdated as far as this country is concerned, while acknowledged to be a foremost concern for the United States (which, luckily for China, knows better than China where the latter's true source of national greatness lies). There, perhaps, is the most genuinely "imperial" aspect of American foreign policy today. This policy talks jubilantly, and perhaps too much, of American power, of how it differs from others', and of what it can accomplish for America and the world. This new, and positive, attitude of the United States vis-à-vis power, especially military force, may or may not be a good thing for the United States. (I personally happen to believe that it runs against the best American traditions, those on which the Atlantic Alliance mostly rests, and that it will be highly detrimental to America and Europe in the long run.) But it is fanciful to imagine that an America loudly professing such attitudes could continue to expect from others that they should stay clear from them and happily confine their own ambitions to "trade and other pursuits of peace."

An additional problem with such pronouncements, as well as with the preventive war doctrine, is that one can understand why the United States would want to do these things (prevent any conceivable competition in the military field or attack other countries before they attacked it), but hardly why it feels a need to boast in advance about them. After all, the prospect of any military competition against the United States is exceedingly remote. The need to implement the preventive war doctrine is certainly more real (*vide* Iraq), but it is demonstrably easier to do it under any other heading than preventive war, which is the one most likely to upset other countries and possibly American public opinion: in the case of Iraq, illegal weapons of mass destruction programs before the war, and regime change after, have been much more acceptable and effective rationales.

That is only talk, though. The truest test of America's imperial intentions will be what it chooses to make of postwar Iraq: either minimize its footprint, and the time its military stays in Iraq, as well as the regional goals their presence is meant to serve, or transform the country through an extensive stay and start to reshape the Middle East from there. This latter goal could itself have two versions: either a "liberal imperial" one aimed at bringing more rule of law, political openness, and fairness, if not democracy proper, to the region or a "hard imperial" one aimed at using the opportunity of a changed power equation in the Middle East to challenge and defeat all of America's potential enemies there. As the U.S. strategy will definitively emerge only over time, it would be premature to offer predictions. The result will no doubt be some combination of the hit-and-run, liberal imperial, and hard imperial scenarios. But of these three options, the one that has most suffered already is the second one, that is, the most genuinely imperial one: the Afghan precedent, the rapid drawdown envisaged for American forces, and the preference for self-appointed structures for the interim period, rather than ones involving the international community and Iraq's neighbors, do not bode well for the liberal imperial scenario.

Assuming the United States stays there, will it rule the Middle East from Iraq? The United States will exert a dominant influence there, just as it did after the first Gulf War, but at the expense of a much greater military presence and political involvement. But now, like then, there will remain nations like Iran, Turkey, Syria, and Israel, who tend to display different views of their national interests from those of the United States. They will presumably continue to do so. The Americans will be more than ever the dominant power in the region, investing themselves even deeper in its day-to-day political management. They will not necessarily own the place, and it must be granted that those most committed to the Iraqi war, such as Paul Wolfowitz, consistently said they did not want to.

The Middle East is the only conceivable place for putting into practice an American neo-imperial agenda. In the Far East, the United

States remains essentially a force balancer. In Latin America, the U.S. imperial role seems now to belong to the past. In essence, the neo-imperial ideology started from the Middle East and extrapolated from there. It is there that it will be tested on the ground. But its consequences are bound to go further. As America talks about its imperial role, the place where such talk is most heard, and is likely to do significant damage to America's image and interests, is Europe.

THE AMERICAN EMPIRE VERSUS THE EUROPEAN REPUBLIC

There is a certain paradox in the neo-imperialists' view of Europe. Some are highly critical of Europe, and especially of its support for international law and organizations. The best and most substantive neo-imperial view of the world was developed in contrast to Europe by Robert Kagan in his "Power and Weakness." Neo-imperialists often make disparaging comments on the Europeans (especially the French) and their alleged lack of taste for, or incompetence at, war in a way that reminds one of ancient American prejudices about the effeminate character of the old continent as opposed to the more manly and authentic American nature. (These characterizations are less than innocent, however. One should remind oneself that the extreme Right's language has always been replete with sexual undertones praising its superior virility and denigrating its adversaries as unmanly.)

For all this low regard for Europe, the neo-imperialists are aware that the imperial idea was born in Europe and knew many reincarnations in European history. They praise the British imperial heritage, which they think befell to America. (They seem to be mostly unaware of the French colonial past, though its universalism and dedication to France's *mission civilisatrice* should make it an interesting forerunner of the kind of disinterested and benign imperial role they advocate for America.) They are not alien to the idea of solidarity of the Anglo-Saxon or English-speaking nations, in a way reminiscent of Kipling himself. Altogether, they seem to desire for their imperial creed some European chic. A "new *raj*" is how they are reported to see the American empire.[13]

What they do not realize is how deep Europe's instincts against the imperial idea run. This is not recent and is in effect as old as European history. The notion of empire or "universal monarchy" has from the start been at odds with the fact that there was in Europe a plurality of political entities. The first ones to become modern states, France and Britain, fought forcefully against the closest thing there was to an empire in Europe, the Spanish king and the house of Austria. Even before the emergence of a Westphalian system of states, the idea of empire was widely rejected in Europe. The will of Charles V, which separated his Austrian from his Spanish possessions, reflected this fact. The Treaty of Utrecht, which confirmed the separation of the French and Spanish realms, confirmed it.

With the Enlightenment, empires came increasingly to be associated with "oriental despotism" and were regarded as a particularly primitive and un-European form of tyranny. At the same time, the Holy Roman Empire was praised (by Rousseau, notably) not for its aspiration to universal dominance, which it had long abandoned, but for being a commonwealth able to preserve the identity and the plurality of its constituent states. To be sure, it was deemed acceptable for European states to subject peoples abroad, because they were less advanced. Empires were permissible beyond Europe. But even so, they were initially more a result of the greed of merchants than a strategic choice of states. And the imperial idea was generally scorned by the *philosophes* whose universalism went hand in hand with a relativism that told how futile one's sense of superiority over foreign cultures was.

Gibbon described Europe as "one great republic." Such a sense that there was a European political construct consisting of states united by manners, religion, and a shared deference to international law (*jus gentium*) was originally developed by Voltaire and Montesquieu, who both used the term "European republic." It was embodied in the eighteenth century "Concert of Europe," which was successfully restored after the revolutionary and Napoleonic episodes (the ultimate demise of the Napoleonic empire itself being the product of these traditional anti-imperial forces, along with a newer one the French themselves had spread throughout Europe, namely nationalism). The European Union today rests on this ancient foundation, which combines unity with plurality and legality. The notion of an American empire thus runs against one of the most ancient and deeply held political traditions of Europe. If an imperial America should go beyond the realm of ideology into real life, it would deeply divide the Atlantic community and alienate America from Europe.

THE REAL AMERICA

America is not an empire. Its power does not translate into either a desire or an ability to rule foreign people, because it would not conform to the prevalent norms of the day both at home and internationally. The talk about an imperial America is an anachronism and is void of any serious policy prescription for the United States.

Such talk is nevertheless dangerous, because it encourages domineering, intractable, and confrontational attitudes that are the preserve not only of imperialism but also of nationalism. These attitudes include the fascination with one's own power, the confidence in one's own right, and contempt for weaker states. These attitudes are encouraged by the positive references to empire and the imperial revival that goes along with it. They run the risk of further alienating America from the rest of the world, especially Europe, where the imperial idea has been discredited, and is, deep down, alien to the political tradition of the continent.

As of now, all this is only talk. It is unlikely that it should ever translate into actual policies. But it is contaminating the style and undertones of American foreign-policy pronouncements. In this sense it matters. It also matters because the outside world's attention is focused on the American foreign-policy debate (despite its self-absorbed quality, of which the "imperial" talk is but a sign) to a degree that is perhaps the ultimate measure of the United States' dominance in foreign affairs today. What this talk adds to American options is unclear, but what it jeopardizes is only too visible: a certain sense of fairness and moderation in America's relationship with power and some of the respect this sense had won for the United States abroad.

Notes

1. An exception may be George Liska's *Career of Empire* (Baltimore: Johns Hopkins University Press, 1978).
2. Walter Russell Mead, *Special Providence: American Foreign Policy and How It Changed the World* (New York: Knopf, 2001).
3. Warren Zimmerman, *First Great Triumphs: How Five Americans Made Their Country a World Power* (New York: Farrar, Strauss and Giroux, 2002).

4. Alexis de Tocqueville, "De la démocratie en Amérique," *Livre II, Partie I*, Chapitre XII .
5. Dana Priest, *The Mission: Waging War and Keeping Peace with America's Military* (New York: Norton, 2003).
6. Robert Kagan, "The Benevolent Empire," *Foreign Policy* (Summer 1998). Kagan has strongly argued against using the word *empire,* however ("it would be a very bad idea and entirely inconsistent with the kind of nation the United States is"). Others, who are normally skeptical of America's imperial role, have recently labeled its global leadership an empire. Michael Ignatieff, "The American Empire: The Burden," *New York Times Magazine,* January 5, 2003; Anatol Lieven, "The Dilemma of Sustaining an American Empire," *Financial Times,* January 2, 2003; Christopher Hitchens, "Imperialism: Superpower Dominance, Malignant and Benign," *Slate,* December 10, 2002.
7. Max Boot, "Arab Street Needs a Signal of Strength," *Australian,* February 7, 2003.
8. On the consequences of U.S. weakness as perceived by bin Laden, see Norman Podhoretz, "How to Win World War IV," *Commentary,* February 2002. On the virtue of force and the need for the United States to have a positive relation to its use, see Robert Kaplan, *Warrior Politics: Why Leadership Demands a Pagan Ethos* (New York: Random House, 2002).
9. Max Boot, *The Savage Wars of Peace: Small Wars and the Rise of American Power* (New York: Basic Books, 2002).
10. Robert Kagan, "Power and Weakness," *Policy Review* 113 (June–July 2002); *Of Paradise and Power: America and Europe in the New World Order* (New York: Knopf, 2003).
11. William Kristol and Robert Kagan, "Toward a Neo-Reaganite Foreign Policy," *Foreign Affairs* 75, no. 4 (July–August 1996).
12. The index in my copy of the *Federalist* does not have an entry for *empire.*
13. The reference to the Raj is attributed to Tom Donnelly by Kevin Baker, "American Imperialism, Embraced," *New York Times,* December 9, 2001.

5

PAX AMERICANA AND PAX EUROPEA

by Wolfgang Ischinger

THE TRANSATLANTIC ALLIANCE has been the most integrated and successful alliance in modern history. Yet time and again, the relationship has gone through crises, and many books and articles have been written on this phenomenon—among them, Henry Kissinger's book *The Troubled Partnership*, published back in 1965.[1] Was Robert Kagan's essay "Power and Weakness"[2] just another contribution to this never-ending story of disputes within the transatlantic community? Or have we actually drifted apart this time, without a return ticket?

Seen from Europe, Kagan represents those U.S. neoconservative intellectuals who criticize Europe in an effort to legitimize American unilateralism. He perceives current differences between Europe and the United States not as transitory but as permanent. According to Kagan, Europeans and Americans no longer share a common view of the world, because they do not share a common view of the role and desirability of power. Kagan asserts that Europe has thus embarked on a Kantian path toward peace based on law and treaties, whereas the United States continues to see the world according to Thomas Hobbes, where order is based on power. Kagan believes Europe can opt for Kant only because the United States is prepared and willing to maintain order through power.

In this essay I attempt to present my own view of the transatlantic relationship and explain why I think Kagan's approach is, at best, incomplete and, in my view, flawed.

WHAT IS POWER ALL ABOUT?

Kagan believes that the "Euro-weenies" can be Euro-weenies because they know that, ultimately, they can rely on Uncle Sam. But do we really live in a Hobbesian world? Can power in the twenty-first century be adequately measured by the number of aircraft carriers or divisions? This is not to suggest that military power per se is no longer necessary. However, "soft power"—including the prudent use of the leverage provided by increased global interdependence—is vastly more important today than, say, a generation ago. Successful leadership today requires more than the ability to win military victories. It requires the ability to build consensus, to lead not through domination but through persuasion, and to make others appreciate such leadership—all in all, a huge challenge. And military power alone is not sufficient to meet this challenge. Let us take a look at the facts.

From Security Dependence to Economic Interdependence

The democratic West, under the unchallenged and unquestioned leadership of the United States, won the Cold War because of its joint strength. Europe and the United States stood shoulder to shoulder as they confronted the Soviet challenge. Each side needed the other. This era of transatlantic mutual dependence came to an end in 1989 when the Berlin Wall fell. The collapse of the Soviet Union in 1991 accelerated the transformation. The breakup of the Soviet Empire was, in fact, a geopolitical revolution. The bipolar system became unipolar. This is the central cause of America's new unilateralist potential. The Cold War played a major role in the formation and development of the transatlantic alliance. It should therefore come as no surprise that its end would have a tectonic effect on transatlantic relations.

No doubt, the end of the Cold War has led to the unprecedented global primacy of U.S. power. Some argue that the United States no longer needs allies to pursue its goals—America can go it alone. By comparison, Europe looks weak. Indeed, total European military expenditures have declined considerably since the early nineties. Kagan argues that the United States sees itself as the world's policeman, whereas Europeans have made themselves comfortable in a world of peace and multilateralism. He says that Americans are from Mars and Europeans are from Venus. But considering the European wars of the twentieth century, Europeans are not from Venus! We are the children of Mars, as German Foreign Minister Joschka Fischer put it, and he is right. Or, as Bob Dole put it, "Through their experience of World War II, the Germans have earned the right to oppose war."

It is true that we may live in a unipolar world when it comes to military power. The same cannot be said, however, of economic power. (Interestingly, Kagan did not devote a single sentence to the role of economics.) Today, power is determined at least as much by economic strength and interdependence as it is by military might. Not surprisingly, economic rivalries have intensified since the end of the Cold War among the transatlantic partners, equal partners in terms of economic power and weight. Numerous indicators for trade, foreign direct investment, and capital flows show that, in economic terms, the transatlantic region is highly integrated. In 1999, 45.2 percent of all U.S. foreign direct investment went to Europe, whereas 60.5 percent of all European foreign direct investment went to the United States. European investments in Texas alone are higher than all Japanese investment in the United States combined. Moreover, intrafirm business constitutes a large part of transatlantic trade. European subsidiaries of U.S. companies import more than one-third of all U.S. exports to the European Union (EU), whereas U.S. subsidiaries of European Union companies import more than two fifths of all EU exports to the United States. Six million jobs on either side of the Atlantic depend on transatlantic economic investments and trade. In addition 500,000 airline passengers cross the Atlantic in each direction on a daily basis.

Together the European Union and the United States account for half of the world's economy. Taken as a whole, the transatlantic market is highly integrated and growing even more so, despite ups and downs in the political relationship. As a result, the current global economic order is largely determined by the transatlantic economic relationship. Together the United States and Europe bear major responsibility for maintaining the contemporary liberal economic world order based on multilateralism and dispute-settlement mechanisms.

Common Values

Kagan argues that Americans today have different visions and aims than Europeans. Yet during the Cold War, the transatlantic alliance was forged not only by the perception of a common threat but also by the conviction that we had common interests to defend that extended beyond direct economic gain or the benefits of peace. These common interests were not exclusively of a material nature but also of reflected common values. Common political–cultural roots bind Americans and Europeans in matters of fundamental principles of human rights, the rule of law, and democracy, an ideal that European philosophers developed in the Age of Enlightenment, drawing on ancient Greek thinking. Europe and America thus share a common heritage that is still foreign to other parts of the world. The abrogation of the use of force as an instrument to advance one's own interests, as stated in the UN charter, has its roots in Euro-American political philosophy, reflected prominently in the Kellogg–Briand Pact of 1928.

Not only during the Cold War but also in the post–Cold War era did the Western community fight for its principles and values on numerous occasions, from the Persian Gulf War to the war in Kosovo. The war in Kosovo and the transformation of most of the former Yugoslavia into a Western protectorate was motivated by a shared interpretation of and commitment to humanitarian principles. Why, if one may ask, should this community of values end now? There is no evidence to support this claim—but much to support the view that 9/11 has, in fact, reinforced the shared belief in common Western values.

Common Challenges

Recent opinion polls by the Pew Center, the Chicago Council on Foreign Relations, and the German Marshall Fund show a remarkable degree of transatlantic consensus with respect to mutual sympathy, threat perceptions, and support for a multilateral order. More than two thirds of the European public sees the United States in the same favorable terms as most Americans view their major European allies. Overall, the United States and Europe continue to feel a strong affinity for each other. Interestingly, threat perceptions in Europe and the United States are also remarkably similar. Terrorism is considered on both sides of the Atlantic to be a top national priority. Europeans and Americans alike agree that religious and ethnic hatred constitutes one of the greatest dangers in the world. Even Iraq under Saddam Hussein's regime was almost unanimously viewed as a threat on both sides of the Atlantic. There was even agreement that Saddam should be removed from power. The big difference here is not about the threat but about how to respond to it.

Support for multilateral institutions is equally high in western Europe and the United States, particularly with respect to the United Nations, which continues to be seen as the sole legitimizing institution for the use of military force. These surveys stand in contrast to Kagan's assertion that Americans in general have become Hobbesian following 9/11. Apparently, only a small segment of the American people fits this profile. I would therefore argue that, on the whole, both Americans and Europeans are still Kantians (or Wilsonians) at heart.

There is, in fact, little evidence of a widening gap in overall views, general foreign-policy objectives, or mutual trust and sympathy. Europeans may resent what they perceive as American arrogance and missionary zeal, but, overall, there is more continuity than change, despite 9/11 and despite Iraq. It would be equally wrong to interpret critical European views of current U.S. foreign policy as a reflection of spreading anti-Americanism in Europe. The current dispute over Iraq is likely, of course, to highlight the differences rather than the areas of agreement. But, most likely, this particular gap will begin to narrow again once the war in Iraq is over.

Common Interests, Different Actions

There is an urgent interest, and even an urgent need, on both sides of the Atlantic to meet the common challenges we face, but there is little consensus on how best to confront them. In his "psychology of weakness," Kagan drew the analogy of a man with a knife who is vulnerable to the threat of a bear, whereas a man with a rifle can effectively deal with the threat. But are those really the only options—shoot or run? Surely, there are other alternatives. How about, for example, building a fence to stop the bear?

PAX AMERICANA?

The United States has been called a hegemonic power and a "hyperpower." But while the United States has been seen as a benign hegemonic power, the Soviet Union was a traditional imperialistic power. Hegemonic power rests on the willingness of the superpower to sustain an international order and to commit itself to the rules of that order. At the same time, it also relies on the readiness of smaller states to accept that order as legitimate. This was clearly the case in the Western world. European countries looked to Washington for leadership. But this was clearly not true in the case of the Soviet Empire. The main difference between imperial power and hegemonic power is that the imperial superpower only plays by the rules when it suits its interests. In other words, an imperial power sets itself above the rules that others have no alternative but to abide by. It is highly unlikely that smaller states will consider such an order legitimate. This was the case regarding the former Eastern Bloc countries, which had no choice but to follow the Soviet lead or be forced to follow it—as we saw, for example, in East Germany in 1953 and in Hungary in 1956. This lack of legitimacy added to Moscow's costs of maintaining its empire and is the reason why the Soviet Empire quickly collapsed once Moscow lost its grip on its constituent parts.

For the allies and for the sustainability of the transatlantic alliance (and also for the transpacific alliances between the United States and Japan and South Korea), the key question today is: What will the United States wish to be—a benevolent hegemonic power or an imperial power? Europeans are willing to continue to look to Washington for leadership. But what Kagan postulated is that the United States should act unilaterally if necessary, without taking the interests of its European (and other) allies into consideration. In effect he wants the United States to become an imperial power. That, to me, would, indeed, appear to be a recipe for creating and accelerating transatlantic drift, of which we have just had a taste during the Iraq crisis of 2002–2003.

Engaging in multilateral negotiations does not seem to be a natural reflex for the one remaining superpower, which is virtually a continent unto itself. But it is my strong belief that the United States should not, through unilateral action, weaken the legitimacy of the international order that it has helped to forge. By following the Kagan recipe, the United States could fall prey to the "arrogance of power," ignoring the warnings of Joseph S. Nye, Samuel Huntington, Senator Chuck Hagel, and others that even the powerful depend on cooperation by the less powerful.

Pax Europea?

The European Union is the only power in history whose geographical enlargement has not caused fears among nations or the formation of counteralliances. From the original six member states of 1951 and 1957, it grew to fifteen nations and now comprises twenty-five. Instead of inspiring resentment in nonmembers, it is regarded as the most attractive club to join. Why? Because the European Union is not a traditional strategic power.

The European Union has (not entirely correctly) been called a "civilian power," whose vision is to build a federation of democratic states and to strengthen the international rule of law through strong multilateral institutions. The European track record in the promotion of human rights, peace building, and conflict prevention, as well as in the protection of the global environment—that is, in key areas of "global governance"— is second to none in the world. There is a widely shared belief among Europeans that the root causes of transnational terrorism, the proliferation of weapons of mass destruction, and other current security threats are a lack of prosperity, democracy, human rights, and social justice in the crisis regions of the world. Europe is a leader in responding to these challenges—which, by the way, are the same challenges identified by President Bush in his 2002 National Security Strategy.

The notion of "civilian" or "soft power" sounds Kantian, but what is wrong with that? European Kantians are not pacifists. They do support the use of military force as a last resort. In 1998 one of the very first decisions taken by the newly elected German coalition government headed by Gerhard Schröder and Joschka Fischer was to participate in the military campaign in Kosovo in order to avoid a humanitarian disaster. After 9/11 Chancellor Schröder risked his political future to ensure German participation in the war in Afghanistan. He won the mandate in the German parliament by a majority of two votes. By becoming the lead nation of the International Security Assistance Force in 2003, Germany has assumed prime responsibility for stabilizing Afghanistan. But it is a widely shared view in Europe that military power has to be embedded in a clear political and diplomatic strategy and that military power alone will not resolve political conflicts.

In the Balkans, particularly in Bosnia and Kosovo, it became evident that the European Union was not able to look after its own strategic interests. The beginning of the Balkan wars revealed a disunited Europe. Today, there is consensus not only on that issue but also on relations with Russia, as well as with Africa, Latin America, and Asia. Although the foreign policies of the bigger member states—Germany, France, the United Kingdom, and Italy—still differ on procedure and style, they are quite similar in substance. Recent disagreements and demonstrations of European disunity in the case of Iraq will again, I am sure, have a sobering and revitalizing effect. We are in a very early stage in terms of creating a mechanism that turns alignment of interests into operational reality. But a coherent and common European foreign policy is not an impossible dream. Yes, European governments have been divided over Iraq; however, European publics have not. In fact, the Iraq crisis probably for the very first time created something resembling European public opinion, a consistent majority view. This may actually be quite useful in the effort to create a more coherent common European foreign policy.

The European Union is not a state with an army and a defense budget. Military and security issues are still largely in the hands of nation-states and subject to consensual voting in the European Council of Ministers and the committees of the European Security and Defense Policy. But a EU military role is evolving, as can be seen in Macedonia, where the European Union has taken over the task from NATO of stabilizing this country, which not long ago was on the brink of civil war. The European Union is getting ready to do the same in Bosnia.

Kagan asserts that Europe's weakness and its lack of international ambition is due to European integration. But Europe appears to be militarily weak only when compared with the United States. The European member states that belong to NATO spend as much on defense (about $160 billion) as Russia, China, and Japan combined. Britain, France, and Germany rank fifth, sixth, and seventh, respectively, in total defense spending in the world. Europe maintains substantial military forces. Germany has taken on ever-greater roles in both peacekeeping and peacemaking, sending more than ten thousand soldiers abroad since its landmark Constitutional Court decision in 1994 permitting deployments outside of the NATO region.

The remarkable shift in German attitudes and policy toward the use of force outside Germany, first in the Balkans and then in Afghanistan, goes completely unnoted by Kagan. Germany stresses peaceful, long-term treatment of the root causes of instability through foreign aid and development. But, when necessary, it is prepared to act militarily with allies to thwart terrorists or other threats. Yet, mindful of its history, Germany feels a special responsibility to balance leadership and restraint. And, surely, Berlin is justified in looking for clear legal justifications of military action, which should be considered only as a very last resort.

The problem of European defense is not so much a budgetary issue as it is an issue of duplication and redundancy. European defense industries have not yet been able to take sufficient advantage of economies of scale. Indeed, European integration is not the problem here; it is the answer. A European army is not yet in sight, but important efforts to start pooling military resources have already been undertaken. And the intellectual debate about a future European army is beginning.

Pax Europea has worked well. It is important to recall that, when six European countries embarked on the project of European integration, not only was eastern Europe under communist rule but Spain and Portugal (and later Greece) were fascist or military dictatorships. It was the attraction of the emerging European Union that fostered the democratization process in these countries, now all respected members of the European Union. Détente, Germany's Ostpolitik, and, in particular, the Helsinki process, which began in the early seventies with the first Conference on Security and Cooperation in Europe, deserve as much credit for undermining the Soviet bloc as does Ronald Reagan's effort to force Moscow into yet another round of arms buildup and thus push the already weakened Soviet economy into bankruptcy.

With its concept of Pax Europea, our continent is much more progressive than any other region. Economic growth in Europe may be lagging behind the United States and Asia, but, politically, Europe is dynamic and vibrant. The process of EU enlargement is surely the biggest and most ambitious regional security and stability program in history.

RECONCILING PAX AMERICANA AND PAX EUROPEA

No serious political voice in Europe wants to pit Europe against the United States. Pax Europea is not meant to replace Pax Americana but to complement it. America should continue to be a "European" power. Both the European Union and the United States have been and should continue to be integral parts of the transatlantic community.

Some U.S. strategists suggest, on one hand, that international terrorism represents an immediate threat to the survival of highly industrialized societies, while, at the same time, claiming that U.S. dominance in the world does not require allies. This is hard to understand. The events of 9/11 have demonstrated that the United States and other open societies are highly vulnerable both to high-intensity terrorist attacks and to low-intensity attacks, for example, through the use of biological agents. Terrorism, if anything, strengthens the case for alliances and joint action. In fact, new and effective international coordinating mechanisms and institutions to deal with such global concerns as transportation safety, container safety, and airport and airline security operations may be warranted.

Our societies are so uniquely linked by common security concerns, economic ties, and democratic values that the Atlantic region has become the most important zone of peace in the world. The Atlantic community and its achievements can and should serve as a model for the aspirations of societies throughout the world. NATO is an important part of this community, but only one part. Does the Atlantic community need a new institutional framework, a new transatlantic agenda?

In my view the Atlantic community does not need more military power. Instead, what we need is a coherent strategic debate to redefine our objectives, our priorities, and our strategic concepts, in particular, for dealing with the Greater Middle East and facing the challenge of proliferation of weapons of mass destruction.

Vegetius was right: to avoid war, you have to be prepared for war. Nevertheless, the best strategy for tomorrow is not preemptive military intervention but strategic preventive political action. The Atlantic community needs to be able to intervene nonviolently, persistently, and consistently on behalf of stability, democracy, and prosperity. Hasn't the "American way of life" done more for the growth of democracy in the world than the actual wars this nation has fought? But a decision to try to transform the Greater Middle East, to bring democracy to this entire region, should not be made unilaterally in Washington. If our objective is to focus the energies of the West on how best to work with this region and transform it, then we need a strategic debate on this endeavor, which is of Wilsonian dimensions.

The challenges that call for a multilateral, global-governance approach can be met only if Europe and America cooperate. What is urgently needed is a willingness by both the United States and Europe—along with their partners in the G8 framework—to begin a serious debate about our strategic directions and priorities. It is not good enough for Europe to be invited by Washington to participate in the implementation stage of a strategy defined by Washington. Europe has a right to be included in the process of both defining and adopting strategy, and it should say so.

A world order based on the rule of law, democracy, human rights, and market economy cannot be promoted by a superpower that places itself above the rules without being inherently contradictory. If it is a principle of Western democracy that no one—not even the most powerful—is above the law, then this principle should also apply to relations between nations. In my view the International Criminal Court is not so much about the protection of soldiers as it is about world order and, thus, about the values governing a liberal community of states.

Although the United States will need to withstand the natural temptations of unilateralism, Europeans have to understand that building a sustainable multilateral liberal world order is no fair-weather job, as the German scholar Thomas Risse put it. The occasional use of military force may indeed be required, but it should come embedded in an agreed political strategy of conflict resolution. In the words of Henry Kissinger, "The ultimate challenge for U.S. foreign policy is to turn dominant power into a sense of shared responsibility."[2] Europe is willing to pick up its share.

Thus, although the differences between Europe and the United States are substantial, they are not as great, as structural, or as lasting as Robert Kagan would have us believe. This is good news not just for the transatlantic relationship but also for the global community as a whole.

Notes

1. Henry Kissinger, *The Troubled Partnership: A Reappraisal of the Atlantic Alliance* (New York: McGraw-Hill, 1965).
2. Robert Kagan, "Power and Weakness," *Policy Review* 113 (June-July 2002).

6

THE POWER OF THE SUPERPOWERLESS

by Kalypso Nicolaidis

A ESOP, THE MOST POPULAR storyteller of ancient Greece, told the tale of the fox and his beautiful tail.[1] One day, to the fox's horror, a hunter shoots off his tail. The fox does not know which is worse, the pain or the shame. Then he hatches a plan. Proudly he rejoins his friends and announces that he has got rid of his cumbersome and impractical tail. Soon, there are no tails left in the land of the fox.

It is no wonder that Robert Kagan's seminal 2002 essay struck a chord in Europe, where commentators since then have competed to prove him wrong with ever greater vehemence in the wake of the war in Iraq.[2] Kagan assumed that Europeans, brandishing an external policy that seems devoid of all forms of real power, are, like Aesop's fox, simply making a virtue out of necessity. Having lost their power and appetite for war, addicted to welfare state spending and unable to muster the political will to rebuild a credible military capacity, European leaders present their meek civilian power as the ideal instead of the default option it really is. Accordingly, Europeans, rather than humbly and gratefully accepting that their Kantian paradise can only survive in a

Hobbesian world thanks to American military strength, fool themselves into believing that their own naive view of international affairs can and should prevail—thus assuming away the huge power differential that now exists between the two sides of the Atlantic. To many in the United States, Europe is not only irresponsible, indecisive, and irrelevant but also hypocritical.

Of course, Europeans must acknowledge that Kagan's view is right on many counts: that successfully building a zone of peace on their continent colors the way most of them see the world, that Europeans have achieved this peace under the umbrella of the U.S. security guarantee in the past half century, that the end of the Cold War has given Europe a peace dividend in contrast to continued military buildup for the United States, that there are places and instances in the rest of the world where the occasional use of military force by outside actors may be legitimate, and that they, the Europeans, have been unable as of yet to forge a meaningful post–Cold War strategy because of their disagreement over what such use of force means for them in practice.

But what if, beyond these undeniable facts, the tailless fox had a point? What if Europe's story of peace building had more relevance for the rest of the world than the U.S. story of liberal imperialism? What if *not to be the superpower*—or even *a* superpower—was itself the key to Europe's international influence? There is no single narrative in Europe to describe and guide this alternative project. Instead there are debates about a new European Constitution, a new European army, a new European agricultural policy, and, yes, a new transatlantic bargain. Make no mistake: at the dawn of the third millennium, Europe is reinventing itself as a global actor.

The paradox is as follows: for all its brilliant insight, Kagan's essay failed to carry through his own ultimate logic. Kagan believes that material conditions determine the ideological superstructure: the European view of international relations is the reflection, albeit mythologized, of Europe's weakness and its place in the balance of power. Moreover, in this classic (Marxist-realist) logic, European consciousness is blind to the very conditions that have led it to believe in the effectiveness of law and negotiation in the conduct of international affairs.[3] Yet in the end Kagan calls for Europeans to overcome their psychology of weakness and share the burden of global coercive leadership with the United States.[4] This is not a contradiction, as his critics too easily like to point out, if one believes that free agency can transcend determinism. And Kagan does recognize that the ideological gap between Europe and America has its own role to play in explaining the rift. But then because this gap is a function of power differentials, the circle is complete: weakness causes Europe's vision, which justifies its weakness.

If the psychology of nations matters, would it not be more consistent to take the Europeans' claim to relevance seriously? Why assume that causality runs only in one direction, that the ideas Europeans hold about the world are only a product and not a cause of its military weakness? If the latter can be the case, why assume a lack of self-consciousness on the part of Europeans? Why assume that there are no other bases for Europe's philosophy and behavior than power—or lack thereof? Why assume that in the post–Cold War era, Europeans would want, if they only could, to compete militarily with the United States? And why assume that in the rest of the world beyond "the West," a world presumably weaker than Europe itself, the materialist logic of history generally prevails over the institutionalist-idealist logic expounded by Europeans?

When Vaclav Havel wrote *The Power of the Powerless* twenty years ago, he may not have predicted the Velvet Revolution of 1989. But he described a world vying under an oppressive superstructure, where the capacity to connect and communicate with others, the creation of networks of understanding and signs of mutual recognition between apparently powerless individuals shaped an alternative reality where the long hand of the communist state had little purchase. Could the Europeans similarly yield their ultimate from exploiting the potentails of being superpowerless?

My aim in this chapter is to suggest that, whatever its own reckoning with the ambitions of superpowerhood, the United States would greatly benefit from a new division of labor with Europe, grounded on a recognition of the latter's comparative advantage; the real question is whether Europe will want to play. Such comparative advantage rests on three premises that build on and diverge from Kagan's account.

First, today's Europe is no longer Kantian by necessity, as Aesop and Kagan would have it, but by choice. The widening divide between the United States and Europe should not be attributed to some born-again European naïveté about power. Rather the divide is both less and more acute. It is less acute because most Europeans harbor little doubt about the relevance of power to world affairs, in all its forms. Conversely, most Americans believe in multilateral institutions.[5] The divide is more acute, because the European Union (EU), which increasingly shapes Europe's role in the world, is such a radically different entity from the United States.

Second, the rest of the world, far from being Hobbesian, is attuned to this European choice because both power and purpose matter in international relations: legitimacy translates power into effectiveness. In such a world, the promise held up by the "European difference" is great and lies in the legitimacy of the narrative of projection that the European Union seeks to deploy, that is, the consistency between its internal and external praxis and discourse. EU-topia is relevant beyond the shores of its own paradise.

Third, perhaps spurred by the fallout of the Yugoslav wars, 9/11, the Iraq conflict, and Europe's own divisions, Europeans are finally starting to engage in a debate not only on how the use of military power fits the European Union's raison d'être but on the relevance of power to the European project. It has been one of Kagan's great merits to expose the unspoken prejudices, implicit assumptions, and unresolved tensions underlying this debate in Europe.

THE KANTIAN CHOICE

The European Union, like the United States, was born in opposition to empire. But unlike the United States, this opposition was grounded in a colonial past, that of its constituent member states, which rendered suspect any talk of a civilizing mission as a basis for acting in the world. Indeed, the colonial notion of Europe as a vanguard that may have something to teach the rest of the world was the discourse invented to deal with an altogether more powerful underlying factor: Europe's fundamental security dilemma. This dilemma, the internal power rivalry and conflict between its constituent nations that have plagued Europe for the past four centuries, was exported around the globe—and in the process, the European space, self-conceived as the center of the world, became the basis for organizing its periphery.

It took two successive continental wars turned world wars to solve Europe's security dilemma. Initially, with the establishment of the European Community, institutions were created with the ambition of locking European countries in peace forever through supranational constraints on unilateral policies and the progressive development of community norms. These institutions were indeed Kantian in inspiration—the second Kant, who eschewed the first's recourse to a supranational government in favor of autonomous republics committed to relating to each other through the rule of law. Progressively, the new union replaced the old balance-of-power logic with the creation of what Karl Deutsch called a security community: a group of peoples and states integrated to such an extent that they derive their security from each other.[6] Within a few decades, this most ambitious of conflict-prevention projects had made war between European states unthinkable. But only with the end of the Cold War and the last remnant of the old belligerencies as they appeared in the breakup of Yugoslavia was Europe's security dilemma concluded for good. And with it, grounds in Europe for exporting conflict have simply disappeared.

Who denies it? It was the American conventional and nuclear umbrella that allowed Europeans the breathing space for so much fence-mending and fence-removing. Without this external military safeguard, it is unlikely that the European community could have been created—let alone evolved into a political union. The creation of a quasi federation without collective security as a driving force was an aberration of history made possible to a great extent by the United States.

Ironically, it is precisely at this historical juncture, when Europeans freed from their internal security dilemma no longer need this ultimate reassurance, that they seem to want to learn anew to project power externally to Europe's periphery and beyond.[7] But in great contrast with the past era of colonial rivalry, such power projection would be justified and sustained not by the need to maintain an internal balance of power but by the needs and ambitions of Europe as a whole. What are those needs? Are existing global threats sufficient enough to overcome

European historical inhibitions? What can such ambitions be, short of a modernized version of the *mission civilisatrice*? Can any such ambition justify the use of coercive power—by the EU or by its member states? To view Europeans as naive, free-riding wimps preempts the burning questions that are at the heart of our debates today.

To the extent that there exists the beginnings of a European answer, a global European narrative, its seeds have been germinating over the past half century in an ad hoc fashion, through a learning process that led Europe to accept and then embrace its distinctive approach to international affairs. Increasingly, Europe's Kantian approach is not utopian, or second best, but a deliberate choice, the most effective strategy it has found based on hard experience. In short, Europe is no longer Kantian because it is weak (militarily that is); it is now weak because it is Kantian.

The significance of this distinction should not be underestimated. Historically, relative weakness was a condition forced on countries by either domestic breakdown or external forces, or a combination thereof, as with the fall of Soviet Union. In contrast, European taxpayers have the means to provide themselves with stronger defense capabilities, and they already spend more than twice as much per capita on the military as any other power block except the United States. And although part of the reason for Europe's military weakness is no doubt a lingering belief that Uncle Sam can always come to the rescue, Americans consistently exaggerate the importance of this explanation.

CIVILIAN POWER AND THE IMPERATIVE OF CONSISTENCY

Instead, Americans need to understand how Europeans are revisiting and reinventing their own collective view on power. Yes, Europeans have a problem with power. They care about it but are unable (individually) or reluctant (collectively) to project it bluntly. We in Europe have come up with various labels for the Union reflecting this ambivalence, mitigating the bluntness of the assertion: quiet power, middle power, emancipatory power, postnational power, and, of course, civilian power. The labels are not simply exultations of Joseph Nye's soft as opposed to hard power. Nor are they lofty concepts to accommodate the psychology of weakness. Why would Europeans stop at that? Be they the arrogant French, the ambitious British, the cosmopolitan Scandinavians, the globally trading Dutch, the idealist Germans, or the Spanish or Greeks with their far-reaching networks, most European nation-states do not restrict their self-definition to the shores of Europe. The European unease with power is part and parcel of a powerful and compelling narrative still in the making: that of a union of postcolonial nation-states slowly and painfully constructing together the instrument of their collective atonement.

Already in the 1960s and 1970s, some saw the European integration project as evolving into a significant international actor of a type different from the two superpowers, one whose power was based on "civilian forms of influence and action," constructive presence, and the force of persuasion. As Francois Duchene famously argued in 1973:

> Europe as a whole could well become the first example in history of a major centre of the balance of power becoming in the era of its decline not a colonised victim but an *examplar* of a new stage in *political civilisation*. The European Community in particular would have a chance to demonstrate the influence which can be wielded by a large political co-operative formed to exert essentially civilian forms of power [emphasis added].[8]

It is of course tempting to dismiss the idea of civilian power as an oxymoron based on myth (peace through trade) and colonial nostalgia, as well as born of frustration at Europe's inability to become a third superpower during the Cold War. Yet the idea that the European Union can "lead by example" and project its relevance worldwide has been tremendously resilient to global changes, such as globalization and the end of the Cold War.

Perhaps the ambivalence of the concept of civilian power accounts for its longevity and its contestation. It is descriptive and prescriptive— valid as a goal even if not attained. It can refer alternatively to means or ends—*civilian* as *civil* means (e.g., nonmilitary) and as *civilizing* objectives (e.g., diffusing habits of peaceful change). Thus even if the alleged "sea-change in the sources of power" from military to economic was in doubt (as it is today), Europe's power would be sustained by its message. But that message too has been ambiguous or at least multidimensional. On one hand, it is about values, the values held by all its member states and promoted by the European Union, both internally and externally. On the other hand, it is about process. When Duchêne described the Community's "civilian form of influence and action," he not only referred to its economic rather than military strength, or to the democratic credentials of its member states, but also to its precious and transferable experience in intestate cooperation. In short, civilian power is a broader notion than soft power and can be wielded only by a group of states. It rests on the consistency and even synergies between the European Union's *being,* its political essence, and its *doing,* its external actions.[9]

There has been, since the beginning, a straightforward version of this story: the notion of European integration as a model for other regions around the world seeking to engage in deep economic and political co-operation. But with time, the European pretension to universal relevance has been chastised in light of the obvious idiosyncratic character of the whole affair and reaffirmed in light of its success in enlarging to a continent with half a billion people.

Accordingly, the European Union is the entity in the world that has the longest and deepest experience in aggregating collective preferences among nations. It is a grand-scale experiment engaging nation-states who seek on a continuous basis to accommodate each other's interests and reach consensus in two dozen policy areas at once. And somehow, in spite of the haggling, it works. Therefore, shouldn't European habits of cooperation and institutional frameworks be built on, not only in other regional contexts but also in tackling global issues? Why not see the European Union as a microcosmos, an explorer of new kinds of political deals between and beyond states? And isn't EU enlargement, with the concurrent dramatic increase in the differences of size, wealth, and political system within the Union, added evidence for the expansionary potential of the EU model?

Europeans like to argue that their continent is a microcosm precisely because, while European nation-states in the colonial era exported their internal conflicts, Europe has now become the place where many of the world's problems crystallize and get played out: refugee inflows and socioethnic tensions, transnational economic inequalities between north and south, the enlargement between west and east and the calls for redistribution and the pursuit of justice beyond the state, the controversial balancing of social standards and trade liberalization, the two-edged sword of free movement of people and capital, and the tension between liberal and conservative values in coordinating police and justice systems. So, Europeans have not only the institutional capital but also the substantive know-how to promote a shift in the global agenda toward better management of our commons. In fact, they have credibility.

It may be that such an ambition to act as a model beyond Europe can serve to compensate for the danger of the overly introverted nature of the EU. But the notion of "model" is too one-dimensional to capture the spirit of civilian power, at least in its sophisticated version. Such Euromorphism also makes many inside and outside Europe ill at ease. There is a fine line between ambition and arrogance, and arrogance is especially embarrassing when the model suffers all too many defects. As Clyde Prestowitz wrote about his own *Rogue Nation,* "a good mythology can cover a multitude of sins."[10]

How can its narrative of projection be reconciled with the postcolonial character of the EU project? In part, by systematically banishing the kind of dual standards that underpinned colonialist thinking, even on the part of such enlightened figures as Alexis de Toqueville. In his *Travail sur l'Algerie* (1841), the same man who explored with exquisite insight the requirements for a truly democratic polity on either side of the Atlantic came to advocate, albeit as a necessary evil, crop destruction, the kidnapping of children, and mass terror—in short, "total domination" and "devastation"—in the lands beyond civilization. More than a century later, the European Community would be the vehicle not only for solving Europe's internal security dilemma but also for addressing, modestly at first, the continued fallout from this historic shame and schizophrenia. The European Community both inherited the postcolonial guilt of its member states and provided an institutional venue to assuage that guilt, a venue that would be less vulnerable to accusations of neocolonialism than individual member states' diplomacy. Irrespective of the relevance of the EU model for the rest of the world, the narrative of projection associated with civilian power refers to the praxis of the European Union and the exigency of anti-Tocquevillian consistency between norms of internal and external action. Duchene saw the European Community's raison d'être "as far as possible to *domesticate* relations between states including those of its own members and those with states outside its frontiers. This means trying to bring to international problems the sense of common responsibility and structures of contractual politics which have in the past been associated almost exclusively with 'home' and not foreign, that is alien, affairs." Treating abroad as home could be taken as the ultimate promise of civilian power thinking in the post–Cold War era.[11]

The imperative of consistency helps highlight the commonalities and the profound differences between European and American exceptionalism, their respective sense of being in a unique position to guide humanity toward a better future. There is of course a common "Western agenda" in the spread of a political model, whether or not its dominance has heralded the end of history. Indeed, historians like to point out how the most intense transatlantic rivalry, that between France and the United States, is rooted in their similar sense of mission, of being the upholders of political and philosophical models for the world through the avowedly universal reach of their respective eighteenth-century revolutions. Both the United States and the EU think of themselves as normative powers promoting externally the adoption of their internal norms of democracy and human rights. Although there may be significant differences in their respective versions of these norms, their views of state-society relations, of secularism, or of the acceptable limits of institutionalized violence like the death penalty, it can be argued that these differences are but variants of shared core beliefs.[12]

Nevertheless these two competing exceptionalisms are of a different kind. Their respective founding myths—the escape from despotism and the escape from nationalism, tyranny from above and tyranny from below—led both entities to elevate commitment to the rule of law as their core. But this was domestic law in the United States, supranational law in the European Union; this meant checks and balances between branches of government on one side, between states on the other. While the United States progressively became a federal state, the European Union, admittedly still in its infancy, is braced to remain a federal union of nation-states.[13] In the past two decades, while the United States and the European Union have been fertile grounds for exploring "subsidiarity" and multilevel governance, the European Union alone has explored ways of doing this without coordination by a centralized state, through methods that might one day be relevant to global governance. U.S. exceptionalism is a national project; European exceptionalism is a postnational one.

As there were two Kants, there are also two Fukuyamas, and Europeans are closer to the pessimist one: the need for mutual recognition and separateness endures. The European Union's real comparative advantage lies less in engineering convergence among its members' policies and more in its capacity to manage enduring differences between nations. At its core, the European Union is about institutionalizing tolerance between states.[14] A byword for the European project may be empowerment, mutual empowerment by all actors in the system. This is why contrary to the United States, the European Union is less interested in exporting democracy in ready-made packs than in seeking ways to empower local actors to determine their destiny, even if and when they mess it up. And this is why, although the European Union could never hope to rival the United States in effectiveness and decisiveness, it can surpass it in legitimacy.

We are back to the old adage: the medium is the message. Americans believe that their example is so powerful that the use of soldiers and guns to implement it is legitimate. Europeans believe that their example is so powerful that its promotion requires neither soldiers nor guns.

One may in the end dismiss it as a product of weakness, but one must first do justice to this European narrative of projection. It is on the basis of its own trajectory that the European Union can claim or aspire to influence international relations. And this trajectory in turn may be about curbing the capacity of states to do harm. But it is not beyond power. There is no doubt that this half-century affair has accustomed Europeans to the belief that pooling sovereignty with other states is not only a constraint but an empowerment. Yet, to describe the European Union as having taken Europe into a post-Westphalian era devoid of power politics is closer to myth than reality. In the European Union, power is mediated—not eliminated. Institutions mandated to pursue the common good have been created to balance those where the size of a member country's budget, population, and, indeed, army, matters. And European multilateralism does not easily work without leadership, be that of the Franco-German couple, of a Tony Blair or of a Jacques Delors.

Pushed to its ultimate logic, the European Union is less a model to be emulated than an experience, a laboratory where options are explored for politics beyond the state, a toolbox for non-state-based governance, a pioneer in long-term interstate community building. In this vision the European Union is one of the most formidable institutional machines for peacefully managing differences ever invented; there is no reason to think that nothing in this experience is relevant to other regions, or indeed to governance at the world level.

This does not mean that Europeans should display moral certainty about their "gift" to the world. Actually, their enterprise is predicated on a great degree of moral and political doubt. For the imperative of consistency between "who we are" and "what we do" is a tall order—as Americans have come to better recognize since their abroad came home to haunt them on September 11, 2001.

Indeed, Europeans are far from having taken such a postcolonial vision of their role in the world to its ultimate logic. This would entail that the internal development of the European Union be guided by the kind of inspiration it wants to provide. It would also mean that everyone of its internal decisions be checked and corrected for its external impact, starting with its agricultural policy. It would mean granting significant voice in our own affairs to those most affected by our actions, thereby implementing a philosophy of reciprocal intervention and mutual inclusiveness with our partners around the world. It would mean setting an example in the global politics of mutual recognition.

Ultimately, absolute consistency is about our treatment of others as we move from our relationship with the "other" European to our relationship with the non-European "other." It is grounded on the cosmopolitan belief that there is no radical separation between a national, European, and universal community of fate, even if there is indeed a gradation in the amount and range of common uncertainties to be faced and managed. Europeans are not there yet, but they have the potential, through the European Union, to move beyond the relationships of dominance and exploitation with the rest of the world that have characterized much of their history.

CIVILIAN TOOLS AND TIES

As they stand today, the European Union's external relations (as distinct from that of its member states) pertain more to the biology of reproduction, contagion, and osmosis than to the physics of force, action, and reaction favored by the United States. Consistency requires that the European Union follow its own guiding principles when acting beyond its borders: integration, prevention, mediation, and persuasion. It tries, more or less, consistently.

In the EU lexicon negotiated integration through free trade is the tool of choice, but it leads to and is predicated on other types of integration—between regulators, judges, administrations, political parties, trade unions, and civil societies. Integration also has meant giving structural aid to poorer regions to compensate for the pains of adjustment to a common market. The European Union has similarly structured its external relations. Although still wanting, its growing aid budget, technical assistance, and nation-building programs reflect the expectation of its citizens that the state should fulfill a wide range of socioeconomic and political functions—abroad as well as at home.[15] Enlargement, perhaps the most successful instance of EU foreign policy, has been predicated on the combination of selective aid and the forging of multilevel partnerships with potential new members. In its so-called wider neighborhood, the European Union has sought to apply its model of multifaceted integration including through the forging of a Euromed region—which admittedly has fallen pray to the Israel-Palestinian conflict. Beyond, it engages in preferential trade deals with political significance, from the Lome conventions renewed since the 1960s to its latest free trade initiative toward least developed countries, "Everything but Arms" (everything except, of course, agriculture). And its approach to integrating markets through mutual recognition of norms and regulations has become contagious worldwide, largely through its own proselytizing zeal supported by conditional access to its 8 trillion euros interval-market.

Second, like the United Nations, the European Union was invented as a conflict prevention machine. On the external front, it has been engaged in developing civilian capacities capable of preventing conflicts and managing their aftermath, using diplomacy combined with economic and technical assistance to avert crises (because the highest predictor of future conflict is the occurrence of past conflict, the latter can be considered as part of the overall strategy of prevention). The civilian element of the EU's defense policy—exporting capacity in policing, the rule of law, civilian administration, and civil protection—represents a sophisticated attempt to anticipate the requirements of nation building in conflict-prone regions. The EU's expertise in monitoring compliance is a key to the success of conflict prevention regimes, be they related to arms trade, weapons of mass destruction, or money laundering.

Third, the EU's reputation as a civilian rather than military power makes it a mediator of choice, where peacekeeping forms part of a more integrated mediation process. Its claim to impartiality (if not always neutrality) is the more credible given that European states have often found themselves on different sides of a conflict on historical grounds, whereas the European Union is seen as having incorporated and transcended these differences. Moreover, this reputation is strengthened by the rising prominence and access to decision-making on the part of "development" nongovernmental organizations in the European Union (which funds three thousand of them) and their insistence that intervention abroad reflects ethical and sustainable development imperatives. In the past decade EU representatives have engineered new approaches to bottom-up national reconciliation processes in a number of war-torn societies, from the Balkans to Central America and the great lakes of Central Africa, through inter alia the funding of institution building and action by nongovernmental organizations on a previously unprecedented scale.

Finally, with its culture of compromise and debate (to the point of indecision), the European Union is bent on acting through persuasion. Even internally it operates increasingly through publicity and emulation rather than mandatory law (a process know as the Open Method of Coordination). Similarly, externally, persuasion is at the heart of constructive engagement. For instance, the European Union has become a norm setter through multifaceted persuasion campaigns in the past few years, using its financial muscle to give a voice to transnational civil society—such as in the case of its multifaceted campaign for the abolition of the death penalty, which has already claimed success in several dozen countries.[16]

Obviously, none of these policy tools are specific to the European Union. More often than not its dealings with the rest of the world are a reflection of asymmetric power, rather than a cosmopolitan ethos that would require significant sacrifices in the name of global solidarity. Nor does the European Union's increasingly assertive role as a mediator and peace builder within states reflect the notion that the rights of people must now trump the rights of states internationally. Nevertheless, the European Union is unique precisely because it brings to its relations with the world the multiple ties borne by its different member states, cultures, and histories. Beyond the panoply of civilian power tools, the EU's claim to the title of normative power may just about withstand its colonial connotation if the core norm it seeks to promote through negotiated integration and mediation is that of peaceful coexistence between groups or nations.

A HOBBESIAN WORLD?

Meanwhile, Americans cannot be faulted for dismissing the European Union when European leaders are only now coming to recognize what an effective European foreign policy could and should look like. And it would be naive to believe that strategies of integration, prevention, mediation, and persuasion are always enough.

In tragic-realist mode, Kagan argued that consistency between who we are inside and what we do outside is a luxury, reserved for those who have removed themselves from our Hobbesian world, a world in which practicing the kind of double standards the United States is accused of practicing is a matter of survival. In such a world a lone policeman cannot afford to behave in civilian ways. Negotiation gives way to coercion, and multilateralism gives way to unilateralism. Those who analyze the world in this way pride themselves on realism—their ability to see and understand what is really going on out there. But the

European approach is not less realistic; it is simply predicated on a different diagnosis about the world and how to deal with it.

To be fair, Kagan is not an absolutist. He sees the coherence of concurrent worldviews by strong and weaker powers. It is true that Americans and Europeans disagree on the nature of the threats, not only on the ways to address them, as wishful thinkers would have it. It is true that Europeans may discount threats they feel powerless to address. It is true even that Europeans tend to focus on failed states whereas the United States focuses on rogue states. But does this mean there is no fact of the matter here? Does this mean that neither side is ready to argue for the validity of its understanding of the world? Kagan did not go that far in his relativism. Realities of the world beyond are not all in the eyes of the beholders. In the end the United States must be relied on to deal with the real threats to us all: "only the hammer sees the nails."

There is an alternative liberal-institutionalist view, a view that is not only European. Accordingly, the current U.S. government has become focused in a curious Schmittean way entirely with the exceptions, those relatively few states that flaunt totally the norms of the international systems. Yet although Iraq, North Korea, and Zimbabwe make the headlines, the simple fact of the matter is that the number of countries in the world where relationships cannot be managed through the rule of law has been shrinking since the end of the Cold War. Our world is not a Hobbesian landscape beyond the Kantian European island, full of rogue states bent on destroying the civilized West. Instead, democratization, even if imperfect, even if too often illiberal (as if mass elections alone could mean democracy), has been the trademark of the past decade. A great majority of countries in the world have affirmed their commitment to European arguments, particularly about the importance of international institutions and international law. They must at least be given the benefit of the doubt. In short, and in this third millennium, much of the world has embraced, if not mastered, bourgeois politics— a politics beyond violent death.[17] The progressive socialization of governing elites as well as the growing interconnections between civil societies around the world has meant that zones of democracy by contagion and democratic peace coexist with zones of chronic instability. And indeed, conflict and instability in these zones are more often than not due to the idleness and despair spurred by the chronic poverty, un-employment, and corruption associated with failed states and corrupt governments than to the provocations of rogue states. The revolt of the alienated, which defines our era like so many others, cannot be put down with guns.[18]

Of course, this does not make the threats of terrorism and weapons of mass destruction less real. For the current U.S. administration, this Schmittean focus on the exceptions is justified because the greatest danger to humanity today are the few hard cases the United States is bent on tackling by force if need be. Clearly, Europeans must recognize more explicity that rogue states and other Hobbesian realities need to be dealt with. But they are right not to see these threats in isolation. Having learned from their own historical experience, they fear negative spillovers and the spread of conflict as much as they value positive spillovers and the spread of cooperation. They imagine scenarios—as many did in the case of Iraq—in which our very actions in these cases contribute to an enlargement of the Hobbesian zones. Acting as if the world is Hobbesian can be a self-fulfilling prophecy, increasing the likelihood that it would be so. Their fears may sometimes be misplaced, but they are not unrealistic. It was wrong to forecast an explosion of the Middle East after the war in Iraq, but instead Americans have created a magnet for terrorism.

Moreover, even when dealing with rogue states, terrorism, and weapons of mass destruction, civilian tools are of central importance. Rogue states often start as failed states, captured by dictators and thugs, and they become failed states after their downfall. As the situation in postwar Iraq amply demonstrates, the challenge of rebuilding societies takes more than military force. And here too the European Union's experience, the design of loose federations and the concept of limited sovereignty, refined over the years by the very states who invented sovereignty four centuries ago, can inspire the reconstruction of troubled countries and regions.[19]

In this debate suspicions of false consciousness can be turned onto the United States. Do Americans (or at least some in the U.S.) need to overemphasize the new terrorist threat and the Hobbesian quality of the world because with the end of the Cold War they lost that "other" that was necessary to their own unity? Do they need to undervalue the effectiveness of international institutions because classical external sovereignty is the only collective cause they can agree on? How is it that the pursuit of moral certainties happens to never contradict American economic and geostrategic interests? The world may indeed look different seen through the lenses of power or weakness, but power does not buy lucidity.

FROM MILITARY TO EMANCIPATORY POWER

The question remains, Where do Europeans stand on waging war? Their version may differ with Americans' version of a Hobbesian world. But the wars in Yugoslavia and beyond in the past decade have served as a stark reminder of the Hobbesian faultlines that the European Union cannot ignore. As a result, the end of the Cold War has led to a profound rethinking of the civilian power concept, stretching its elasticity and ambiguity to its limits, without yet making it obsolete.

Here, as elsewhere, let us not exaggerate change over continuity. Individual member states such as France, the United Kingdom, or Greece have never eschewed military power, commensurate of course to their size. The postcolonial echo, whether in Africa or the Middle East, has led to continued arms sales and military agreements with countries around the world, including on the part of states such as Germany. In the past decade, the defense establishments in European capitals have been willing to deploy military forces to respond to humanitarian needs or state failure, such as Sierra Leone or the Ivory Coast. And they have been largely supportive of the U.S. line on fighting terrorism—as witnessed by NATO's invocation of Article 5 after 9/11.

The real *new* question today for Europeans lies with their common post–Cold War project, the EU banner. The European Union pertains to a different logic than that of member states, even if it is the result of their interaction. During the Cold War it anchored Europe to the United States by serving as its regional pacifier.[20] By channeling existing disagreement among member states (often France versus the rest) as to the extent to which Europe should rest content to play second fiddle to the United States, it enhanced the predictability of its member states' foreign policies providing not only the European but also the transatlantic glue. We have come to a historical juncture, however, where this logic is reversed, and it is the very existence of the European Union that is making the prospect of Europe as an autonomous power a plausible proposition. Europe's new constitutional treaty is one more small step in this direction. Should it worry Washington?

To be sure, there is no consensus in Europe today on the necessity of giving the EU the capacity to defend itself outside NATO—a European Article 5—not only because there is still a majority of governments in Europe who believe that the United States is and should remain a European power but also because direct threats to the territory of European states seem so remote. At the same time, most of the political spectrum in Europe (even formally neutral member states) calls for a greater capacity for autonomous military intervention around the world, a view shared by a majority of European public opinion. Indeed, as of 2003, the European Union did have its own rapid reaction force (even if falling short of its own headline goals), as testified by its presence in Macedonia and Congo.

It is therefore more urgent than ever to ask how can the European Union's broader civilian mission to tame the capacity of states to harm others born from Europe's pre-1945 history can be made compatible with the use of force in the twenty-first century. Only with the aftermath of 9/11 has this question been conflated with Europe's relationship to the power of the United States.

Obviously, Europeans have not reached a collective answer and are not likely to for some time. Nevertheless, the terms of their debate do not boil down to an old pro-autonomy versus a new pro-American Europe. Most Polish supporters of the United States in Iraq would welcome a European defense, whereas many Europeans opposed the war in the name of pacifism, not anti-Americanism.

Arguably, the most important divide in Europe today is between those loyal to civilian power thinking who view any European military involvement beyond peacekeeping with suspicion and those among European elites, especially in Britain and France, who extrapolate from today's incipient common security policy and envision the European Union moving beyond the confines of civilian power altogether:

l'Europe puissance, or superpower Europe. For the latter, as for Kagan, civilian power was but a second best, and the European Union should now learn to behave like a military power and magnify the power of its member states—be it to supplement and restrain (i.e., the United Kingdom) or balance (i.e., France) American power.

Is there a middle way? Can enhanced military power be compatible with civilian power?[21] Indeed, it is hard to see how the projection of credible military power would not entail the kind of collective exclusivist identity, power hierarchies, and unified centralized leadership eschewed until now by the European project. Europe is not and should never become a state writ large. But too many in Europe still confuse their *exigence d'Europe* with such a goal. In this regard, the current constitutional moves to provide the European Union with a president is exemplary of a trend to replicate the national model on a European scale and put at its apex a *directoire* of big states à la de Gaulle: a trend worrisome to smaller countries in the European Union as well as to those among us attached to the unique nonstatelike character of the union.[22]

And yet, spurred in great part by the schism within Europe over Iraq, all sides of the debate recognize the need today to try to forge a common EU strategy, a response to the annual *National Security Strategy* of the United States. "As a union of 25 States with over 450 million people producing a quarter of the world's GNP," affirmed the first ever EU security strategy paper, "the European Union inevitably is a global actor… it should be ready to share in the responsibility for global security" and address the main threats of our era, namely, "terrorism," proliferation of weapons of mass destruction, regional conflicts, failed states and organized crime.[23] While an early mention of "pre-emptive engagement" was replaced in the final draft by a milder appeal to "preventitive action," the new strategy paper signalled a definite commitment on the part of the EU not to shy away from forceful intervention. How should this be done in the spirit of civilian power? For one, it can be done by making military means one among a panoply of means, and in fact derivative. The document advocated widening the EU's spectrum of missions in addition to the Petersberg task (peacekeeping and reconstruction), including "joint disarmament operations, support for third countries in combating terrorism, and security reform in the broader context of institution building."

Most important, there cannot be "war ends" or war aims per se for today's Europeans. Instead, military force must be used only to increase the international community's capacity to pursue civilian ends, as in the case of Kosovo, after all other means in the aforementioned panoply have been tried. This is what Europeans mean when they speak of force "as a means of last resort." The European divisions over Iraq obviously reflected different national attitudes toward American power; they also reflected different assessments of such a "last resort" threshold: Had all other means been exhausted? If war was the only means left, for what ends? Would it not be more legitimate to frame this intervention as humanitarian, even if international law lagged behind?

Some of us may never reconcile ourselves with the fact that more on either side of the debate did not see the issue of war in Iraq as a truly agonizing choice. Nevertheless, lessons from this crisis will continue to be drawn for years to come as the consequences of the war unfold. How much transatlantic convergence can there be on the use of force? Can the two sides agree that military means make sense when (for Europeans), if and only if (for Americans), they constitute the only way to create a space for meaningful civilian presence and the pursuit of goals largely shared locally and internationally, and that the judgment involved in determining last resort must be validated by the international community, lest it be tainted by the narrow pursuit of narrow geopolitical or economic self-interest?[24] The EU must stubbornly keep on the table the core bargain eschewed by the United States in the case of Iraq: acceptance by the United States on limitation of its power in exchange for legitimation.

Just as Americans may come to admit that it is impossible alone to label a war "liberation" and to win the peace, Europeans will wrestle with that other possible world without regime change where Iraqis would have continued to be tortured en masse. Were Europeans right to derive an uncompromising antiwar stance from the rightful precept that democracy cannot be imposed by force, should "come from below" and be earned and learned collectively? Or on the contrary, is war not sometimes necessary to unlock the door for democracy, create the possibility of home-grown democracy and the rule of law? Either way, the right—and, beyond, the duty—to intervene, the fragile emerging notion that sovereignty must be deserved, is too precious to be left hostage to our well-founded distrust of American motives.[25]

But if the crucial issue for Europeans is not the use of force per se but its legality under international law, then they must do something about the law, not about the use of force. In this vein, bringing together the human rights and security wings of the United Nations, adapting the need to use force to circumstances not foreseen in 1945, would be central to a future global European agenda.[26] Actually, Europeans should be the first to applaud a thorough revisiting of the Westphalian principles of sovereignty under the UN aegis as they have done under the aegis of the European Union. But will Americans contemplate institutionalizing a concept of limited sovereignty they would never apply to themselves? And is the international community likely to embrace this agenda? Let this then be the European Union's lone battle.

In fact, Europeans, if consistent, cannot rest content even with such prospect. It is not enough for intervention to be blessed by a multilateral stamp in order to qualify as nonimperial. Its results, its substance, matter. If truly postcolonial, Europeans must continue to render symmetric the relationships established by intervention, military or financial for that matter, to systematically free such intervention from elements of domination. If the European response to American liberal imperialism is to become an emancipatory power, whose goal is to allow peoples beyond its shores to forge their own destiny, it must define (or redefine) power as the capacity to empower others.

But then again, the most fundamental divide between Europeans and Americans no longer concerns constraints on the use of force but on its possession. Today, just as Europeans converge toward American assessment of significant threats, the U.S. government has already moved on to declare its plan to build up beyond threats. Europeans ask: Is this the way we can agree to be jointly responsible for global security? Is bailing out of the Comprehensive Test Ban Treaty, the Anti-Ballistic Missile Treaty, or obligations under the Non-Proliferation Treaty the most effective way to guard against a resumed nuclear arms race? The transatlantic security community symbolized by NATO should still be the core of world order. But as Europeans see it, it is not their own desire for some modest autonomy but the American insistence on its own immunity that is shaking its foundations.

LIVING WITH OUR DIFFERENCES

Contrary to the cries of many Americans in the wake of the Iraq war, Europeans have not forgotten World War II. But in non-American eyes, there is a world of difference between the righteous might of Roosevelt's era and the self-righteous might of George W. Bush. At the very least, as the Clinton administration understood so well, style, rhetoric, and due process matter. More substantively, well-intentioned liberals on both sides of the Atlantic have been right to insist on the shared values and interests that must continue to guide transatlantic cooperation on all fronts. But what the European story of civilian powerhood also suggests, even in its latest version, is that differences between Europe and the United States must be valued, and reinforced, if we are to counter the challenges facing us in the decades ahead.

Geographically, the global impact of progressively expanding the European Union's zone of peace and prosperity cannot be underestimated. This does not mean confining the European Union to a local role: both the United States and the European Union are global actors with regional strategies. Indeed, the prospect of EU membership for Turkey would constitute the most powerful signal yet that the European Union is a world partner that will not banish the Muslim world as Europe's "other." And clearly, the European Union bordering Iraq and Russia is not irrelevant to the supply of global order. Beyond enlargement, the construction of a Euromed region constitutes the best hope for the peoples bordering the *Mare Nostrum*—notwithstanding the crucial role of U.S. arbitration in the Middle East in the immediate future.

Functionally, there is nothing wrong with Europeans continuing to invest in reconstruction and stabilization when the United States is not up to it. Good cop–bad cop routines can be effective, as can competition in winning hearts and minds. Why shouldn't Europeans accept doing the dishes if Americans consult on the menu? At its best, the United States can create worthy recipients for Europe's constructive engagement. At its worst, it will alienate more renegades whose impulses the European Union can seek to moderate.

Crucial to their respective roles, the United States and the European Union also have different temporal horizons. Europeans are turtles, Americans are hares. The long-term horizon is the European Union's comparative advantage, and ongoing preventative action is its response to the U.S. strategy of preemptive strike. Whereas Americans like to drop by, Europeans have staying power (there is widespread acknowledgment in the Middle East that it is the Europeans' long-term presence on the ground that prepared the ground for the Quartet and American public diplomacy). Since the measure of success in the prevention field is that there is nothing to report, this strategy is not likely to win many votes. Similarly, microinvolvement and assistance requiring the acquisition of detailed local knowledge is unglamorous and painstaking. But the less-democratic European Union can afford slow and discrete results. Its machinery is subject not to short-term unionwide electoral cycles but to the long-term constraint of its own civilian logic. And even as the European Union becomes more accountable with time, European public opinion might stay more patient.

What do these differences amount to? How should they be translated politically? Perhaps it is best to take an external viewpoint when addressing these questions. And indeed, seen from the rest of the world, transatlantic rows must appear very parochial.

There is no single "rest of the world," of course. But it is fair to assume that most countries know what they do not want the U.S.–EU relation to be: allout rivalry or western hegemony. Heighted and continued rivalry between them would be bound to spell global instability. It would weaken the reach and effectiveness of international organizations – above all, the UN – which would most probably be increasingly deemed irrelevant by the U.S. And on an issue-by-issue basis, most countries usually resent being asked to take sides as we have seen with the disput over the International Criminal Court.

At the same time, there is little appetite in the developing world for the kind of "western hegemony" that characterized the heydays of neo-liberalism. The combined economic power of the two sides already overwhelms the rest of the world. And while the U.S. does not need the

EU on the military front, the latter's growing military capacity is not ir-relevant to NATO. The prospect of the U.S. and the EU "making up" through exclusive trans-atlantic economic deals, or of NATO supplant-ing the UN (or filling the vacuum) in the role of global policman, con-jures up a world entirely shaped by "western" interests.

A European strategy must be inspired by the imperative of avoiding these two pitfalls, destructive rivalry and hegemonic arrogance. But the diversity of issues and actions involved make it impossible to presc-cribe a magic formula to encaptulate such a middle strategy. Insead, and most likely, the European strategy that is likely to develop in the near future will oscillate between two poles for the European strategy—call this schizophrenia, ambivalence, or simply differentiation. On one hand, our longstanding transatlantic partnership will need to be revis-ited based on a multifaceted division of labor between the two sides that draws on our complementary strengths and inclinations.[27] On the other hand, and to satisfy the yearning for a new kind of international rela-tions inspired by a Kantian Europe, the European Union should not hes-itate to take stands as an alternative to the United States, with its different methods, policy concerns, and priorities and its own ways of making friends and indeed enemies: parallel with the United States "port of call" rather than with or against. At its best, this alternative would lend its know-how and resources to the advocacy and imple-mentation of alternative approaches to social, economic, and political management, as is currently the case in the genetically modified organ-isms affair under the World Trade Organization. It would preferably not refer to itself in terms of power at all, but as an intervener, a global part-ner, a "vanishing mediator."[28]

There is little doubt that these two middle strategies will continue to coexist in Europe, along with the more extreme temptations of rivalry and Western hegemony. They will coexist not only because some mem-ber states are more inclined toward one or the other or because, in fact, the choice between them needs to be issue specific but because the em-phasis will depend, to no small extent, on the attitude of the United States. In any event, actors who shape the European Union's role in the world are far from having articulated the meaning of this "European al-ternative," a global role for the EU that does not aim to replicate traditional parameters of powerhood. The test here for Europeans lies not with U.S. appreciation but with their ability to do their own thing in a world characterized, whether they like it or not, by U.S. hegemony. Upholding the values of pluralism and multilateralism in today's world order requies no less.

Nonetheless, those in the United States intoxicated with the prospect of a new American century, this time of unconstrained global power, may want to pause for a moment and consider the cunning of their European cousins. What if the new transatlantic division of labor was based on the same basic logic that governed the U.S. presence in Europe during the Cold War: the shaping of institutions of governance and justice beyond the state, under an American security umbrella, but this time beyond Europe? That is, the new U.S. liberal imperialism, turned wittingly or unwittingly into the instrument for the extension of Europe's model to the rest of the world—while the United States dealt with the spoilers at the margin of the system, the European Union would progressively position itself as the alternative power, treating its many partners as equals engaged in a dialogue on the ins and outs of global governance, whether in the World Trade Organization, the UN Security Council, or the International Criminal Court. Thankfully, even the most messianic among Europeans do not dare articulate such a scenario!

The more pragmatic will simply argue that if only they can learn to live with their differences, exploit their complementarity, and learn to agree to disagree, both the United States and the European Union should be better off for it. Politicians in the United States should not scold but applaud their European counterparts for not having followed the U.S. path after the end of the Cold War. Americans and Europeans should not be surprised by the Iraqi crisis. Both are the order of things to come and a reflection indeed of different worldviews. As they watch their young American cousins fall prey to the attraction of power, Europeans will and must continue to opt for Venus, or the power of attraction.

Notes

1. This article is based on several recent publications on related topics, including, Kalypso Nicolaidis and Robert Howse, "This Is My EU-topia: Narrative as Power," *Journal of Common Market Studies* (October 2002); Kalypso Nicolaidis and Justine Lacroix, "Order and Beyond the Nation-States: Europe's Competing Paradigms," in *Order and Justice in International Relations,* ed. Rosemary Foot (Cambridge: Oxford University Press, 2003); Anand Menon, Kalypso Nicolaïdis, and Jennifer Welsh, "In Defense of Europe," Working paper, 2003, ESC, Oxford University ; Kalypso Nicolaidis, "Living with Our Differences," in Nikos Kotzias and Petros Liacouras, eds., *EU–ES Relations: Repariing the Transatlantic Riff* (London: Palagrave, 2004). I would like to thank Thierry Fabre, Robert Howse, Andrew Hurrell, Dimitri Nicolaidis Michael Petrou, Simon Saunders, and Keith Thompson for their comments.
2. Robert Kagan, "Power and Weakness," *Policy Review* 113 (June–July 2002).
3. For a discussion see Etienne Balibar, *L'Europe, l'Amerique, la Guerre: Reflexions sur la mediation europeénne* (Paris: Editions La decouverte, 2003).
4. This ultimate twist is more prevalent in the publication expanding on the essay, Robert Kagan, *Of Paradise and Power* (New York: Knopf, 2003).
5. The Pew Research Center, The Pew Global Attitudes Project, (Washington, D.C.: March, 2003).
6. Emanuel Adler and Michael Barnett, eds., *Security Communities* (Cambridge: Cambridge University Press, 1998).
7. Obviously I do not mean to say that the end of colonial wars in the 1970s spelled the end of neocolonial politics and wars.
8. Francois Duchêne, "The European Community and the Uncertainties of Interdependence," in *A Nation Writ Large? Foreign Policy Problems before the European Communities,* ed. Max Kohnstamm and Wolfgang Hager (London: Macmillan, 1973).
9. See Nicolaïdis and Howse; for an early post–cold war discussion, see Christopher Hill, "Power Bloc, Civilian Model—or Flop?" in *The Evolution of an International Actor—Western Europe's New Assertiveness,* ed. Reinhardt Rummel (Boulder, Colo.: Westview, 1990).
10. Clyde Prestowitz, *Rogue Nation: American Unilateralism and the Failure of Good Intentions* (New York: Basic Books, 2003).
11. Ian Manners, "Normative Power Europe: A Contradiction in Terms?" *Journal of Common Market Studies* 40, no. 2 (2002): 235–58.
12. For a forceful argument on this point, see Tod Lindberg, "The Atlanticist Community," in *Beyond Paradise and Power: Europe, America, and the Future of a Troubled Partnership,* ed. Tod Lindberg (New York: Routledge, 2004 [this volume]).
13. See Kalypso Nicolaïdis and Robert Howse, eds., *The Federal Vision: Legitimacy and Levels of Governance in the US and the EU* (Oxford: Oxford University Press, 2001).
14. For a discussion in the context of constitutional debates see J. H. H. Weiler, "Federalism without Constitutionalism: Europe's *Sonderweg*," in *The Federal Vision,* Nicolaidis and Howse, eds.
15. The United States may outspend the Europeans on defense by a factor of four, but Europeans (member states and the EU combined) outspend the United States on development aid by a factor of seven.
16. "The Future of Freedom: Illiberal Democracy at Home and Abroad" 2003.
17. Tod Lindberg, "September 11 & September 10," *Policy Review* 109 (October–November 2001).
18. Chris Patten, Cyril Foster Lecture, Oxford University, January 30, 2003.
19. Robert Keohane, "Ironies of Sovereignty: The European Union and the United States," *Journal of Common Market Studies* 40, no. 4 (2002): 743–65.
20. Josef Joffe, "Europe's American Pacifier," *Foreign Policy* 54 (Spring 1984).

21. Stelios Stavridis, "Why the 'Militarizing' of the EU is Strengthening the Concept of a Civilian Power Europe " (working paper) (Florence: European University Institute, 2001); Karen E. Smith, "The End of Civilian Power Europe: A Welcome Demise or a Cause for Concern?" *International Spectator* 35, no. 2 (April–June 2000).

22. See Nicolaidis and Weatherill, *Whose Europe: National Models and the EU Constitution* (Oxford, 2003). Javier Solana, the EU foreign policy chief, followed an initiative of the Greek presidency. The paper was approved in its initial version by European heads of states in June 2003.

23. For a cogent defense, see International Development Research Council, *The Responsibility to Protect: Report of the International Commission on Intervention and State Sovereignty* (Ottawa: Author, 2001).

24. An interesting variant would be the setting up of an association of democraticc states which would issue considered opinions on the legitimacy of the use of force against a tyrannical government or refer it to the Hague, not as a replacement but as a support to the UN. See Stanely Hoffman, *L'Amerique vraiment Imperiale? Entretiens sur le vif avec Frederic Bozo* (Paris: Audibert, 2003).

25. Anne Marie Slaughter, "A Chance to Reshape the U.N.," *Washington Post,* April 13, 2003. A. U.N. commission has now been set up to investigate this agenda.

26. See, for instance, Declaration by the Center for International Studies; see also the response by Jacques Delors's Notre Europe in Le Monde.

27. See, for instance, Andrew Moravcsik, "Striking a New Transatlantic Bargain," *Foreign Affairs* 82, no. 4 (July–August 2003).

28. This term is used by Etienne Balibar, op.cit.

7

THE NEW ANTI-EUROPEANISM IN AMERICA

by Timothy Garton Ash

I N THE YEAR THE UNITED STATES went to war against Iraq, readers saw numerous articles in the American press on anti-Americanism in Europe. But what about anti-Europeanism in the United States? Consider the following:

> To the list of polities destined to slip down the Eurinal of history, we must add the European Union and France's Fifth Republic. The only question is how messy their disintegration will be. (Mark Steyn, *Jewish World Review*, May 1, 2002)

And,

> Even the phrase "cheese-eating surrender monkeys" is used [to describe the French] as often as the French say "screw the Jews." Oops, sorry, that's a different popular French expression. (Jonah Goldberg, *National Review Online*, 16 July 2002)

Or, from a rather different corner,

"You want to know what I really think of the Europeans?" asked the senior State Department Official. "I think they have been wrong on just about every major international issue for the past 20 years." (quoted by Martin Walker, UPI, November 13, 2002)

Statements such as these brought me to the United States—to Boston, New York, Washington, and the Bible Belt states of Kansas and Missouri—to look at changing American attitudes toward Europe in the shadow of a possible second Gulf War. Virtually everyone I spoke to on the East Coast agreed that there is a level of irritation with Europe and Europeans higher even than at the last memorable peak, in the early 1980s.

Pens are dipped in acid and lips curled to pillory "the Europeans," also known as "the Euros," "the Euroids," "the 'peens," or "the Euroweenies." Richard Perle, then chairman of the Defense Policy Board, said Europe has lost its "moral compass" and France its "moral fiber."[1] This irritation extends to the highest levels of the Bush administration. In conversations with senior administration officials I found that the phrase "our friends in Europe" was rather closely followed by "a pain in the butt."

The current stereotype of Europeans is easily summarized: Europeans are wimps. They are weak, petulant, hypocritical, disunited, duplicitous, and sometimes anti-Semitic and often anti-American appeasers. In a word: Euroweenies.[2] Their values and their spines have dissolved in a lukewarm bath of multilateral, transnational, secular, and postmodern fudge. They spend their euros on wine, holidays, and bloated welfare states instead of on defense. Then they jeer from the sidelines while the United States does the hard and dirty business of keeping the world safe for Europeans. Americans, by contrast, are strong, principled defenders of freedom, standing tall in the patriotic service of the world's last truly sovereign nation-state.

A study should be written on the sexual imagery of these stereotypes. If anti-American Europeans see "the Americans" as bullying cowboys, anti-European Americans see "the Europeans" as limp-wristed pansies. The American is a virile, heterosexual male; the European is female, impotent, or castrated. Militarily, Europeans can't get it up. (After all, they have fewer than twenty "heavy lift" transport planes, compared with the United States' more than two hundred.) Following a lecture I gave in Boston, an aged American tottered to the microphone to inquire why Europe "lacks animal vigor." The word "eunuchs" is, I discovered, used in the form "EU-nuchs." The sexual imagery even creeps into a more sophisticated account of American-European differences, that of Robert Kagan of the Carnegie Endowment for Peace titled "Power and Weakness."[3] "Americans are from Mars," wrote Kagan approvingly, "and Europeans are from Venus"—echoing that famous book about relations between men and women, *Men Are from Mars, Women Are from Venus*.

Not all Europeans are equally bad. The British tend to be regarded as somewhat different and sometimes better. American conservatives often spare the British the opprobrium of being Europeans at all—a view with which most British conservatives, still mentally led by Margaret Thatcher, would heartily agree. And Tony Blair, like Thatcher before him, and Churchill before her, is cited in Washington as a shining exception to the European rule.

The worst abuse is reserved for the French—who, of course, give at least as good as they get. I had not realized how widespread in American popular culture is the old English pastime of French bashing. "You know, France, we've saved their butt twice and they never do anything for us," Verlin "Bud" Atkinson, a World War II veteran, informed me at the Ameristar casino in Kansas City. Talking to high school and college students in Missouri and Kansas, I encountered a strange folk prejudice: the French, it seems, *don't wash*. "I felt very dirty a lot," said one college student, recalling her trip to France. "But you were still cleaner than French guys," added another.

Two prominent American journalists, Thomas Friedman of the *New York Times* and Joe Klein of the *New Yorker,* back from extensive book tours around the United States, separately told me that wherever they went they found anti-French sentiment—you would always get a laugh if you made a dig at the French. The *National Review Online* editor and self-proclaimed conservative "frog-basher" Jonah Goldberg, who also can be seen on television, has popularized the epithet quoted previously—cheese-eating surrender monkeys—which first appeared in an episode of *The Simpsons*. Goldberg told me that when he started writing

24T

anti-French pieces for *National Review* in 1998 he found "there was a market for it." French bashing became, he said, "a shtick."

WHAT IS ANTI-EUROPEANISM?

Clearly it will not do to throw together neoconservative polemics, Kansas City high school students' prejudices against French bathroom behavior, and remarks of a senior State Department official and senior administration officials, and then label the whole bag "anti-Europeanism." As a European writer I would not want to treat American anti-Europeanism in the way American writers often treat European anti-Americanism.

We have to distinguish between legitimate, informed criticism of the European Union or current European attitudes and some deeper, more settled hostility to Europe and Europeans as such, just as American writers should, but often do not, distinguish between legitimate, informed European criticism of the Bush administration and anti-Americanism or between legitimate, informed European criticism of the Sharon government and anti-Semitism. The difficult question in each case, one on which knowledgeable people may reasonably disagree, is, Where's the dividing line?

We also need to keep a sense of humor. One reason Europeans like to laugh at President George W. Bush is that some of the things he has said—or is alleged to have said—are funny. For example: "The problem with the French is that they don't have a word for entrepreneur."[4] One reason Americans like to laugh at the French is that there is a long Anglo-Saxon tradition—going back at least to Shakespeare—of laughing at the French. But there's also a trap here. Conservative writers such as Jonah Goldberg and Mark Steyn make outrageous statements, some of them obviously humorous, some semiserious, some quite serious. If you object to one of the serious ones, they can always reply "but of course I was only joking!" Humor works by exaggeration and playing with stereotypes. But if a European writer were to describe "the Jews" as "matzo-eating surrender monkeys" would that be understood as humorous banter? Of course the context is very different: there has been no genocide of the French in the United States. Yet the thought experiment might give our humorists pause.

Anti-Europeanism is not symmetrical with anti-Americanism. The emotional leitmotifs of anti-Americanism are resentment mingled with envy; those of anti-Europeanism are irritation mixed with contempt. Anti-Americanism is a real obsession for entire countries—notably for France, as Jean-François Revel recently argued.[5] Anti-Europeanism is very far from being an American obsession. In fact, the predominant American popular attitude toward Europe is probably mildly benign indifference, mixed with impressive ignorance. I traveled around Kansas for two days asking people I met, "If I say 'Europe' what do you think of?" Many reacted with a long, stunned silence, sometimes punctuated by giggles. Then they said things such as, "Well, I guess they don't have much huntin' down there" (Vernon Masqua, a carpenter in McLouth); "Well, it's a long way from home" (Richard Souza, whose parents came from France and Portugal); or, after a very long pause for thought, "Well, it's quite a ways across the pond" (Jack Weishaar, an elderly farmer of German descent). If you said "America" to a farmer or carpenter in even the remotest village of Andalusia or Ruthenia, he would, you may be sure, have a whole lot more to say on the subject.

In Boston, New York, and Washington—"the Bos-Wash corridor"— I was repeatedly told that even people who know the continent well have become increasingly indifferent toward Europe since the end of the Cold War. Europe is seen neither as a potent ally nor as a serious potential rival, like China. "It's an old people's home!" said an American friend who attended school and university in England. As the conservative pundit Tucker Carlson remarked in an exchange on CNN's *Crossfire:* "Who cares what the Europeans think. The European Union spends all of its time making sure that British bologna is sold in kilos not pounds. The whole continent is increasingly irrelevant to American interests."[6]

When I asked a senior administration official what would happen if Europeans went on criticizing the United States from a position of military weakness, the gist of his response was, "Well, *does it matter?*"

Yet I felt this claim of indifference was also overstated. Certainly, my interlocutors took a lot of time and passion to tell me how little they cared. And the point about the outspoken American critics of Europe is that they are generally not ignorant of or indifferent to Europe. They know Europe—half of them seem to have studied at Oxford or in Paris—and are quick to mention their European friends. Just as most European critics of the United States fiercely deny that they are anti-American ("don't get me wrong, I love the country and the people"), so they will almost invariably insist that they are not anti-European.[7]

Anti-Americanism and anti-Europeanism are at opposite ends of the political scale. European anti-Americanism is mainly to be found on the left, American anti-Europeanism on the right. The most outspoken American Euro-bashers are neoconservatives using the same sort of combative rhetoric they have habitually deployed against American liberals. In fact, as Jonah Goldberg acknowledged to me, the Europeans are also a stalking horse for liberals. So, I asked him, was Bill Clinton a European? "Yes," said Goldberg, "or at least, Clinton thinks like a European."

There is some evidence that the left–right divide characterizes popular attitudes as well. In early December 2002 the Ipsos-Reid polling group included in their regular survey of U.S. opinion a few questions formulated for the purposes of this chapter.[8] Asked to choose one of four statements about American versus European approaches to diplomacy and war, 30 percent of Democratic voters but only 6 percent of Republican voters chose "The Europeans seem to prefer diplomatic solutions over war and that is a positive value Americans could learn from." By contrast only 13 percent of Democrats but 35 percent of Republicans (the largest single group) chose "The Europeans are too willing to seek compromise rather than to stand up for freedom even if it means war, and that is a negative thing."

The divide was even clearer when respondents were asked to pick between two statements about "the way in which the war on Iraq should be conducted." Fifty-nine percent of Republicans as opposed to just 33 percent of Democrats chose "The US must remain in control of all operations and prevent its European allies from limiting the States' room to maneuver." By contrast, 55 percent of Democrats and just 34 percent of Republicans chose "It is imperative that the United States allies itself with European countries, even if it limits its ability to make its own decisions."

It seems a hypothesis worth investigating that actually it's Republicans who are from Mars and Democrats who are from Venus.

For some conservatives, the State Department is also an outpost of Venus. William Kristol, one of America's hereditary neoconservatives, wrote of "an axis of appeasement—stretching from Riyadh to Brussels to Foggy Bottom."[9] Down the Bos–Wash corridor, I was several times told of two groups competing for President Bush's ear over Iraq: the "Cheney–Rumsfeld group" and the "Powell–Blair group." It is rather curious for a British citizen to discover that our prime minister has become a senior member of the State Department.

Atlanticist Europeans should not take too much comfort here, for even among lifelong liberal state department Europeanists there is an acerbic edge of disillusionment with the Europeans. A key episode in their disillusionment was Europe's appalling failure to prevent the genocide of a quarter of a million Bosnian Muslims in Europe's own backyard.[10] Since then, there has been Europe's continued inability to "get its act together" in foreign and security policy, so that even a dispute between Spain and Morocco over a tiny, uninhabited island off the Moroccan coast had to be resolved by Colin Powell.

"They are not serious" was the lapidary verdict on the Europeans delivered to me by George F. Will over a stately breakfast in a Washington hotel. Though Will is very far from being a state department liberal, many in the department would agree. Historically, the tables are turned. For what was Charles de Gaulle's verdict on the Americans? *"Ils ne sont pas sérieux."*

DEEPER CAUSES

So there is, in significant quarters of American life, a disillusionment and irritation with Europe, a growing contempt for and even hostility toward the Europeans, which, at the extreme, merits the label anti-Europeanism. Why has this come about?

Some possible explanations have emerged already; to explore them all would take a book. Here I can indicate only a few more places to look. For a start, there has always been a strong strain of anti-Europeanism in the United States. "America was created as an antidote to Europe," Michael Kelly, the late editor of *Atlantic Monthly,* observed. "Why," asked George Washington, in his Farewell Address, "by interweaving our destiny with that of any part of Europe, entangle our peace and prosperity in the toils of European ambition, rivalship, interest, humor or caprice?" For millions of Americans, in the nineteenth and twentieth centuries, Europe was the place you escaped from.

Yet there was also an enduring fascination with Europe, famously exemplified by Henry James; a desire in many respects to emulate, and then outdo, European countries, above all, England and France. Arthur Schlesinger Jr. quoted to me the old line "when Americans die, they go to Paris." "Every man has two countries," said Thomas Jefferson, "his own and France." When was it that American attitudes toward England and France diverged so sharply? Was it 1940, the year of France's "strange defeat" and England's "finest hour"? Thereafter de Gaulle recovered French self-esteem in opposition to the Americans, whereas Churchill conjured a "special relationship" between his parents' two nations. (To understand the approaches of Chirac and Blair to the United States today the key names are still de Gaulle and Churchill.)

For fifty years, from 1941 to 1991, the United States and a growing fellowship of Europeans were engaged in a joint war against a common enemy: first Nazism, then Soviet communism. This was the heyday of the geopolitical West. There were, of course, repeated transatlantic strains throughout the cold war. Some of today's stereotypes can be found fully formed in the controversies of the early 1980s about the deployment of cruise and Pershing missiles and American foreign policy toward Central America and Israel.[10] They were formed in the minds of some of the same people: Richard Perle, for example, then widely known as "the prince of darkness" because of his hardline views. These transatlantic arguments often were about how to deal with the Soviet Union, but they also were finally constrained by that clear and common enemy.

Now no longer. So perhaps we are witnessing what the Australian writer Owen Harries foresaw in an article nearly ten years ago in *Foreign Affairs:* the decline of the West as a solid geopolitical axis, owing to the disappearance of that clear and common enemy.[11] Europe was the main theater of World War II and the Cold War; it is not the center of the war against terrorism. The gap in relative power has grown wider. The United States is not just the world's only superpower; it is a hyperpower, whose military expenditure will soon equal that of the next fifteen most powerful states combined. The European Union has not translated its comparable economic strength—fast approaching the U.S.$10 trillion economy—into comparable military power or diplomatic influence. But the differences are also about the uses of power.

Robert Kagan argued that Europe has moved into a Kantian world of "laws and rules and transnational negotiation and cooperation," whereas the United States remains in a Hobbesian world where military power is still the key to achieving international goals (even liberal ones). The first and obvious question must be, Is this true? I think that Kagan, in what he admitted is a caricature, is actually too kind to Europe, in the sense that he elevated to a deliberate, coherent approach what is, in fact, a story of muddled seeking and national differences. But a second, less obvious question is: Do Europeans and Americans wish this to be true? The answer seems to be yes. Quite a lot of American policymakers like the idea that they are from Mars—on the understanding that this makes them martial rather than Martian— whereas quite a lot of European policymakers like to think they are, indeed, programmatic Venusians. So the reception of Kagan's thesis is a part of its own story.

As the European Union searches for a clearer identity, there is a strong temptation for Europe to define itself against the United States. Europe clarifies its self-image by listing the ways in which it differs from America. In the dread jargon of identity studies, America becomes "the other." Americans do not like being othered. (Who does?) The impact of the September 11 terrorist attacks increases their own readiness to accept a martial and missionary account of America's role in the world.

Stanley Hoffmann observed that France and the United States are nations that see themselves as having a universalizing, civilizing mission. Now there is a European, rather than a merely French, version of the *mission civilisatrice,* a "EU-topia" of transnational, law-based integration, and it clashes most acutely with the latest, conservative version of an American mission.[12] Thus, for example, Jonah Goldberg quoted with irritation the claim by the veteran German Atlanticist Karl Kaiser that

"Europeans have done something that no one has ever done before: create a zone of peace where war is ruled out, absolutely out. Europeans are convinced that this model is valid for other parts of the world."

Each side thinks its model is better. This applies not only to the rival models of international behavior but also to those of democratic capitalism: the different mix of free market and welfare state, of individual freedom and social solidarity, and so on.[13] For the political scientist Charles A. Kupchan, the author of the recent book *The End of the American Era*, this presages nothing less than a coming "clash of civilizations" between Europe and America. Whereas Kagan thinks Europe is characterized by enduring weakness, Kupchan sees it, not China, as the United States' next great rival.[14] Many Europeans would love to believe this, but in the United States I found Kupchan almost alone in his view.

There is, I think, one other, deeper trend in the United States. I have mentioned already that for most of the nineteenth and twentieth centuries American suspicion of things European was mixed with admiration and fascination. There was, to put it bluntly, an American cultural inferiority complex. This has gradually faded. Its fading has been accelerated, in ways that are not easy to pin down, by the end of the Cold War and the United States' consequent rise to a unique preeminence. The new Rome no longer feels in awe of the old Greeks. "When I first went to Europe in the 1940s and 1950s, Europe was superior to us," a retired American diplomat with long European experience wrote to me recently. "The superiority was not personal—I never felt demeaned even by condescending people—but civilizational." Not any more. America, he wrote, "is no longer abashed."[15]

A DOWNWARD SPIRAL?

All these trends were somewhat obscured for eight years after the end of the Cold War by the presence in the White House of an honorary European, Bill Clinton. In 2001 George W. Bush, a walking gift to every European anti-American caricaturist, arrived in the White House with a unilateralist agenda, ready to jettison several international agreements. After September 11, he defined his new presidency as a war presidency. The post–September 11 sense that America is at war persisted more strongly in Washington than anywhere else in America, including New York.[16] It persisted, above all, in the heart of the Bush administration. The war against terrorism strengthened an existing tendency among the Republican elite to believe in what Robert Kaplan called "Warrior Politics," with a strong seasoning of fundamentalist Christianity—something conspicuously absent in highly secularized Europe. As Walter Russell Mead of the Council on Foreign Relations put it in his book *Special Providence*, it brought back the "Jacksonian" tendency in American foreign policy.[17] Al-Qaeda terrorists are the new Creek Indians.

The American question to Europeans then became, as the conservative columnist Charles Krauthammer put it to me, "Are you in the trenches with us or not?" At first, the answer was a resounding yes. Everyone quotes the *Le Monde* headline *"Nous sommes tous Américains."* But a year and a half later, on the eve of the Iraq war, the only European leader who most Americans thought was in the trenches with them was Tony Blair.[18] Many in Washington feel that the French have reverted to their old anti-American attitudes, and that the German chancellor, Gerhard Schröder, won his reelection last September by cynically exploiting anti-Americanism.

When and where did European and American sentiment start diverging again? It started in early 2002, with the escalation of the Israeli–Palestinian conflict in the Middle East. The Middle East is a source and a catalyst of what threatens to become a downward spiral of burgeoning European anti-Americanism and nascent American anti-Europeanism, each reinforcing the other. Anti-Semitism in Europe, and its alleged connection to European criticism of the Sharon government, has been the subject of the most acid anti-European commentaries from conservative American columnists and politicians. Some of these critics are themselves not just strongly pro-Israel but also "natural Likudites," one liberal Jewish commentator explained to me. In a recent article Stanley Hoffmann wrote that they seem to believe in an "identity of interests between the Jewish state and the United States."[19] Pro-Palestinian Europeans, infuriated by the way criticism of Sharon is labeled anti-Semitism, talk about the power of a "Jewish lobby" in the

United States, which then confirms American Likudites' worst suspicions of European anti-Semitism, and so it goes on and on.

Beside this hopeless tangle of mutually reinforcing prejudice—difficult for a non-Jewish European to write about without contributing to the malaise one is trying to analyze—there are, of course, real European-American differences in approaches to the Middle East. For example, European policymakers tend to think that a negotiated settlement of the Israeli–Palestinian conflict, rather than war on Iraq, would be a bigger contribution to the long-term success of the war against terrorism. The larger point, for our purposes, is that although the Cold War against communism in Middle Europe brought America and Europe together, the war against terrorism in the Middle East is pulling them apart. The Soviet Union united the West; the Middle East divides it.

Coolly examined, such a division is extremely stupid. Europe, just next door and with a large and growing Islamic population, has an even more direct vital interest in a peaceful, prosperous, and democratic Middle East than the United States does. Moreover, I found two senior administration officials in Washington quite receptive to the argument—which is beginning to be made by some American commentators—that the democratization of the greater Middle East should be the big new transatlantic project for a revitalized West.[20]

But that's not how it looks at the moment. Instead, the Middle East looks like the vortex in which real or alleged European anti-Americanism fuels real or alleged American anti-Europeanism, which in turn fuels more anti-Americanism; both being aggravated by sweeping charges of European anti-Semitism. A change might come through a major conscious effort on both sides of the Atlantic or with a new administration arriving in Washington. Yet a lot of damage can be done in the meantime, and the current transatlantic estrangement is also an expression of the deeper historical trends I have mentioned.

One might say that to highlight American anti-Europeanism, as I have done in this chapter, will contribute to the downward spiral of mutual distrust. But writers are not diplomats. American anti-Europeanism exists, and its carriers may be the first swallows of a long, bad summer.

Notes

1. Richard Perle, *The Guardian,* November 13, 2002.
2. Jonah Goldberg believes he coined this term, and he relates it etymologically to a wiener sausage—as a metaphor for the European spine. However, an earlier coinage seems to be P. J. O'Rourke's *Rolling Stone* essay "Terror of the Euroweenies," reprinted in *Holidays in Hell* (New York: Atlantic Monthly Press, 1988), 186–203.
3. Robert Kagan, "Power and Weakness," *Policy Review* 113 (June/July 2002); *Of Paradise and Power* (New York: Knopf, 2003).
4. Attributed to him by the *London Times* (July 9, 2002), quoting what someone told the *Times* journalist that Shirley Williams said that Tony Blair said that President Bush said to him. Blair's spokesman, Alastair Campbell, denied that Bush said anything of the sort.
5. Jean-François Revel, *L'Obsession Anti-Américaine* (Paris: Plon, 2002).
6. Tucker Carlson, *Crossfire,* June 12, 2001. For an Englishman this does raise an urgent question: What on earth is "British bologna"?
7. Jonah Goldberg was the only person I met who was prepared to accept that he was "anti-European," as long, he explained, as one means by "European" a certain kind of know-it-all, bureaucratic, liberal internationalist in Paris or Brussels.
8. *Weekly Standard,* August 26, 2002.
9. See my "Bosnia in Our Future," *New York Review of Books,* December 21, 1995. In this case the British government was very much among the Europeans.
10. The *Economist* ran a cover drawing in 1984 titled "How to Recognise a European through American Eyes." Distinguishing characteristics of the European were "An Angry Eye on Reagan. A Blind Eye on Russia. Limp-wristed. Weak-kneed. No Guts. Cold Feet. Snooty. Too Big for His Boots. But in Need of US Support."
11. Owen Harries, "The Collapse of 'The West,' " *Foreign Affairs* 72, no. 4 (September–October 1993).
12. See Kalypso Nicolaïdis and Robert Howse, " 'This is my EUtopia …': Narrative as Power," *Journal of Common Market Studies* 40, no. 4 (2002).
13. See, for example, Will Hutton, *The World We're In* (London: Little, Brown, 2002), and my debate with him in *Prospect* (May 2002).
14. See Charles A. Kupchan, "The End of the West," *Atlantic Monthly,* November 2002, and his *The End of the American Era: US Foreign Policy and the Geopolitics of the Twenty-first Century* (New York: Knopf, 2002).
15. E-mail to the author from Ambassador Thomas W. Simons, May 16, 2002, quoted with his kind permission. Michael Ledeen put it less kindly: "Conversation is much better in America," he wrote, and "Europeans have gone brain dead." This in the journal of the American Enterprise Institute, the *American Enterprise* (December 2002). The issue, titled "Continental Drift: Europe and the U.S. Part Company," is a veritable anthology of American right-wing views of Europe, including Mark Steyn's remarkable comment, "I find it easier to be optimistic about the futures of Iraq and Pakistan than, say, Holland or Denmark."
16. See my "The Capital Makes Up Its Mind," *New York Times,* December 12, 2002. This impression is confirmed by an August 2002 opinion poll by the Pew Research Center for the People and the Press.
17. Walter Russell Mead, *Special Providence: American Foreign Policy and How It Changed the World* (New York: Routledge, 2002).
18. This is borne out by the IPSOS US-Express, December 3–5, 2002, poll. When asked, "Out of the following six countries, which one, in your opinion, exhibits the strongest reaction of solidarity with the United States in its efforts against Iraq?" 59 percent said Britain. This was followed by Israel, 11 percent; Canada, 7 percent; France, 4 percent; Germany, 3 percent; and Russia, 3 percent.
19. Stanley Hoffmann, "The High and the Mighty," *American Prospect,* January 13, 2003.
20. See, for example, Ronald D. Asmus and Kenneth M. Pollack, "The New Transatlantic Project," *Policy Review* 115 (October–November 2002).

PART THREE

AMERICAN POWER AND ITS DISCONTENTS

8

DOES "THE WEST" STILL EXIST?

by Francis Fukuyama

IN A PROPHETIC ARTICLE written back in 1993, Owen Harries suggested that the concept of the West as it existed during the Cold War
did not reflect a natural or enduring community of interests but was
rather the product of a common, overarching Soviet threat and could
not be expected to endure for long past the Cold War's close.[1] This Cold
War West was conceived of in civilizational terms as a group of countries sharing common institutions and values, which saw the world in
similar ways and would readily seek collective action. Such a political
unit did not exist in the interwar period or indeed during any other historical period prior to the onset of the Cold War. Although institutions
and habits persist out of inertia, it was only a matter of time, according
to Harries, before the international system reverted to something resembling nineteenth-century Europe, with the countries of the former
West entering into a series of shifting alliances.

We have not yet made a return to the nineteenth century, but
American responses to the terrorist attacks of September 11 have

opened up a chasm between the United States and many of its European friends and allies that is not likely to heal soon. Chancellor Gerhard Schröder of Germany took the unprecedented step of campaigning on an overt platform of opposition to American foreign policy during the campaign leading to his reelection in September 2002, and French President Jacques Chirac sought to stake out a role for France as leader of a coalition opposing American hyperpower during the debate in the UN Security Council in the winter of 2002–2003. Together with Belgium, France and Germany took the extraordinary step of vetoing NATO support for fellow alliance member Turkey when the latter was thinking of assisting the United States in its strike against Iraq.

All of the familiar Cold War institutions remain in place, and it is not clear as of this writing that dramatic shifts, such as the rebasing of U.S. forces out of Germany and into countries of the new Europe like Poland or Romania, will take place. But a number of important changes have already occurred in the way Americans and Europeans think about one another that will have lasting political effects. The sense of automatic moral community that existed within the West during the Cold War no longer exists. Americans feel betrayed by the actions of European states, particularly France, in the buildup to the war, whereas many Europeans no longer see the United States as a benevolent protector but as the chief source of international instability. In the words of Dominique Moïsi, Europeans increasingly dislike not just American policies but what America represents. What makes the post-Iraq situation different from earlier periods of transatlantic discord (e.g., Suez, the intermediate range nuclear forces missile deployments, the gas pipeline deal) is that a certain kind of fashionable anti-Americanism has engulfed not just the usual suspects on the European Left but many of America's traditional supporters on the Right. This reflects, in turn, not just power disparities, as Robert Kagan argued, but deeper differences in historical self-perceptions between Europeans and Americans that may be patched over in the short run but will continue to be sources of continuing discord in the longer run.[2] It seems doubtful that an institution such as NATO will be able to survive under such conditions.

THE POST–SEPTEMBER 11 RIFT

The ostensible issues raised in the U.S.–European disputes since President Bush's "axis of evil" State of the Union speech in January 2002 for the most part revolve around alleged American unilateralism and international law. There is by now a familiar list of European complaints about American policy, including but not limited to the Bush administration's withdrawal from the Kyoto Protocol on global warming, its failure to ratify the Rio Pact on biodiversity, its withdrawal from the ABM (antiballistic missile) treaty and pursuit of missile defense, its opposition to the ban on land mines, its treatment of al-Qaeda prisoners at Guantánamo Bay, its opposition to new provisions of the biological warfare convention, and most recently its opposition to the International Criminal Court (ICC).

The most serious act of U.S. unilateralism in European eyes concerns the Bush administration's war to topple Iraq's Saddam Hussein. This conflict marked the first full implementation of the very important change in American foreign policy, announced in the White House's 2002 *National Security Strategy of the United States,* from deterrence to a policy of active preemption of terrorism. As explained in Bush's West Point speech of June 2002, "The war on terror will not be won on the defensive. We must take the battle to the enemy, disrupt his plans, and confront the worst threats before they emerge. In the world we have entered, the only path to safety is the path of action."

Europeans by and large did not buy the Bush administration's arguments that Iraq and its weapons of mass destruction(WMD) programs represented a uniquely dangerous threat that could not be met through conventional means of deterrence. Indeed, many Europeans dismissed the administration's security-related arguments altogether, believing instead that the United States was motivated by a desire to control oil or to make the Middle East safe for Israeli interests. But the most serious problem for Europeans was American unilateralism, its willingness to go ahead with the war despite the evident failure of the UN Security Council to back a second resolution authorizing the use of force.

The European view is that Europe is seeking to create a genuine rule-based international order suitable to the circumstances of the post–Cold War world. That world, free of sharp ideological conflicts and large-scale military competition, is one that gives substantially more room for consensus, dialogue, and negotiation as ways of settling disputes. Adherents to that view are horrified by the Bush administration's announcement of a virtually open-ended doctrine of preemption against terrorists or states that sponsor terrorists, in which the United States and the United States alone decides when and where to use force. In Europe the nation-state to an increasing extent has been dissociated from military power, despite the fact that the modern state built on centralized power was born on that continent.

Robert Kagan put the current difference between the United States and Europe as follows. The Europeans are the ones who actually believe they are living at the end of history, that is, in a largely peaceful world that to an increasing degree can be governed by law, norms, and international agreements. In this world, power politics and classical realpolitik have become obsolete. Americans, by contrast, think they are still living in history and need to use traditional power-political means to deal with threats from Iraq, al-Qaeda, and other malign forces. According to Kagan, the Europeans are half right: they have indeed created an end-of-history world for themselves within the European Union (EU), where sovereignty has given way to supranational organization. What they do not understand, however, is that the peace and safety of their European bubble is guaranteed ultimately by American military power. Absent that, they would be dragged backward into history.

IS THE RIFT GENUINE?

This, at least, is the popularly accepted account of American unilateralism and European emphasis on international law and institutions. We need to ask, however, whether it is in fact accurate and whether the United States has consistently been more unilateralist than Europe. The truth of the matter here is far more complicated, with the differences between the United States and Europe being much more nuanced.

Liberal internationalism, after all, has a long and honored place in American foreign policy. The United States was, after all, the country that promoted the League of Nations, the United Nations, the Bretton Woods institutions, the General Agreement on Tariffs and Trade, the World Trade Organization, and a host of other international organizations. There is a huge number of international governance organizations in the world today in which the United States participates as an active, if not the most active member, from standards setting, nuclear power safety, and scientific cooperation to aviation safety, bank settlements, drug regulation, accounting standards and corporate governance, and telecommunications.

It is useful here to make a distinction between those forms of liberal internationalism that are primarily economic and those that have a more political or security dimension. Particularly in recent years the United States has focused on international institutions that have promoted international trade and investment. It has put substantial effort into creating a rule-based international trade regime with stronger and more autonomous decision-making authority. In addition, it has promoted uniform rules on investment and capital flows under the banner of the "Washington Consensus." The motives for this are obvious: Americans benefit strongly from and indeed dominate the global economy, which is why globalization bears a "made in the USA" label.

In the realm of economics, both Americans and Europeans are sinners and it is hard to argue that the latter have a notably better record with regard to respect for multilateral rules. In 2002 the Bush administration announced a series of measures to protect domestic steel producers, while Congress passed and the president signed a highly protectionist agriculture bill. On the other hand, the administration managed to use these concessions to protectionist interests to wring so-called Trade Promotion Authority out of the Congress, and U.S. trade representative Robert Zoellick argued that the agriculture bill allowed him to put something on the table to bargain with in fulfillment of the Doha round's agenda of lowering agricultural subsidies. It was the Europeans who already had the biggest stack of chips on the table with their Common Agricultural Policy. It is the Common Agricultural Policy rather than the new American subsidies that at this moment appear to be the less moveable obstacle to freer trade.

There are a number of areas where the Europeans have acted unilaterally in economic matters, and in ways that at times contravene the existing legal order. The European Union resisted unfavorable decisions against them on bananas for nine years, and beef hormones for even longer. They have announced a precautionary principle with regard to genetically modified foods, which is very difficult to reconcile with the World Trade Organization's sanitary and phytosanitary rules—a principle has hurt poor consumers in Africa and that the Bush administration decided to challenge before a World Trade Organization panel in 2003. Indeed, the Europeans have been violating their own rules with regard to genetically modified foods, with certain member states setting standards different from those of the community itself. The European Competition Commission under Mario Monti successfully blocked the merger of GE and Honeywell, after the deal had been approved by American and Canadian regulators, in ways that promoted suspicions that the European Union was simply acting to protect specific European interests. Finally, the European Union has succeeded in exporting its data privacy rules to the United States through its Safe Harbour requirements.

For all their talk of wanting to establish a rule-based international order, the Europeans have not done that well within the European Union itself. As John van Oudenaren argued, the Europeans have developed a decision-making system of Byzantine complexity, with overlapping and inconsistent rules and weak enforcement powers.[3] The European Commission often does not have the power to even monitor compliance of member states with its own directives, much less the ability to make them conform. This fits with an attitude toward law in certain parts of Europe that often sees declarative intent as greater in importance than actual implementation and that Americans tend to see instead as undermining the very rule of law.

The second type of liberal internationalism has to do with politics and security. With the exception of the two environmental agreements (Rio and Kyoto), all of the U.S.–European disputes in recent years have concerned security-related issues (the International Criminal Court may not seem like a security matter, but the reason that the United States does not want to participate in it is out of fear that its soldiers and officials may be held criminally liable by the Court in the conduct of their duties). It is in this realm that the tables are turned and European charges of American unilateralism are made.

It is possible to overstate the importance of these disputes. A great deal of European irritation with the United States arises from stylistic matters, and from the Bush administration's strange failure to consult, explain, justify, and cajole in the manner of previous administrations. The administration could have let ratification of the Kyoto Protocol languish in Congress as the Clinton administration did, rather than casually announcing withdrawal from the pact at a luncheon for NATO ambassadors. American conservatives tend not to take global warming seriously and fail to see why those who do find the U.S. unwillingness to tax energy infuriating. This perhaps more than any other act cemented in the mind of many Europeans the image of George Bush as a self-serving unilateralist. Europeans did not like the religious language of the "axis of evil" speech. The United States has had a consistent record of using strong-arm tactics to shape international agreements to its liking and then to walk away from them at the last moment. This pattern goes all the way back to Woodrow Wilson and the League of Nations and was continued in negotiations over the Rio Pact, the Kyoto Protocol, and the International Criminal Court. Even those people skeptical about the value of international institutions should not have difficultly seeing why non-Americans might get a little irritated at this kind of behavior.

The Bush administration also failed to put much effort into elucidating its new national security doctrine.[4] The doctrine alarmed Europeans because it sought to justify not simply preemption (i.e., disrupting an imminent attack by another power) but also what amounts to preventive war (i.e., intervening to head off a threat months or years down the road). When combined, as in the 2002 "axis of evil" speech, with a list of at least three proliferators apparently targeted by the administration, they were led to conclude that Iraq was simply the first in a series of planned military actions.

But Iraq for the United States was in many respects a unique case, combining internal dictatorship, a history of external aggression, WMDs, and a high degree of vulnerability and isolation. The new doctrine, it appears, was written largely to justify the pending attack on Iraq and not as an open-ended declaration of a series of preventive wars. Evidence for this was soon forthcoming when North Korea admitted that it had violated the 1994 Framework Agreement and pursued a nuclear weapons program. The administration did not shift into high gear of war preparations as in the case of Iraq, because it had no prudent military option against North Korea. Nor did it have plans to launch military campaigns against other supporters of terrorism like Iran or Syria, despite some threats in their direction at the end of the Iraq war. All of this was probably self-evident to the formulators of the doctrine, but they did not bother to explain the kinds of prudential limits to which American foreign policy would continue to be subject. All of this would have been simple enough to do, but the administration did not make the effort.

The foregoing suggests that much of the European-American rift concerned style rather than substance. The Clinton administration talked a multilateralist game, whereas the Bush administration has at times asserted what amounts to a kind of principled unilateralism; in fact, policy between the two administrations did not differ in substance all that much. Clinton may have signed the Kyoto and ICC treaties, but he knew he would not spend much political capital in a hopeless effort to get them through Congress.

But although it is tempting to say the problem is simply stylistic, I think that this is a fundamentally wrong interpretation. There is in fact a deeper issue of principle between the United States and Europe that will ensure that transatlantic relations will remain contentious through the years to come. The disagreement is not over the principles of liberal democracy, which both sides share, but over where the ultimate source of liberal democratic legitimacy lies.

Americans, to put it rather schematically and simply, tend not to see any source of democratic legitimacy higher than the constitutional democratic nation-state. That any international organization has legitimacy is because duly constituted democratic majorities have handed that legitimacy up to them in a negotiated, contractual process. Such legitimacy can be withdrawn at any time by the contracting parties; international law and organization have no existence independent of this type of voluntary agreement between sovereign nation-states.

Europeans, by contrast, tend to believe that democratic legitimacy flows from the will of an international community much larger than any individual nation-state. This international community is not embodied concretely in a single, global democratic constitutional order. Yet it hands down legitimacy to existing international institutions, which are seen as partially embodying it. Thus, peacekeeping forces in the former Yugoslavia are not merely ad hoc intergovernmental arrangements but rather moral expressions of the will and norms of the larger international community.

Kant and Hobbes are thus relevant in a slightly different way from what Kagan suggested. For Hobbes, the Leviathan's legitimacy comes because it ultimately reflects the contractual choice of the people. For Kant, the rules of morality exist in a noumenal realm that transcends the physical world; they would be true and perceivable even if democratic majorities consistently rejected them.

One might be tempted to say that the stiff-necked defense of national sovereignty of the type practiced by Senator Jesse Helms is a characteristic only of a certain part of the American Right, and that the Left is as internationalist as are the Europeans. This would be largely correct in the security-foreign policy arena but dead wrong with regard to the economic side of liberal internationalism. That is, the Left does not grant the World Trade Organization or any other trade-related body any special status with regard to legitimacy. The Left is very suspicious of the World Trade Organization when it overturns an environmental or labor law in the name of free trade, and it is just as jealous of democratic sovereignty on these issues as Senator Helms was.

Between these two views of the sources of legitimacy, I suggest, is that the Europeans are theoretically right but are wrong in practice. They assert that they and not the Americans are the true believers in liberal universal values. It is in fact impossible to assert as a theoretical matter that proper liberal democratic procedure by itself inevitably results in outcomes that are necessarily legitimate and just. A constitutional order that is procedurally democratic can still decide to do terrible things to other countries, things that violate human rights and norms of decency on which its own democratic order is based. Indeed, it can violate the higher principles on which its own legitimacy is based, as Lincoln argued was the case with slavery. The legitimacy of its actions is based not, in the end, on democratic procedural correctness but on the prior rights and norms that come from a moral realm higher than that of the legal order.

The problem with the European position is that although such a higher realm of liberal democratic values might theoretically exist, it is very imperfectly embodied in any given international institution. The very idea that this legitimacy is handed downward from a willowy, disembodied international level rather than handed upward from concrete, legitimate democratic publics on a nation-state level virtually invites abuse on the part of elites who are then free to interpret the will of the international community to suit their own preferences.[5]

The second important practical problem with the European position is that of enforcement. The one power that is unique to sovereign nation-states and to them alone, even in today's globalized world, is the power to enforce laws. Even if existing international laws and organizations did accurately reflect the will of the international community (whatever that means), enforcement remains by and large the province of nation-states. A great deal of international and national law coming out of Europe consists of what amount to social policy wish lists that are completely unenforceable. Europeans justify these kinds of laws by saying they are expressions of social objectives; Americans reply, correctly in my view, that such unenforceable aspirations undermine the rule of law itself.

The only way that this circle of theory and practice could be squared would be if there were a genuine democratic government at a level higher than that of the nation-state. Such global democratic government could then be said to truly embody the will of the international community while containing procedural safeguards to make sure that that will was not misinterpreted or abused by various elites or interest groups. It would also presumably have enforcement powers that do not today exist, apart from the specific ad hoc arrangements made for peacekeeping and multilateral coalitions.

Some Europeans may believe that the steady accumulation of smaller international institutions like the International Criminal Court or the various agencies of the United Nations will someday result in something resembling democratic world government. In my view the chance of this happening is as close to zero as you ever get in political

the biggest gamble of his political career by supporting George Bush as firmly as he did in the face of widespread skepticism about the war.

There are multiple Europes in another sense as well. Much of the most strident criticism of the United States has come from European elites, and particularly from the left-of-center chattering classes that define what is and is not politically correct. Poll data on any number of issues show that there are significant differences between elite and mass opinion on issues from gay rights to the death penalty to the war in Iraq throughout Europe. A poll sponsored by the Chicago Council on Foreign Relations and the German Marshall Fund taken in mid-2002 showed that similar majorities in Europe and the United States favored a policy of disarming Iraq, but doing so on a multilateral basis.[6]

Political correctness exists in the United States and Europe, of course, but it tends to be more pronounced in the latter. That is, there are certain issues (almost always, ones raised by the Right) that are deemed so inflammatory that even to bring them up demonstrates that one is not part of respectable opinion. For example, it has been very difficult in Europe to talk openly about the relationship between immigration, race, and crime in societies that have been experiencing steadily increasing levels of social disorder. In the United States there were similar sensitivities in broaching a discussion of race, crime, and immigration, but public pressure to do something about crime forced public authorities to confront the issue squarely in the 1980s. As a result, many European societies are just now beginning to talk about these issues openly and getting tough on crime, a good fifteen to twenty years after the United States.

There are good reasons for the reluctance of European elites to enter into this discussion too openly, because the Right there includes extremist groups like the Front National in France, the Vlaams Blok in Belgium, or Jörg Haider's Freedom Party in Austria. The alienation of Europe's Muslim populations is one of the most sensitive issues today and clearly limits the freedom of action of many European politicians when it comes to policy in the Middle East. This is a problem for European democracy that promises to get worse over time as the birthrates of white Europeans fall and the proportion of Muslims increases.

THE REASONS FOR THE DIFFERENCES

Robert Kagan in the article mentioned previously provided a realpolitik explanation for U.S.–European differences with regard to international law. The Europeans like international law and norms because they are much weaker than the United States, and the latter likes unilateralism because it is significantly more powerful than any other country or group of countries (like the EU) not just in terms of military power but in economic, technological, and cultural terms as well.

This argument makes a great deal of sense as far as it goes. Small, weak countries that are acted upon rather than that influence others naturally prefer to live in a world of norms, laws, and institutions, in which more powerful nations are constrained. Conversely, a sole superpower like the United States would naturally like to see its freedom of action be as unencumbered as possible.

But although the argument from the standpoint of power politics is correct as far as it goes, it is not a sufficient explanation of why the United States and Europe, not to mention other countries around the world, differ. As noted previously, the pattern of U.S. unilateralism and European multilateralism applies primarily to security and foreign policy issues and secondarily to environmental concerns; in the economic sphere, the United States is enmeshed in multilateral institutions despite (or perhaps because of) its dominance of the global economy.

Moreover, to point to differences in power is merely to beg the question of why these differences exist. The EU before enlargement on May 1, 2004 collectively encompassed a population of 375 million people and has a gross domestic product of $9.7 trillion, compared with a U.S. population of 280 million and a gross domestic product of $10.1 trillion. Europe could certainly spend money on defense at a level that would put it on a par with the United States, but it chooses not to. Europe spends barely $130 billion collectively on defense—a sum that has been steadily falling—compared with U.S. defense spending of $300 billion, which is due to rise sharply. The post–September 11 increment in U.S. defense spending requested by President Bush is larger than the entire defense budget of Britain. Despite Europe's turn in a more conservative direction in 2002, not one rightist or center-right candidate campaigned on a platform of significantly raising defense spending. Europe's ability to deploy the power that it possesses is of course greatly weakened by the collective action problems posed by the current system of EU decision making. But the failure to create more useable military power is clearly a political and normative issue.

Moreover, not every small, weak country is equally outraged by American unilateralism. In a curious role reversal from Cold War days, the Russians were actually much more relaxed about the American withdrawal from the ABM treaty than were many Europeans, because it made possible deep cuts in offensive strategic nuclear forces. Australia, although of course wanting the United States to abide by international trade rules, was strongly supportive of the U.S. war in Iraq.

This brings us to other reasons why Europeans see the international order so differently from Americans. One critically important factor has to be the experience of European integration over the past generation. The loss of sovereignty is not an abstract, theoretical matter to Europeans; they have been steadily giving up powers to Brussels, from local control over health and safety standards to social policy to their currency. Having lived through this masochistic experience repeatedly, one imagines that they are like former smokers who want to put everyone else through the same withdrawal pains that they have endured.

The final important difference between the United States and Europe with regard to international order has nothing to do with European beliefs and practices but with America's unique national experience and the sense of exceptionalism that has arisen from it. The sociologist Seymour Martin Lipset has spent much of his distinguished career explaining how the United States is an outlier among developed democracies, with policies and institutions that differ significantly from those of Europe, Canada, Australia, New Zealand, or Japan.[7] Whether in regard to welfare, crime, regulation, education, or foreign policy, there are constant differences separating America from everyone else: it is consistently more antistatist, individualistic, laissez-faire, and egalitarian than other democracies.

This sense of exceptionalism extends to its own democratic institutions and their legitimacy. Unlike most of the old societies of Europe, the United States was founded on the basis of a political idea. There was no American people or nation prior to the founding of the country:

national identity is civic rather than religious, cultural, racial, or ethnic. There has been only one American regime that, as the world's oldest continuously existing democracy, is not viewed as a transient political compromise. This means that the country's political institutions have always been imbued with an almost religious reverence that Europeans, with more ancient sources of identity, find peculiar. The proliferation of American flags across the country in the wake of September 11 is only the most recent manifestation of Americans' deeply felt patriotism.

Moreover, for Americans, their Declaration of Independence and Constitution are not just the basis of a legal-political order on the North American continent; they are the embodiment of universal values and have a significance for mankind that goes well beyond the borders of the United States. The American dollar bill has the inscription *novus ordo seclorum*—"new order of the ages"—written under the all-seeing eye of the great pyramid. When President Reagan repeatedly quoted Governor Winthrop in speaking of the United States as a "shining city on a hill," his words had great resonance for many Americans. This leads at times to a typically American tendency to confuse its own national interests with the broader interests of mankind as a whole.

The situation of Europe—as well as of developed Asian societies like Japan, for that matter—is very different. Europeans were peoples with shared histories long before they were democracies. They have other sources of identity besides politics. They have seen a variety of regimes come and go, and some of those regimes have, in living memory, been responsible for very shameful acts. The kind of patriotism that is commonplace in America is highly suspect in many parts of Europe: Germans for many years after World War II taught their children not to display the German flag or cheer too loudly at football matches. Although the French and, in a different way, the British continue to feel a sense of broader national mission in the world, it is safe to say that few other European countries regard their own political institutions as universal models for the rest of the world to follow. Indeed, many Europeans regard their national institutions as having a much lower degree of legitimacy than international ones, with the European Union occupying a place in between.

The reasons for this are not hard to fathom. Europeans regard the violent history of the first half of the twentieth century as the direct outcome of the unbridled exercise of national sovereignty. The house that they have been building for themselves since the 1950s called the European Union was deliberately intended to embed those sovereignties in multiple layers of rules, norms, and regulations to prevent those sovereignties from ever spinning out of control again. Although the European Union could become a mechanism for aggregating and projecting power beyond Europe's borders, most Europeans see the European Union's purpose as one of transcending power politics. They do, in other words, see their project as one of finding comfortable accommodations for the last man at the end of history.

THE PALESTINIAN QUESTION AND TERRORISM

There is a final abiding area of disagreement between the United States and Europe, which concerns attitudes toward Israel and the Palestinians. The Bush administration accepted the Israeli interpretation of the failure of the Oslo Accords promoted under the Clinton administration. By that view, the Israelis were ready to offer the Palestinians a remarkably generous two-state solution that, by the time of the Taba talks in January 2000, included turning over nearly two-thirds of the Old City of Jerusalem to Palestinian control. It was Yasser Arafat who decided that he could not abide this offer and who turned away from it by raising the nonnegotiable "right of return" issue at the last moment. By this view, it was Arafat as well who deliberately encouraged the use of suicide bombers as a means of upping the ante and who had to be removed from power before any further progress could be made toward peace. More broadly, many people within the Bush administration believed that any solution to the Palestinian problem that did not fundamentally endanger Israel's security would be insufficient to appease Arab opinion and that it was therefore better to stick to a hard line of no compromise with suicide terrorists. A number of administration supporters have argued that Arab anti-Americanism was rooted less in anger over the Palestinian question than in the lack of democracy throughout the Arab world.[8]

Many Europeans have argued, by contrast, that failure to achieve a final peace settlement between the Palestinians and Israel is a continuing source of instability and terrorism throughout the Middle East and that efforts to resolve this conflict should take precedence over dealing with rogue states like Iraq. They do not accept the Israeli account of the failure of Oslo, beginning with the view that the Taba settlement was a fair one from the Palestinian point of view. Europeans tend to blame the onset of Intifada II on Ariel Sharon's visit to the Temple Mount in September 2000 and his subsequent use, as prime minister, of preemptive attacks and assassinations against the Palestinian leadership. There is little inclination in Europe to take seriously the view that apparent Arab anger over the Palestinians is actually a displacement of rage over their own lack of voice.

In the bitter debate prior to the Iraq war, both sides voiced, usually *sotto voce,* caricatured interpretations of the other side's motives. In Europe it was common to hear the view that U.S. foreign policy had been hijacked by the Israel lobby and by fundamentalist Christians, which was leading Washington to policies directly counter to U.S. national interests. In the United States there were accusations that anti-Semitism had been resurrected in countries like France and Germany or that European politicians were simply playing for Muslim votes or oil contracts.

These contrasting views on the Middle East conflict reflect far more than style or diplomatic emphasis; on the other hand, it is not clear that they are based on deep structural differences between Europe and America. There is no question that Israeli views get a more sympathetic hearing in the United States, whereas Arab perspectives are more pervasive in Europe. This much is evident simply in watching the media coverage of the conflict in Palestine, which often diverges to such an extent as to present mutually unrecognizable accounts of the same events. To some extent the differing policy views reflect the relative strengths of these various ethnic lobbies in the respective political systems on both sides.

But Europeans who charge that American policy has been captured by the Israel lobby fail to understand certain key facts about American politics. There has been something of a convergence of American and

Israeli strategic views over the past several decades, not because of some nefarious Jewish influence but because of the Cold War. American and Israeli hard-liners are highly realist in their belief in the need to use power forthrightly in pursuit of security and national interest, both stress the offensive and the need to take the initiative and control events, both have a rather jaundiced view of arms control and negotiated deals between fundamentally hostile parties, and both are skeptical about international institutions generally and the United Nations in particular.

There has of course been some Israeli influence on American strategic thinking. But the views of most American hard-liners were bred during the Cold War, when the enemy was not the Arab world but the Soviet Union and its allies. And what many Europeans fail to recognize is that this hard-line strategic view had a great deal of merit—indeed, it was responsible in large measure for the Cold War ending on the positive terms it did (i.e., a Europe "whole and free"). Like George W. Bush's administration, the Reagan administration took a moralistic view of the conflict in which it was engaged (the "axis of evil" had precedent in Reagan's "evil empire"), made apparently outlandish and one-sided proposals (e.g., Richard Perle's "double-zero" in the INF negotiations), and undermined various arms control deals with the dying Brezhnev regime. This perspective became deeply entrenched precisely because it was perceived at the time to be highly politically incorrect but in the end vindicated. Being right once when the rest of the world was wrong has reinforced a tendency to believe in one's own judgment and to disregard world opinion.

ARE WE AT THE END OF HISTORY?

The fact that a particular strategic worldview is appropriate for one historical period does not mean that it will be right for another. After the collapse of the Soviet empire, there was tangible nostalgia on the part of many American hard-liners for the Cold War and the moral clarity that it provided. During the 1990s there were efforts by some, such as William Kristol and Robert Kagan, to promote China as a new strategic competitor in place of the former Soviet Union. In this respect

September 11 was a godsend insofar as it presented a clear enemy capable of directly threatening the U.S. homeland in a way that China never did.

Kagan is right that there are significant differences in strategic culture between the United States and Europeans today. But many of the contrasts he cited do not reflect deep differences between the United States and Europe as societies but rather are consequences of recently experienced history. The "Martian" policy favored by the Bush administration came into vogue because of the way the Cold War ended and will continue to be favored as long as it appears successful. But it can turn "Venutian" very quickly if, for example, U.S. forces get bogged down in an occupied Iraq that looks more and more like the West Bank than a liberal democracy. Similarly, the Venutian Europeans could turn Martian in short order should they experience a mass-casualty terrorist attack. Martian policies do not make sense in Venutian worlds, and vice versa.

This brings us back full circle to the initial question with which we started, which is also one of the important sources of U.S.–European disagreement. The Europeans are certainly right that they are living at the end of history; the question is, where is the rest of the world? Of course, much of the world is indeed mired in history, having neither economic growth nor stable democracy nor peace. But the end of the Cold War marked an important turn in international relations, because for the first time the vast majority of the world's great powers were stable, prosperous, liberal democracies. Although in history there could be skirmishes between countries, such as Iraq, and those beyond it, such as the United States, the prospect of great wars between great powers had suddenly diminished.

There are certainly no new nondemocratic great powers to challenge the United States; China may one day qualify, but it is not there yet. But a terrorist organization armed with weapons of mass destruction is a different matter: although the organization itself may be a minor historical player, the technological capability it can potentially deploy is such that it must be taken seriously as a world-class threat. Indeed, such an organization poses graver challenges in certain ways than nuclear-armed superpowers, because the latter are for the most part deterable and not into the business of committing national suicide.

The question about the threat is, then, whether the world has fundamentally changed since September 11, insofar as hostile terrorist organizations armed with weapons of mass destruction will become an ongoing reality. Many Americans clearly think so and were led to believe that once a leader like Saddam Hussein possessed nuclear weapons, he would pass them on to terrorists as a poor man's delivery system. They, like President Bush, came to believe that this is a threat not just to the United States but also to Western civilization as a whole. The acuteness of this perceived threat is what then drives the new doctrine of preemption and the greater willingness of the United States to use force unilaterally around the world.

Many Europeans, by contrast, believe that the attacks of September 11 were a one-off kind of event where Osama bin Laden got lucky and scored big. But the likelihood that al-Qaeda will achieve similar successes in the future is small, given the heightened state of alert and the defensive and preventive measures put into place since September 11. Even Britons sympathetic to the United States, such as Michael Howard[9] or David Owen, tend to see the World Trade Center attacks as part of a low-level campaign of terrorism akin to the IRA bombing attacks in Britain, welcoming Americans in a slightly patronizing tone to a club of which they have been members for a long time. Most Europeans simply disbelieved American claims about the dangers posed by Iraqi WMD programs; they felt that the chance of Saddam Hussein passing nuclear weapons to terrorists was small and that he could be deterred. And finally, they tend to believe that Muslim terrorists do not represent a general threat to the West but are focused on the United States as a result of U.S. policy in the Middle East and Gulf.

DEMOCRACY'S FUTURE

Assuming we get past these near-term threats, there is a larger principle at issue in the current U.S.–European rift that will continue to play an important role in world politics for the foreseeable future. That principle has to do with the nature of democracy. In an increasingly globalized world, where is the proper locus of democratic legitimacy? Does it now and forever more exist only at the nation-state level, or is it possible to imagine the development of genuinely democratic international institutions? Will the existing welter of international rules, norms, and organizations someday evolve into something more than a series of ad hoc arrangements, in the direction of genuine global governance? And if so, who will design those institutions?

My own view, as stated earlier, is that it is extremely hard to envision democracy ever emerging at an international level, and many reasons for thinking that attempts to create such international institutions will actually have the perverse effect of undermining the real democracy that exists at a nation-state level. A partial exception to this is the European Union, which continues to move ahead as a political project with the introduction of the euro and expansion under the Nice Treaty. But in a way, the experience of the EU proves my point: there is a significant democracy deficit at the European level, one that exacerbates existing democracy deficits at the member-state level. This is the source of much of the backlash against further European integration, which is seen as weakening local powers in favor of unmovable bureaucrats in Brussels. The problem will become even more severe with enlargement, as states from eastern Europe enter the Union with very different expectations and experiences.

But if the United States refuses, rightly, to concede the principle that there is a broader democratic international community providing legitimacy to international institutions, it needs to consider carefully the consequences and perceptions of its behavior as the world's most powerful democratic nation-state. Its own self-interest dictates the need for reciprocity across the broad range of cooperative agreements and institutions within which it finds itself enmeshed. The opportunities for unilateral action that exist presently in the military realm are not nearly as broad in the realm of trade and finance. There are a large number of global public goods, such as standards, free trade, financial flows, and legal transparency, as well as public bads, such as environmental damage, crime, and drug trafficking, that create difficult collective-action problems. Some of these problems can be solved only if the world's most powerful country takes the lead in either providing those public goods or in organizing institutions to provide them—something the United States was eager to do in earlier periods.

The enormous margin of power exercised by the United States, particularly in the security realm, brings with it special responsibilities to use that power prudently. Robert Kagan spoke of the need to show what the American founders labeled a "decent respect for the opinions of mankind." But for him that seems to consist of nothing more than not gratuitously rejecting offers of support for American aims and objectives. It is not clear that those aims and objectives should in any way be shaped by the opinions of non-Americans.

This kind of unilateralism would be justified if the Bush administration were correct in its assessment of the threat posed by Iraq. It is not possible to argue in principle that if a nation is threatened with terrorists armed with weapons of mass destruction it does not have a right to defend itself with whatever means it has at its disposal. But with the failure to find virtually any significant evidence of WMDs in Iraq following the invasion, it would appear that the European position that Iraq simply was not as dangerous as the Americans said was correct. The world appears to be a bit more Venutian in hindsight, which should then temper American anger at its Europeans allies for not providing sufficient support in its hour of need. On the question of who is right about the severity of the future terrorist threat, it is hard to say because we simply do not know what the empirical state of the world is at present. But the European view that the United States has overreacted to the September 11 attacks and has thus become a source of instability is not, on the face of it, absurd.

What would an American foreign policy that did show a real degree of decent respect involve? It seems to me that a realist foreign policy can nonetheless show some deference to multilateral institutions without having to concede the principle of their legitimacy. That is, even if the United States does not believe in the superior legitimacy of a body like the United Nations to its own constitutional government, it can at least recognize the fact that much of the rest of the world does and use that legitimacy for its own national purposes.

The Bush administration made a gesture in that direction by going to the UN Security Council in September 2002 and winning unanimous passage of Resolution 1441. But it also made clear that it would accept no UN outcome that did not support its desire to forcibly disarm Iraq.

The United States dismissed French, Russian, and German suggestions that a stronger inspections regime could have been made to work and started a war mobilization that made it very difficult to stand down. It now appears that the Iraqis did in fact destroy the vast bulk of their earlier WMD programs, which would imply that international pressure was effective in derailing them. Hence a bit more deference to the opinions of mankind would not have seriously injured American interests here.

This should not in any way imply that the United States needs to go to the United Nations on every occasion to legitimize its activities. The Kosovo war was carried out under a NATO banner rather than that of the United Nations because the Russian veto would have prevented collective action. Perhaps the world needs a variety of different institutional forums to meet different security needs, which would permit a certain amount of forum shopping tailored to the circumstances of the crisis. But Americans should not fool themselves that "coalitions of the willing" are a substitute for such institutions; these will never be perceived as anything but covers for American unilateralism.

The United States can show greater respect for the opinions of mankind by simply making a better effort to explain itself. If the United States is going to shift to a preemptive policy toward international terrorism, there ought to be a thinking through and enunciation of a broader strategy that among other things indicates the limits of this new doctrine. What kinds of threats, and what standards of evidence, will justify the use of this kind of power? A more realistic appraisal of future threats will mean raising the bar to preemption, while keeping it in the arsenal.

Finally, the United States needs to take some responsibility for global public bads like carbon emissions. The Kyoto Protocol is a very flawed document for any number of reasons, and a link between carbon emissions and observed warming has not been conclusively proved. On the other hand, it has not been disproved, either, and it would seem only prudent to hedge against the possibility that it is true. Apart from global warming, there are any number of good reasons why the United States ought to tax energy use much more heavily than it does: to pay for the negative externality of having to go to war every decade or so to keep open access to Middle Eastern oil, to promote development of alternative energy sources, and to create some policy space in dealing with Saudi Arabia, which does not seem to be a particular friend of the United States after September 11. Americans may not ever be convinced that they should make serious economic sacrifices for the sake of international agreements, but they may be brought around to an equivalent position if they see sufficient self-interest in doing so.

The U.S.–European rift that emerged after September 11 is not just a transitory problem reflecting the style of the incumbent U.S. administration or the world situation in the wake of September 11. It is a reflection of differing views of the locus of democratic legitimacy within a broader Western civilization whose actual institutions have become remarkably similar. The underlying principled issue is essentially unsolvable because there is ultimately no practical way of addressing the democracy deficit at the global level. But the problem can be mitigated by a degree of American moderation, even as it carries on a realist foreign policy within a system of sovereign nation-states.

Notes

1. Owen Harries, "The Collapse of 'The West,' " *Foreign Affairs* 72, no. 4 (1993).
2. Robert Kagan, "Power and Weakness," *Policy Review* 113 (June–July 2002).
3. John Van Oudenaren, "E Pluribus Confusio," *National Interest* 65 (Fall 2001).
4. This doctrine was first elaborated in Bush's 2002 State of the Union message, then in his June 2002 West Point speech, and finally in The National Security of the United States (Washington, September 2002).
5. For an elaboration of this argument, see Jeremy Rabkin, *Why Sovereignty Matters* (Washington: American Enterprise Institute, 1998).
6. Views on this issue may have changed in the United States as a result of the conflict in the Security Council over a second resolution.
7. Seymour Martin Lipset, *American Exceptionalism: A Double-Edged Sword* (New York: W. W. Norton, 1995). This theme appears also in his books *Political Man: The Social Bases of Politics*. 2nd ed. (Baltimore: Johns Hopkins University Press, 1981); *The First New Nation* (New York: Basic Books, 1963); and *Continental Divide: The Values and Institutions of the United States and Canada* (New York and London: Routledge, 1990).
8. See for example Barry Rubin, "The Real Roots of Arab Anti-Americanism," *Foreign Affairs* 81, no. 6 (2002).
9. Michael Howard, "What's in a Name? How to Fight Terrorism," *Foreign Affairs* 81, no. 1 (2002).

9

AMERICAN ENDURANCE

by Walter Russell Mead

A MERICANS MAY BE FROM MARS, and Europeans from Venus; the trouble is that both sides must live on planet Earth and, somehow, learn to manage their common affairs.

The recent series of transatlantic rows over the U.S.- and U.K.-led war in Iraq, climaxing in perhaps the bitterest interalliance squabble since the Suez crisis of 1956, exposed the degree to which Europeans and Americans have lost what was once a common view of how the transatlantic partnership should work. Indeed, it is not too much to say that currently the United States and Europe (or at least the Franco-German partnership at the core of "Old Europe") have radically different visions of what the relationship should look like—and that neither side has a vision that could realistically serve as the basis for a partnership of equals.

Many observers on both sides of the Atlantic are in danger of concluding that the partners are too far apart in their basic views of the world for the partnership to prosper. I am more optimistic, believing that at the end of the day the necessities of international life will compel the two sides to keep overcoming their differences. Americans will discover that allies—even obstreperous and vacillating ones—have their uses; Europeans will find that for all its faults and irritating habits, the United States makes a better security and economic partner for Europe than any possible alternative.

The two sides will grumble and snipe at one another but unless one or both sides lose sight of their true interests, the partnership should endure into the future. Nevertheless, difficult adjustments are now underway as Europe and the United States respond to the prospect of continuing declines in Europe's economic and political weight in the world.

THE SPECTER OF ROOSEVELT

The Bush administration's assertion of a right of preemptive attack around the world was unwelcome but not completely surprising to informed European observers. One way to read U.S. foreign policy since World War I is to see it as a progressive globalization of the American principles that, before World War I, had been developed in the Western Hemisphere.

Through this lens, the determination of Franklin Roosevelt and his successors to destroy the European colonial empires around the world looks like a globalization of the Monroe Doctrine that opposed European colonial adventures in Latin America. The Bush administration now seems to be completing the process, recapitulating on a global scale both Secretary of State Richard Olney's famous 1895 declaration that "the United States is practically sovereign on this continent, and its fiat is law upon the subjects to which it confines its interposition,"[1] and Theodore Roosevelt's so-called Corollary to the Monroe Doctrine, which in 1904 asserted that the United States had an "international police power" to enforce the standards of international law and good governance within its hemisphere.

From a European standpoint, few policy doctrines could be more detestable. The combination of Franklin Roosevelt's global Monroe Doctrine and George W. Bush's global Roosevelt Corollary portends, one can easily see, a sort of "Latin Americanization" of international life. Not only do these doctrines expose Europe to all the anxieties and unpredictabilities of American interventions around the world but they also strike at the international standing and even the independence of Europe itself. True, the United States does not (yet) assert the view that France is a banana republic, but the Bush Doctrine certainly presupposes a world in which the United States has no equals and recognizes no institutional constraints on its freedom of action.

Europe cannot accept this without condemning itself to second-class status in the world; the firmness of its rejection is however undercut by so-called New Europe's felt need to maintain transatlantic ties on almost any terms.

THE MIRACULOUS MANTLE

A great deal of attention has been paid to the political deficiencies in the American concept of the Atlantic Alliance, and properly so. Less attention has been paid to the equally severe problems with the way much of European opinion has come to define a desirable relationship with the United States.

A cardinal element in the European position is that for the relationship to be satisfactory, Europe—or at least a critical mass within Europe—must be able to veto American military adventures under certain circumstances. For the United States to go ahead with military action in the face of strong European opposition is unilateralism, and it is radically unacceptable to many European states.

On the other hand, if European states propose some global initiative—an International Criminal Court, for example, or a Kyoto Protocol—the United States has no legitimate right of veto. Forget interposing a veto. For the United States simply to seek an abstention from such initiatives is a sign of unacceptably unilateral behavior. In other words Europe wants a nonreciprocal veto over American initiatives worldwide.

To make the nonreciprocal veto more palatable, Europeans point to their ability to provide substantial financial and peacekeeping assistance for U.S. ventures. Such a Paris, they argue, is well worth a Mass. Beyond that, they often argue that accepting these constraints will vest American foreign policy with a wonder-working garment known as the "mantle of legitimacy." A statesman wrapped by this marvelous robe will, Europeans tell Americans, achieve much more success than one wearing ordinary street clothes. Perhaps the price is high—but the virtues of this garment are such that no self-respecting superpower can be seen in public without one. The significance of symbolic European support is so great that the United States should willingly concede Europe a substantial measure of control over American policy to get it.

Yet when Americans inquire more closely into the specific characteristics and powers of the miraculous textile, the mysteries only deepen. It turns out that the mantle of legitimacy is not efficacious everywhere. In East Asia and the Middle East, European support for American policies does not confer additional legitimacy upon them. Al-Jazeera would not have supported the war in Iraq if French troops were part of the Crusader armies. Indeed, by calling up memories of the imperial past, a united front of Europeans and Americans looks in much of the world like a revival of the old and unlamented effort of the white races to dominate the rest of the world.

The wonder-working powers of the mantle of legitimacy, it appears, are largely confined to Europe. Europeans will like American foreign policy more and support it more fervently if America accepts the non-reciprocal veto—which is to say that Europeans promise to like American foreign policy if Americans adopt only those foreign policies that Europeans like.

There was one other item that Europeans were prepared to supply the United States if it agrees to pay full retail price for the mantle of legitimacy: political wisdom. Europeans are convinced that Americans are generally too impatient, too brash, and too given to black-and-white characterizations ("axis of evil," for example), and they are willing, at no additional charge, to supply the perspective and insight so sadly lacking in America's foreign policy.

It is perhaps not surprising that Americans have generally been unwilling to pay the manufacturer's suggested retail price for this estimable mantle; it is a little more surprising that Europeans are so repeatedly astounded by American resistance to the sale. However, it ought to be clear that European-style multilateralism is at least as unbalanced and a good deal less realistic than America's proposed Bush Corollary.

HAGGLING OVER PRICE

Old Europeans and Americans have fundamentally different assessments of the degree to which the United States benefits from alliance with Europe. To put it another way, they disagree about the proper pricing of the mantle of legitimacy. Europeans genuinely believe that their ability to provide economic assistance and to blunt the edge of anti-Americanism in the developing world by the strength of their moral suasion and prestige is so valuable that the Americans will fail without it and should be glad to purchase it even at the cost of allowing Europe a veto over substantial American initiatives.

Americans are still debating the value of the mantle. The Bush administration, and behind it a gradually growing portion of the American public and foreign policy establishment, believes that the mantle is worth much less than Europe wants for it. Neoconservatives argue that the value is close to zero; many liberal internationalists are ready to pay something close to the asking price. Most American opinion is somewhere in between, with a general tendency since the Cold War to revise its value estimate slowly downward.

Both sides are now testing their views. The Bush administration attacked Iraq without the support of Germany and France, and events will determine whose assessment was correct. Should the United States have tried harder to win their support, even at the cost of a delay of months or even years? Or can the United States proceed to restructure the power and the politics of significant Middle East countries in the face of vigorous opposition from the two leading powers of Old Europe? If the result is a disaster, a chastened United States can be expected to stick closer to its partners and pursue a somewhat more cautious foreign policy. If the outcome is reasonably successful, the asking price for the mantle of legitimacy may drop in future crises.

Either way, this difference over price suggests that the root issue between America and Europe today is more like a disagreement over terms than the breakup of a partnership. We may come to a parting of the ways; it is more likely that we will find a way to compromise and adjust. In the end, Europe needs to sell the mantle and America would like to have it; a market-clearing price is likely to be found.

EUROPE IN DECLINE

Whatever proves to be the proper political value of the mantle of European legitimacy, one of the underlying issues in the relationship is that much European opinion—and some American opinion, principally in the old Europhile northeastern foreign policy establishment—has dramatically misread the European condition. Europe's progress toward economic integration and political union, and its decreased dependency on American protection following the collapse of the Soviet Union, have led many observers to conclude that Europe has begun to reverse its long decline. That is alas probably not true, and the mistake accounts for much of Europe's tendency to misprice its value to the United States.

The secular trend of declining European power on the global stage is one of the oldest and best established trends in world politics. Since 1914 the European empires have melted away. Since 1975 the dramatic rise of East Asia—and the Arab world's liberation from the unequal oil arrangements imposed in an earlier, more imperialistic era—have led to a steady drop in Europe's economic importance. Europe's share of the global population peaked at the turn of the century at 25 percent; by 2000 it had fallen to 12 percent and by 2050 is expected to drop to 7 percent.[2]

Different European countries have adjusted (or not adjusted) to this decline in different ways; nevertheless it remains one of the common truths of the European condition.

During the Cold War, Europe's decline was masked by its central role in America's Cold War strategy. Europe was the central battleground and the location of key allies in the struggle. American policy makers needed to win European consent for significant strategic decisions in the conflict, and Americans constantly examined the effect of their decisions on European opinion and power realities.

This very naturally led both sides to see Europe as centrally important in the world. However it had another result; Europeans—who in reality had almost no direct impact on important events beyond the shores of Europe—assessed their power not by their global influence but by their influence on Washington.

As the colonial empires disappeared and as Europe's economic and military reach shortened, Europe's influence in Asia sank to its lowest level since the sixteenth century. From Singapore and Vietnam to Argentina, Chile, and Brazil, new generations of developing country elites forsook their fathers' and grandfathers' universities in Paris, Heidelberg, and Oxbridge to study on the Charles and in Chicago.

Yet Europe was not watching these trends—it was watching Washington. Europe came to define its world power by its ability to influence world events through influencing Washington. This helped conceal the actual extent of Europe's continuing decline—but also made Europe extremely vulnerable to changes in its relationship with Washington. A loss of influence in Washington was not only disconcerting in itself; it had the effect of underlining Europe's powerlessness in the world as a whole.

The end of the Cold War did not immediately lead to a revaluation of Europe's place in the world. Institutional inertia and the Balkan crises kept Washington's attention on Europe. The widespread belief that "the end of history" had arrived led many observers to overestimate the future importance of the economic and political dimensions of international politics, where Europe is relatively strong, and to underestimate the importance of military and other dimensions, where Europe is weak.

At the same time, Europe misdiagnosed not only the extent of its weakness but also the cause of it and, therefore, the efficacy of the strategies it has employed to strengthen itself. Even before the attacks of September 11 announced the definitive end of the relatively stable (and Eurocentric) post–Cold War period in world history, the gap between European and American perceptions of Europe's importance was growing. After those attacks, when the United States felt itself (rightly or wrongly) to be engaged in a struggle as desperate and deadly as the Cold War, the speed of American reassessment of Europe dramatically increased.

It was not simply that Americans reacted like Martians to September 11 and its aftermath while the European reacted like Venusians. Mars noted that Venus had little help to offer in the crisis. The Venusian armed forces were weak; the vaunted Venusian political links with the

Arab and Muslim worlds were not particularly reliable, helpful, or strong. And, of course, it quickly became clear that Venusian assistance would only be forthcoming at a higher price than Mars was willing to pay.

Looking down the road, many Americans—not only neoconservatives and members of the Bush administration—suddenly realized that Europe was unlikely to loom as large either as a source of problems for the United States or as a source of help. Its problems no longer demanded intensive American engagement; its strengths were of little help in dealing with the new types of international crises and conflict taking shape after September 11. The United States did not initially become more hostile to Europe after September 11; it simply concluded that, in the future, Europe would play a less central role in American planning.

When Americans contemplate the causes of Europe's long decline in world politics, they see a multitude of causes at work. Some are beyond European control—such as the continuing industrialization of non-European parts of the world. Just as Britain's hegemony was doomed once great continental states like the United States and Germany began to industrialize, so Europe's global position could not survive the industrialization of Asia.

In addition Americans increasingly see cultural and social forces at work in Europe's decline. The loss of religious faith and the "debellicization" of European peoples make it much more difficult for Europe to compete in a world where most people are neither secular nor instinctively pacifist. Europeans have reached John Lennon's utopia sketched out in his famous song "Imagine": "Nothing to kill or die for / And no religion, too." The rest of the world is not there yet and unlikely to get there quickly, Americans think; until it does, Europeans will be less energetic, less willing to risk life and limb for God or country, than people in other parts of the world. Like posthistorical France and Britain confronting the still very historical Germany of Adolf Hitler in the 1930s, Europe as a whole today is a little too pure to cut an effective figure in the sad and sorry world we actually have.

Traumatized by the hideous experiences of the twentieth century, Europeans are skeptical of populist and nationalist politics and emotionally committed at virtually all costs to international institutions based on consensus and compromise. Cultural attitudes to work, compensation, and the role of the state in providing welfare and pension payments to individuals have led to proliferating and interlocking formal and informal obstacles to economic growth. The European cultural preference for a strong state—rooted partly in the outcome of the bitter class struggles of modern European history and partly in even deeper historical forces—puts European society at a permanent disadvantage as capitalism accelerates and transforms itself into forms that require ever more flexible practices and autonomous markets and corporations. The deep cultural roots that fortify European social solidarity and social peace make assimilating immigrants difficult or impossible; given Europe's low birth rates, the rise of an alienated, mostly Muslim, disaffected population seems inevitable.

From the American perspective, these preferences and attachments are too deeply rooted for Europeans to change them anytime soon. Moreover, although Americans can and do respect the ethical aspirations embodied in these preferences, Americans tend to believe that this complex of European values commits Europe irrevocably to its own decline and increased irrelevancy. In every case, Americans think, these preferences doom Europe to a choice of present comfort over future greatness.

Behind these specific arguments for European decline, Americans operate from a set of assumptions about the future that they rarely articulate but that nevertheless inform a great deal of American strategic and economic thought. Americans—educated and uneducated, elite and nonelite alike—tend to be profoundly convinced that the United States is on the cutting edge of world history. To put this unspoken, emotional conviction into words is inevitably to distort it, but one way to express it is to say that Americans believe that the capitalist transformation of human society has proceeded farthest and fastest in the United States and that the America of today is the tomorrow of the rest of the world. Although Americans have never consciously embraced Marxist philosophy, they have come very close to embracing Marx's vision of capitalism as an irresistible, world-conquering force that will sweep the entire human universe into a single system of production and exchange based on market relations. America's willingness to open itself to the sometimes painful transformation that capitalism entails is, in this view, a sign of strength and promise for the future. As long as Americans are willing to live with fewer restraints on the destructive as well as the creative aspects of market capitalism, American society will continue to generate new technologies, new companies, new social patterns, and new ideas that will keep the United States ahead of the rest of the world.

Married to an idea of revolutionary, ever-accelerating progress, American society responds to challenges not by compromise or caution but by renewed determination to take risks, increase efforts, liberalize markets, and, in general and overall, let capitalism rip—"to let the black flower blossom as it may," as American conservatives like Nathaniel Hawthorne might sardonically say. When old institutions, alliances, and patterns of behavior no longer serve, Americans remain quicker than most others to set them aside and try something new.

EUROPEAN RESURGENCE

Although many Europeans see some truth in some of the American analyses of European problems, on the whole most Europeans reject most of this criticism. Where Americans see defects, Europeans see the distinctive achievements and institutions of a culturally and humanistically more advanced civilization than what often appears to be an atomized, deracinated, inhuman, and culturally sterile American pattern.

Europe's view of its relative decline in world importance looks to European disunity as the root cause of European decline—and to unification through the European Union as the road to recovery. Disunity and, especially, the Franco-German rivalry led Europe to divide its forces, waste its substance, and deliver itself ultimately over to the United States and the Soviet Union. Unity based on Franco-German reconciliation will enable Europe to reemerge and assume its rightful place as a great power.

And because despite all obstacles—and despite the continuing prophecies of doom by Anglo-Saxon skeptics—the European Union continues to progress, many Europeans believe that their long decline has halted and a great recovery has begun.

Like Americans, Europeans see the rise of what was once called the developing world as a key theme of the twenty-first century, but they believe that this will make the Americans more dependent on European support. A superpower beset with rivals on every continent and every sea will need all the help it can get, and despite their differences Europe and America are part of the same Western civilization and share a common heritage of values. Should world history move toward a clash of civilizations—and Europeans generally think that if there are clashes in the future they will be along civilizational lines—Europe will be America's most important and possibly only potential ally.

Europe also sees a key advantage for itself in that its social and economic models are more compatible with the values of much of the developing world than are those of the United States. The European vision of a strong social welfare state, a relatively stable, slowly changing economic structure, and a large role for the state in economic planning and social administration meshes well with the values of a large number of developing countries. Indeed, by many measures the Jacobin model of the French state—centralism, militant secularism, and state capitalism—has already been more influential as a model for state creation and economic development around the world than the American model. This is certainly true in the Islamic world, where modernizers from Ataturk to the Ba'ath movement have instinctively looked to Paris rather than Washington for a model. It also has been historically true in Latin America and Africa.

Europeans often believe that Europe can serve as bridge between the excessively capitalist United States and the developing world. Europe's values are midway between those of the Americans and the others; Europe will emerge as a world leader because it can be the trusted interlocutor between the two camps, working out the details of the new world order because it has a unique perspective that enables it to grasp and reconcile the aspirations of the two sides.

Europe sees itself as a postmodern society competing with the modern or partially premodern social model of the United States. If the American state benefits from the religiously motivated willingness of many of its citizens to kill and die for the flag, it suffers from a foreign policy deeply deformed by the sympathy of superstitious fundamentalists for Israel. If the American state is relatively small and its burden on the economy light, the neglect of such basic social services as education will cripple the United States in the long run. The very openness to immigration on which the Americans pride themselves will in the long run prove to be a weakness; American society will fall apart into a post–melting pot clash of cultures and civilizations, exacerbated by American culture's historical racism and the low levels of public investment in the education and health of the mostly low-income immigrants.

If America's self-image reflects a revolutionary society that achieves success by giving capitalism increasingly free reign, Europe sees itself shaped by a marriage of the dynamic processes of capitalism to values that have very different roots. European conservatives look to the preservation of precapitalist values of solidarity and justice; European progressives look to a synthesis of the admittedly successful economic processes of capitalism with a set of social and human values that in the twentieth century were represented by social democratic and socialist forces. Europe aspires to lead the world by successfully domesticating capitalism; America aspires to lead the world by letting capitalism run wild and free. Europe believes that its achievements will conquer the world through the irresistible appeal of a successful social model; America believes—in a way that Marx would have recognized—that capitalism is irresistible and that societies that try to control or limit it will always be weaker, more backward, less efficient, and less dynamic than those who rush enthusiastically to meet it.

The United States tends to see an America moving from strength to strength in the twenty-first century, while Europe continues to fade into relative obscurity. Europe tends to see an America weakened from within, dealing with hostile non-American and non-European powers such as China and the Muslim world; this America will increasingly need help from the growing wealth, sophistication, and power of a European Union that has overcome the divisions of the twentieth century.

MANAGING THE GAP

It goes without saying that the simplified archetypal positions presented previously do little justice to the subtleties, reservations, and shades of difference on both the European and American sides of the debate—and, of course, it is also true that what is presented previously as a debate between Americans and Europeans is also and perhaps most intensely a debate within each of the sides of the transatlantic alliance. And it must be equally clear that neither of these oversimplified analyses of world history can be wholly right—that the twenty-first century will to some degree frustrate and fulfill the hopes of Americans and Europeans.

Two basic elements of the future do, however, seem reasonably clear. First, European hopes for an end to the long decline will not, in general, be fulfilled. Even on the assumption that European integration and expansion will continue to go forward, Europe's relative decline in world influence will continue at least through the first half of the new century. Second, although the United States is likely to fend off any and all challenges to its position of global leadership, it will be unable to bring about the democratic peace for which it longs—and that many observers thought they had glimpsed in the first hopeful years after the end of the Cold War. The future relationship of the United States and its Cold War allies in Europe will unfold against a background of significant frustration for both sides.

Europe's hopes to stop its decline will not be fulfilled for three basic reasons: economic, political, and military. Economically, a combination of demographic and structural factors put Europe firmly in the slow lane in the global economy. Demographically, Europe's population will both age and shrink in the coming half century. According to recent projections from the European Commission, the population of the current members of the European Union will shrink from 376 million to 364 million by 2050. As Europe's population ages, the workforce will shrink even faster—dropping by 20 percent from 246 million to 203 million.[3]

If correct, these projections doom Europe to substantially slower economic growth than the world average. The long-term economic growth rate for any country or region equals the change in productivity plus the change in the size of the workforce. A country where each worker is becoming 3 percent more productive per year, and where the total number of workers is growing at 2 percent per year has a long-term growth potential of 5 percent per year. But if the workforce is shrinking at, say, 1 percent per year, the long-term economic growth rate falls to 2 percent per year—productivity growth minus workforce shrinkage.

These differences quickly add up. With 5 percent per year growth, an economy will double in size roughly every fourteen years. At 2 percent growth, an economy doubles every thirty-six years. Take two economies of $9 trillion per year in 2004. By 2040 the 5 percent economy will have an annual gross domestic product (GDP) of $36 trillion. The 2 percent economy will be at $18 trillion.

The coming divergence between the United States and Europe will not be this dramatic, but it will be considerable. U.S. population is now projected to grow to 403 million by 2050[4]—and the workforce will increase by 27.8 percent, or roughly 0.5 percent per year.[5] Assuming that productivity growth in Europe and the United States is roughly equal, and that structural factors do not mean that either Europe or the United States underperforms its long-term potential, the U.S. economy is projected to grow from $10 trillion today to $31 trillion in 2050. The EU economy will grow from $9 trillion to $14 trillion by that year.[6]

These projections point to different trends in the share of each power in global economic activity. Currently, the European Union produces 18 percent of all goods and services in the world economy each year, and the United States produces 23 percent. By 2050 the European Commission forecasts that the United States will produce 26 percent of global GDP, whereas Europe's share will fall to 10 percent.[7]

Incidentally, these trends do not project that the average European will be less rich by American or world standards. Because so much of the growth gap reflects population trends, Europeans will not lose much ground to their American counterparts. They may even grow richer on an individual basis compared with individuals in developing countries. Europe will remain one of the richest places in the world in 2050 on these projections—but the European market and the European economy will be substantially less important in global terms than they are now.

Progress toward political union is also likely to be somewhat disappointing. Even on the assumption that the European Union continues to deepen and that recent divisions do not long delay progress toward a common foreign policy, the European Union is likely even over the longer term to remain a somewhat awkward player on the international scene. The divisions inside Europe are too deep, the constitutional processes of the European Union likely too cumbersome, and the rights of minorities too strong for the Union to be as effective in foreign policy as other great powers. When the European Union reaches a consensus, its voice will be effective, but it is likely to reach consensus less fully and less easily than powers with a longer tradition of unity.

Europe's military standing is also likely to remain relatively low—even with greater integration. The budget problems of European states will grow greater as the population ages and shrinks. It is extremely unlikely that Europe will develop the political will to significantly increase the percentage of its income that it devotes to defense. Although technological prowess rather than soldiers on the ground will probably be a leading source of military strength in the future—and so make Europe's demographic and cultural problems with finding ground troops less of a barrier to great power status—financial constraints are likely to keep Europe out of the front rank of military powers as its relative economic weight continues to decline.

The European Union is and must remain a relatively inefficient military power. Differences in language, the difficulties of coordinating planning and expenditure across so many countries and cultures, and the inevitable wastage that occurs as political expediency directs military spending toward less militarily significant but more politically powerful channels will all help ensure that Europe gets less bang for each buck than other powers. Europe would need to spend more, absolutely and as a percentage of its GDP, than other powers to substantially increase its military standing; it is likely to spend less.

At the same time, it is unlikely that Europe's ideological weight in the world will increase. The United States will become increasingly less impressed by the European elements in its heritage as new immigrants from non-European countries continue to change its demographic balance—and as the descendents of European immigrants gradually lose touch with their pre-American roots. Indigenous populations and the descendents of Africans and Indians brought over in past centuries will continue to gain cultural importance in Latin America and the Caribbean. Non-Muslim East Asia will continue to gain cultural self-confidence and self-consciously begin to shake off what many Asians see as the ideological shackles of European and American tutelage. The Islamic world is unlikely to turn to European-style democratic secularism as its evolution continues; Fabian socialism and other Western ideas seem fated to continue to lose ground in India.

None of this is to suggest that European culture, ideology, technology, science, or economic power will disappear from the world stage. But Europeans must probably gird themselves for another half century of declining world influence. Europeans can make progress toward political and economic integration through the European Union to retard the decline; they probably will not halt and almost certainly will not reverse it.

Americans, on the other hand, will be disappointed in their quest for a new world order on American lines. The complexity and dynamism of the increasingly active and complicated global society of the twenty-first century will defeat the efforts even of a hyperpower to limit or control. This is likely to be true even if American efforts succeed in building a democratic *Pax Americana* in the Arab world. If those efforts fail, Americans will quickly perceive the new century as chaotic and out of control.

This is not a problem that good American policy can prevent. Rather, inherent in the American program for the world—to accelerate its capitalist transformation—is a program for instability and change. The more Americans succeed at shaping the world in their image, the more the titanic forces that are continually reinventing and sharpening American capitalism will break free to transform the rest of the world. The result, especially for cultures not as habituated or disposed to capitalism, must inevitably be resistance, rapid change, instability, and, often, resentment against the United States. Thus American success breeds challenges for American foreign policy. It is this dynamic that will keep the United States in need of allies, and, ultimately, it is this dynamic that imposes limits on American power. A world increasingly energized and enlivened by intensive capitalist development is a world in which technology will constantly cheapen the price of new weapons of mass destruction—even as capitalism introduces political upheavals into various societies, which will make it more likely that extreme or deformed political tendencies will seize power. More and more societies will dispose of more and more power—and individuals and nongovernmental organizations, including terrorist organizations, will increasingly find ways to challenge and displace the will of the superpower.

The world of the twenty-first century, therefore, is neither the hell Europeans fear—untrammeled, unaccountable American domination—or the heaven Americans seek—stable democratic peace under American leadership. Yet both Europe and the United States will retain a certain need for each other. Even if Europeans lose their hopes that the United States will impose the kind of order Europe seeks in the world, Europeans will still by and large prefer an imperfect American order to the conflicts that would arise without it. Europe may not always approve of the way the United States manages affairs in the Middle East or in Asia, but at the end of the day Europe is unlikely to have a viable alternative of its own. In addition, if American mismanagement should create regional crises, Europe will find that the United States will turn to Europe in its hour of need.

It seems likely that over time the Europeans are likely to lower the asking price for the mantle of moral legitimacy—or perhaps to offer the Americans a cheaper, generic substitute at a lower price: the mantle of moral adequacy.

Europeans will once again, as after World War II, accept that the price of getting the United States into world organizations is a series of sovereignty-saving loopholes and escape clauses. Both the NATO founding documents and the UN Charter contain these opt-outs. The Treaty of Versailles did not. Neither did the International Criminal Court and Kyoto Protocol contain the adjustments needed to ensure ratification in the Senate. It might not be pleasant to modify the International Criminal Court and the Kyoto Protocol to meet U.S. objections, but as the twenty-first century wears on, Europe is likely to feel that even with the opt-outs, it is better to have the United States in the organizations than outside.

On the other hand, the domestic political pressure on American administrations, even on conservative American administrations, to embrace international organizations and build multilateral alliances will not disappear. Since September 11, Jacksonian America—traditionally the most hostile current of American opinion vis-à-vis both Europe and global institutions—has been highly mobilized. Although continuing threats will keep Jacksonians engaged with foreign policy, over time the domestic political balance in the United States is likely to shift away from extreme views. The mantle of legitimacy will still be seen as a useful part of the American wardrobe.

At the end of the day, common interests and values still bring the United States and Europe together. The partnership has seen many shocks since 2001, but in a way this is a comfort. Few future periods are likely to contain this many controversies and shocks; if for no other reason, we can be reasonably hopeful that the three years following September 11 are not indicators of the tenor of transatlantic relations in the years ahead.

Notes

1. Paul Lagasse et al., eds., *Columbia Encyclopedia.* 6th ed. (New York: Columbia University Press, 2000). Also, George B. Young, "Intervention under the Monroe Doctrine: The Olney Corollary," *Political Science Quarterly* 57, no. 2 (1942).
2. United Nations, "World Population Growth from Year 0 to 2050," in *1998 Revision of the World Population Estimates and Projections* (New York: United Nations Population Division, Department of Economic and Social Affairs, 2000). Also, *U.S. Census Bureau, Statistical Abstract of the United States* (Washington, D.C., 2002), 823.
3. European Commission, Economic Policy Committee, "Budgetary Challenges Posed by Aging Populations" (Brussels, October 24, 2001).
4. Population Projections Program, Population Division, U.S. Census Bureau, *Projections of the Total Resident Population by 5-Year Age Groups, and Sex with Special Age Categories: Middle Series*, 1999 to 2100. NP-T3. (Washington, D.C.: Author, 2002), http://www.census.gov/population/www/projections/natsum-T3.html. Also see the *2002 U.S. Statistical Abstracts*, 9. The current U.S. population is 290 million.
5. In 2001 the U.S. labor force (population between the ages 16–64) was 185 million. By 2050 the labor force is projected to be 236 million. *2002 U.S. Statistical Abstracts*, 15, 18.
6. These numbers come from Werner Röger and Kieran Mc Morrow of ECFIN at the European Union. The 2050 GDP projections are based on 2002 growth rates and are in 1995 constant dollars.
7. European Commission, Commission of the European Communities, "The EU Economy: 2002 Review" (Brussels, December 11, 2002), 198–99 .

10

COOPERATION OR FAILURE

by Simon Serfaty

ONCE AGAIN WE ARE MOVING though a defining moment in the history of America's relations with Europe. Once again we are pursuing a major debate that is said to be separating Americans and Europeans from each other. Once again we are debating the relevance of our alliance and the significance of our ties.

There have been many other such debates in the past. But with the Cold War a full decade behind, and with many years of the wars against terrorism looming ahead, the transatlantic juncture has rarely seemed to be so critical. Divisions within the Atlantic Alliance over and beyond the war in Iraq, it is argued, have marginalized the role and significance of the North Atlantic Treaty Organization (NATO), notwithstanding some real achievements in providing NATO with an increasingly global relevance since the ambitious agenda adopted at the Prague summit in November 2002. No less significant are new and profound ruptures within the European Union, where the process of unification had been entering a final phase when it was overwhelmed by a bitter and divisive debate over the use of force in Iraq. Worse yet, there seems to be some resignation, and even indifference, to an erosion of the institutional order that has shaped relations within Europe and across the Atlantic. In short, this is a defining moment, meaning that its consequences are likely to extend beyond the next electoral cycles in the United States and in Europe—from the elections in Spain, for the European Parliament, and in the United States in 2004 to national elections in Great Britain, Germany, and France by 2007.

Admittedly, no consensus can be expected to emerge quickly at such moments. After 1945 neither Americans nor Europeans agreed, among themselves as well as with each other, on the threat that confronted them and on the most effective ways to address it. President Truman's bold ideas for the rehabilitation and reconstruction of prewar Europe, including the defeated states, were dismissed as naive, and even dangerous. Rebuild and rearm Germany? Stay in and unite Europe? Contain the USSR until such a time as communism would be toppled and Eastern Europe liberated? Americans, Europeans feared, would not have the endurance needed to lead the West. Europeans, Americans countered, would not have the resilience needed to master their own past and refashion their continent as a cohesive whole. These concerns were misplaced. Periodic Atlantic (and European) crises stalled but never derailed the community of converging interests and compatible values that progressively emerged between the United States and an ever more united Europe. Confronted with the complete weakness of its allies—institutional, military, and economic—the United States relied on its own complete power to build a lasting security order in and with Europe.

How are we to account, then, for the increasingly bitter tone of the transatlantic dialogue—if that is what it has been—since the emotional outbursts of complete solidarity and shared public grief that followed the dramatic events of September 11, 2001? References to persistent anti-American strains in Europe generally, and an especially hostile attitude toward President George W. Bush specifically, are not enough to explain the intensity of the moment. Some of that intensity is a matter of ideology—the lingering echoes of a European Left that resents the U.S. conservatives' "belief in individualism, liberty and self-reliance" and longs for an allegedly "better America ... liberal, outward-looking, and generous."¹ In early 2001 that passion could already be felt as issues that define the liberal-conservative cleavage in the United States spilled across the Atlantic—the death penalty, the environment, gun control, and others. To make matters worse, differences over societal values were reinforced by deep divergences over national security issues that involved various aspects of strategic weapons (defense, testing, and modernization) and the management of rogue, defeated, and rising powers like Iraq, Russia, and China, respectively. Over these issues, too, forceful European fears were voiced over the unilateralist instincts of an administration that neglected, voided, or withdrew from international agreements, conventions, and treaties negotiated by its predecessors.

Yet beyond the repetitiveness of Europe's anti-Americanism, whatever its causes at any moment, there should be little doubt that the events of September 11 and their aftermath profoundly transformed Europe's vision of America, even as these same events were transforming the U.S. vision of the world and its corresponding views of allies, friends, and adversaries. Faced with the fact and consequences of America's preponderant power, a weak Europe portrays itself as an exercise in self-discipline—the new, Old World that was able to call a time-out from its own history to enjoy the institutional bliss of multilateralism. Europe's goal is ambitious—to save America from itself and, in so doing, save Europeans from the risks of U.S. excesses that are keeping them "deeply suspicious and fearful of us."²

GRAVE NEW WORLD

Neither acts of war proper, nor mere terrorist actions, the assaults of September 11, 2001, pointed to a novel approach to the use of force and, by implication, a novel kind of warfare that threatened to redefine "normalcy" in and for the world.³ Forty years ago, Jean-Paul Sartre called upon Europeans to "listen [to] strangers gathered around a fire; for they are talking of the destiny they will mete out to your trading centers and to the hired soldiers who defend them." Their "suppressed fury" and "irrepressible violence," he added, "at times reviving old and terrible myths, at others binding themselves by scrupulous rites," would not be "the resurrection of savage instincts, nor even the effect of resentment: it is man recreating itself."[4] These words sound more credible now than when Sartre used them to reinforce Frantz Fanon's passionate plea on behalf of the "Wretched of the Earth" who populated the European empires at the time. In a narrow sense, September 11 confirmed the will of some extremists to mobilize Islam against the "distant enemy"—a cultural coalition of U.S.-led Western countries—that protects the "near enemy" at home. The ultimate goal of the "war" conceived by Osama bin Laden and his followers is to restore the purity of the Islamic man, a purity that ceased to exist in the thirteenth century when the rule of the Islamic clerics ended. In an even broader sense, these events point to the nihilistic anger that has been building up in vast areas of the world where the state does not exist or, when it does exist, fails to respond to its citizens' minimal expectations, whether for this life or the life after.

Thus, after three global wars and a near infinite number of regional and civil conflicts fought mainly at the expense of civilian populations, in the twentieth century there was a birth of a new generation of "wretched" people gathered throughout the territorial corpses left behind by these wars—wars of territorial expansion, wars of national liberation, and even wars of ideological redemption. In most cases, these were wars that America did not fight—and in many cases, wars that predate the American Republic—but they are nonetheless wars that American power must end if any sort of international order is to be restored.

The United States is ill at ease in such a disorderly and deregulated world. People whose desperation makes them seek death as relief from life are relying on levels of violence that invite more violence. When the use of absolute means takes precedence over the quest for plausible ends, perpetrators and victims stand as judge-penitents, to use a phrase from Albert Camus. Even as we question the reasons that brought our enemies to such hopelessness, the violence they use defines the beginning of a twisted morality—kill in order to not be killed. Traditional rules of war and peace no longer apply. Internal conflicts and international wars are waged on the same battleground, thereby threatening to void whatever remains of the distinctions that used to be made between civilians and armed combatants.[5] The dangerous paradox is that winning the war somewhere and anywhere may require actions that will prolong it elsewhere and everywhere. "Only the complete destruction of international terrorism and the regimes that sponsor it will spare America from further attack," warned Senator John McCain shortly after September 11.[6] But what will be left to rebuild after everything has been destroyed, including a cultural mind-set that embodies far more than "we" can truly understand and is forced to absorb much more than "they" can forget? The mythical "day after"—when winners attend to the losers for absolution of their respective sins—may prove to be long and dark. Memories of postwar Germany and Japan, and their subsequent fate, are meant to reassure on the basis of assumptions that sound benign or naive when describing the scope and nature of the conflicts ahead. By 2004 the debate is not just about war in Iraq (a police operation, really) but also about the commitments made to end it by changing the regime, disarming the state, and reinventing the country, there, in Iraq, but also and most ominously elsewhere in and beyond the region. Or else, historians will uncover that the analogy that was most apt was not that of defeated Germany in 1945 but the more ominous analogy of revanchiste Germany in 1919.

NEITHER WAR NOR TERROR

Coming soon after the sharp criticism that had greeted the arrival of the Bush administration earlier in the year, Europe's emotional response to the events of September 11 and the subsequent war in Afghanistan was extraordinary. It involved not only the unprecedented invocation of Article 5 of the North Atlantic treaty but also an equally impressive display of "total solidarity" from the fifteen members of the European Union, as well as the use of European influence to ensure swift and unanimous UN support for the United States. Indeed, even with the hindsight of later quarrels, America's surprise in the face of the institutional triple play managed by its closest allies was itself surprising: if not from Europe, from where? In fall 2001 like-minded countries on both sides of the Atlantic reaffirmed that the transatlantic community of values they had come to form over the previous fifty years could reason and act as one when these values were at risk.

That did not last long, however. For one, the dust in New York had barely settled when the allies in Europe began to question the scope and goals of the U.S. reaction. With the history of the Old World serving as reference for the events that had transpired in the New World, many in Europe tended to minimize their significance and emphasize instead the normalcy of pain in interstate relations as they had known it over the years. After all, war is remembered as a way of life for the former European great powers, and terror is a recurring accident that can be defeated when it erupts and must be forgotten after it has been defeated.

To be or not to be at war? The semantic contest that erupted almost at once across the Atlantic pointed to a strategic transatlantic gap—a clash of history—that has intensified since.[7] But for Americans who lived the horrific events of September 11, that debate made little sense. Whatever word might be used to call this attack, and however well it might be said to fit the tragic ways of history, it dramatically exposed the United States to a territorial vulnerability that had been historically confined to other countries. In other words, now at last, the "over there" of yesteryear's wars seemed to be moving "over here" on U.S. soil. Accordingly, Bush insisted that such a threat would have to be defeated without conditions, and even preempted without compassion, to the obvious satisfaction of Americans whose approval of their president remained high but to the visible dismay of a worldwide public opinion whose opposition to U.S. policies kept rising dramatically even where national governments remained supportive. The point that could not be understood abroad, if only because it seemed to be self-evident at home, was less a change in the reality we knew than changes in the realities we feared: for the new arithmetic of risk-taking that followed the horrific spectacle of September 11, 2001, whatever risks might have been acceptable the day before ceased to be acceptable the day after, as a matter of morality—the "burden of leadership"—more than as a matter of facts; meaning, the alleged burden of proof that failed to emerge when weapons of mass destruction failed to be uncovered.

If September 11, 2001 changed America's perception of the world, the world's perception of America was changed on January 29, 2002, with President Bush's first State of the Union address. For many, in Europe especially, what seemed to cause offense was the tone as well as the substance of that speech—what Bush said and how he said it, as well as what he might do and to what ends. Coming barely three months after the allies' display of solidarity within NATO, through the European Union, and at the United Nations, the president's failure to mention either institution was astonishing. References to an "axis of evil" between Iran, Iraq, and North Korea left most of continental Europe also fearful of what might come next, whether in terms of other terrorist attacks that would be aimed at soft European targets or in terms of U.S. reprisals likely to be aimed at targets near Europe. To make matters worse, the speech deepened the allies' apprehension that, as had been shown in Afghanistan, they were being moved to a secondary role over issues with which they were directly concerned and which they had explicitly committed to defeat in coordination with their senior partner across the Atlantic.

To combat the new, post-9/11 security conditions, Bush planned to rely on a clear preponderance of U.S. military power to launch the many missions that would have to be assumed before victory could be claimed. Like Truman on the eve of the Cold War, Bush responded to a morality of convictions that presented the world in messianic terms—"with us or against us" to exorcize a new "evil" and "bring him to justice … dead or alive."[8] Like Truman's, too, Bush's strategy was global—"wherever they are"—and time-consuming, as the president urged people to remain "steadfast and patient and persistent." Finally, and also like Truman, Bush's memories of the past strengthened his convictions. Truman had been a product of the earlier dehumanizing brutality of a European war (which he courageously fought) followed by a catastrophic exercise in appeasement (which he unequivocally deplored); Bush was, in his own words, "a product of the Vietnam era," but he had also lived the euphoric years during which the Reagan-Bush administration victoriously completed the strategy started by Truman four decades earlier. As he later confided in order to explain his post-9/11 mind-set, "I remember presidents trying to wage wars that were very unpopular, and the nation split. … I had the job of making sure the American people understood … the severity of the attack."[9] In short, Bush concluded, "This nation won't rest until we have destroyed

terrorism. ... I can't tell you how passionate I feel on the subject. ...
There is no calendar, there is no deadline."[10]

There, however, ends the comparison. Having "scared the hell out of
the American people" Truman ignored his own doctrine—from the
coup in Czechoslovakia to the communist revolution in China—and,
mistakenly hoped to limit the wars he found it necessary to wage in
Korea as a so-called "police operation." Moreover, the multilateral
framework Truman built was a coalition of institutions that included an
Atlantic Alliance built on U.S. power and leadership, and a new Europe
based on Franco-German reconciliation and followership. In truth, if
Truman's America was vulnerable to the new Soviet threat, which it
was, that vulnerability was initially more moral and political than physical and territorial. For Bush, however, the stakes have been higher from
the start: to lead the nation on a mission designed to restore America's
territorial invulnerability and even "to save civilization itself" from a
"global terrorism" inspired by a "vitriolic hatred of America" and also,
by association, of its friends and allies.[11]

FORCE AND CONSENT

After the catalytic events of September 11, President Bush's tone became increasingly firm: "I do not need to explain why I say things.
That's the interesting thing about being the president. Maybe somebody
needs to explain to me why they say something, but I don't feel like I
owe anybody an explanation." And he added, "I believe in results. ...
We're never going to get people all in agreement about force and the use
of force. ... But action—confident action that will yield positive results
provides kind of a slipstream into which reluctant nations and leaders
can get behind."[12] From the moment he was elected, the president of the
United States may not have led with powerful and complex ideas, but
his leadership has been asserted on the basis of overpowering and readily stated beliefs.[13]

This approach to leadership was not well received in Europe, where
it has been viewed as a troubling willingness to take unnecessary risks.
That a world without Saddam would be a safer world, and that an Iraq
without Saddam would be a better country was not at issue. Yet, with
the states of Europe unwilling or unable to develop alternatives to the

U.S. approach, the transatlantic debate over the use of military force in Iraq progressively ignored the reality of the threat raised by Iraq's regime and focused instead on the uses of U.S. power without the consent of its traditional like-minded followers and other major members of the international community.

A world with only one major power to ensure its stability and order is unlikely to remain permanent. However overwhelming America's preponderance is, power never stays in one place. While the hegemon depletes its resources and exhausts its will in a never-ending series of dissymmetrical conflict, coalitions of lesser and ascending states are formed to counter or balance it.[14] Already, most nations (including perhaps, and ultimately especially, the United States) seem ambivalent about the desirability of the current unipolar moment, which means ambivalence over what America is—the sole superpower—irrespective of what it does. But they also seem seriously concerned over the best ways to prepare for the aftermath of that moment, which means a concern over what America does—with and to others—irrespective of what it is. In short, there is concern for what America is, as well as for what it does. Thus, the debate over the use of force in Iraq was a test of the world's ability to impose institutional limits on America's seemingly unlimited access to military power on behalf of an elusive order that it would define unilaterally and, to the extent of the possible, enforce multilaterally.

Nation or empire? As a matter of historical fact, as well as a matter of national conviction, America rose as a world power not to substitute for the European empires but to end the age of empires. Although this condition has not changed—America neither has nor seeks an empire—the question has gained new relevance on grounds of power but also for reasons of necessity. "We have to think new thoughts about how we deal with that threat," repeated Vice President Richard Cheney on March 16, 2003. One of these new thoughts is that containment might no longer be relevant or at least sufficient. "As a matter of common sense and self defense," argued President Bush as part of America's new *National Security Strategy,* "shadowy networks of individuals" and "failing" or "rogue" states intent on perpetrating "premeditated, politically motivated violence … against innocents" cannot be allowed "to strike first"—especially with "weapons of mass destruction as weapons of choice."[15] The strategy is not lacking in logic, but what follows from it may lead to imperial results that will have no logic to them. An occasional and extraordinary need for preemptive action waged because of a clear and imminent danger cannot be worked into a doctrine that can ensure order under a wide variety of unclear and distant risks.

Contrary to what is occasionally assumed, Europe—its nation-states and their union—acknowledges the primacy of American power and the need for American leadership. Europeans also truly understand and appreciate the salutary role played by the United States to revive many of its states after World War II and most of the others after the Cold War. Finally, Europe also comprehends and fears the dangers of a new security environment characterized by the potential dissemination of weapons of mass destruction to revisionist states, or rogue groups within those states, or even loose individuals within these groups. Arguments to the contrary have little basis in fact, and even less basis in history. They are offensive to Europeans, and they should remain irrelevant in the United States.

Concomitantly, but also contrary to what many in Europe seem to believe, most Americans recognize Europe's remarkable transformation since 1945—from a volatile mosaic of national sovereignties into a more cohesive, though still unfinished, union of states. It also is understood that this transformation has benefited not only Europe's but also America's interests in the context of a community of converging values within which transatlantic differences remain far lesser than U.S. differences with any other part of the world outside the Western Hemisphere. Admittedly, America was not born into the world to become a European power. But the Cold War reversed the facts of the nation's birth when the United States developed a presence in Europe, which makes it now a virtual nonmember member of the European Union.

Finally, contrary to what some seem to believe, Americans and Europeans live in the same earthly world, within which they suffer from their respective capabilities gaps—including the patience to wait and the resilience to endure—and to which they can contribute their respective forms of power—which obviously extends beyond military power alone. Within that world, thinking about the United States without the institutional access to Europe provided by NATO is to imagine an isolated America adrift in a hostile world—a power that would remain without peers but also would be lacking the support and comfort of like-minded allies. That is not a happy thought. Nor is it better to imagine an America that would escape such isolation by returning to mixed patterns of relations with one or a few European countries—at the ultimate expense of the European Union. That approach would not be helpful to the United States because, worst of all, it would ultimately be destructive of the European Union. For thinking about Europe without the union—and, for years to come, without NATO—is to imagine the kind of Europe that the United States has endeavored to end over the past fifty years: unsafe without its NATO security blanket and astray without its EU anchor, older because it would be closer to resurrecting its past than to entering the future, and more dangerous because it would become more divided and less predictable.

Past 9/11 and the bitter debates that have followed, a first conclusion is for the United States to continue to assert the complementarity of both of these institutions. Neither would have been conceived without the other, each helped the other deliver on the high expectations that had given them birth, and both are needed for a whole and free Europe to emerge within a strong and cohesive transatlantic partnership. This conclusion is not self-evident in all instances. A good American (or European) idea, especially about security, will not always seem equally good for those in Europe (or the United States) who will be asked to follow or accept it. Nevertheless, the logic of unity transcends the logic of cleavage, across the Atlantic and in Europe. To ignore this logic on either side of the Atlantic is to challenge the most successful policies pursued by the United States and the states of Europe over the past fifty years.

ASCENDING EUROPE

To understand, wrote Isaiah Berlin, "is to perceive patterns."[16] The pattern that has grown out of Europe's history over the past fifty years is compelling: with nation-states reinventing themselves as member states of the Union they form or which they hope to join, Europe is achieving a new synthesis that is making it whole at last. The single currency that was launched in January 2002, the enlargement of the Union with ten new members that was announced in December 2002, and the constitutional debate started in 2003 are the identifiable plays of an endgame known as "finality." Criticism of Europe and exasperation with some of its policies need not stand in the way of its dramatic territorial revolution away from the Westphalian system of nation-states to a more cohesive union of member states. There is nothing old in this new Europe.[17]

The magnitude of Europe's transformation is daunting: not only regarding who does what but regarding what and who is "we"? Nearing finality, Europe's paradox is that it can be "Europe" only by transcending the remnants of its divided past in ways that might make it instead more American. The experience is "oddly schizoid."[18] Even while Europeans become more American every day, they spend more time looking for ways to complain about America. Had there been fewer complaints in Europe, there might have been more satisfaction in the United States: the integration of Europe is a European idea that U.S. power and leadership helped launch more than fifty years ago and have actively sustained ever since. But the idea of a European Union is also, in a deeper sense, an American idea because this is, after all, the idea that gave birth to the American Republic. At last, Europeans are finalizing in their own habitat what other Europeans did on U.S. soil more than two hundred years ago. The calendar is not the same—if only because the U.S. Civil War was fought long after a constitutional convention had been held—but the overall goal, which aims at a territorial consolidation of geographic space, is similar. What began as a mere time-out from European history—a reprieve from wars and conflicts—has evolved into something far more permanent—the end of a prolonged moment in Europe's history.

In short, what the European Union and the Atlantic Alliance need is more, not less, integration. Among themselves, as a mutually shared right of first refusal but also with new associates and partners, the NATO and European Union countries should be able to agree on some immediate priorities and key principles for multilateral action. As Samuel Huntington stated, "the idea of integration" is "the successor idea to containment." More specifically, integration is about locking a group of countries into policies that address common concerns and produce mutually shared benefits, "and then building institutions that lock them in even more." The "halfway integration," which is the current condition of the European Union and the Atlantic community, cannot be sustained and must either move to a higher level of integration, including further levels of supranationality, or regretfully fall back to lower levels.[19]

Admittedly, a call for more integration will be heard with some wariness on both sides of the Atlantic. But if not in and with the European Union, where? If not with the United States and within NATO, with whom? If not now, when? Better to set America's alarm clock at half before the European Union—early enough, that is, for the United States to wake up to the institutional reality it helped launch after World War II. Better also to set Europe's watch at half past NATO—early enough, that is, for the countries of Europe to work toward the finality of their institutions without compromising the organization that brought them security during the Cold War. Some will say, why the rush? As sudden and unpredictable events make history leap forward unexpectedly, as seen most recently on September 11, 2001, opportunities that are spurned may never reappear. The United States and Europe have ample and good reasons to be exasperated with, and even fearful of, their difficult partnership. But neither side wants or can afford a separation, let alone a divorce, because after fifty years of intimacy, there may be less love but there is more dependence—sharing a life that, without both sides of the Atlantic, will not remain as affluent, as safe, and ultimately as satisfying.

Nevertheless, the political consequences of Europe's transformation may be cause for concern. After 1945 Europe was not born out of a single, or even common, vision of the future. Rather, it grew out of the shared vision of a failed past, and there was not any attempt to provide a credible sense of the endpoint to which the process might lead. Instead, an ill-defined logic of integration seemed to unfold, mechanically at first, and state-driven next: deepen in order to widen, widen in order to deepen, and reform in order to do both. As Europe's finality is pursued, therefore, Europeans must now do more to reassure

Americans that the European Union will continue to make the United States feel at home in Europe.[20] Irrespective of Europe's intentions, no such effort has been apparent thus far. Too much of what the European Union begins or does is presented as further evidence of Europe's ability to challenge the United States. More should be done instead to emphasize how U.S. interests are served as the future of Europe continues to evolve toward its finality. It is time for Europe to engage the United States constructively and build with its partner across the Atlantic the same sort of intimacy that the United States built with the states of Europe within the Western Alliance.

LIMITS OF DISCORD

Does America need Europe and its alliance with the states of Europe? That the question would be raised at all is cause enough for distress. Over the intervening years, these ties have become more, much more than emotional. Whether across the Atlantic or within Europe, loosening these ties would be to the disadvantage of all. Paradoxically, the most immediate and greatest danger to transatlantic relations today is not European anti-Americanism, however exasperating that may be, but American anti-Europeanism—the danger, that is, of an America that would no longer feel confident enough to sustain its commitment to an ever closer, larger, and stronger Europe as the U.S. partner of choice.[21]

August 1914, it can be readily agreed, was the defining month for the twentieth century. For the first World War was the event that permitted and conditioned all the events that followed during a century that had opened with hopes that this was a "good time to be alive" but unfolded instead as a century during which too many innocent victims found it to be a time when it was far too easy to be dead. Remarkably enough, a search of all the published cables of foreign ministers, sovereigns, ambassadors, and chancellors during the months leading to that event fails to uncover "a single European diplomat [who] had mentioned the United States, speculated on its strength, or wondered about its attitude."[22] This was Europe's time, not America's. As events came to show, it was not a good time for either. "What have we not seen, not suffered, not lived through?" wept Stefan Zweig in a book he wrote in exile in 1943, away from the Old World that had betrayed him.[23] Seemingly, for

Zweig (and his wife) there had been too much pain—and as had been the case for the continent they loved dearly, both committed suicide upon completing that final testament.

The spring of 1947 nonetheless gave America a second chance at paying the debt it owed history as a result of its past indifference and in return for its past obligations. For the decisions that were made then by the Truman administration—bold, compassionate, and visionary— helped Europe master its past and start anew in ways that seemed to challenge the imagination at the time. These decisions for Europe were made by relatively inexperienced Americans who responded to the explicit invitation of experienced European statesmen who understood all too well that this was their last chance at resurrection. This was now America's time, not Europe's. As events came to show, it proved to be a good time for both: had Zweig written his book after the Cold War rather than during World War II, he would have wanted to live. For where the wasted heroism of World War I produced a peace to end all peaces, the wasteful brutality of World War II proved to be a war to end all wars.

Although most would agree that September 11, 2001, stands as an event of lasting historic significance, there is little agreement yet on its actual meaning. What judgment will historians make of the decade that followed the collapse of the Soviet Union and the traumatic events of September 11? Will they be as distraught as we are still today when reflecting on the murderous insanity of World War I and the twenty-year descent to the war that followed? Or will historians stand in awe of the order that will have been built out of the ruins left by World War II? Writing in 1951, Hannah Arendt evoked the postwar "moment of anticipation" which, she wrote, "is like the calm that settles after all hopes have died. ... Never has our future been more predictable, never have we depended so much on political forces that cannot be trusted to follow the rules of common sense and self-interest. ... It is as though mankind has divided itself between those who believe in human omnipotence ... and those for whom powerlessness has become the major experience of their lives."[24] This is another such moment when the anticipation wavers between common good and sheer insanity. The latter will be denied and cured more effectively if the former is managed by a cohesive and strong transatlantic alliance rather than in spite of or without it. The war in Iraq confirmed that Americans and Europeans will not do everything together, but, beyond Iraq and most of all for the totality of the Greater Middle East, it has not ended the need to ensure that together Americans and Europeans will do everything. Now more than ever before, questions about the future of the Atlantic Alliance are warranted. But now no less than ever before, the answer remains self-evident, not because the absence of an alliance would deny America and Europe a future, but because in the absence of such an alliance the future would be less promising and even more dangerous.

Notes

1. Will Hutton, *The World We're In* (Boston: Little, Brown, 2002), 357, 368–69. Also, Simon Serfaty, "Anti-Europeanism in America and Anti-Americanism in Europe," in *Visions of America and Europe: September 11, Iraq, and Transatlantic Relations,* ed. Christina V. Balis and Simon Serfaty (Washington, D.C.: CSIS Press, 2004), 3–20.
2. Fareed Zakaria, "The Arrogant Empire," *Newsweek,* March 24, 2003, 18.
3. Michael A. Ledeen, *Grave New World* (New York: Oxford University Press, 1985). For a broad and early assessment of the "new normalcy" inaugurated by the events of September 11, see Simon Serfaty, "The Wars of 911," *International Spectator* 36, no. 4 (2001): 5–11; and "The New Normalcy," *Washington Quarterly* 25, no. 2 (Spring 2002): 209–19.
4. Frantz Fanon, *The Wretched of the Earth,* trans. Constance Farrington (New York: Grove Press, 1963); preface by Jean-Paul Sartre, 7–34.
5. Eric Hobsbawm, "War and Peace in the 20th Century," *London Review of Books,* February 21, 2002, 16–18.
6. John McCain, "There Is No Substitute for Victory," *Wall Street Journal,* October 26, 2001, 14.
7. Michael Howard, "Mistake to Declare This a 'War,'" *RUSI Journal* 146 (December 2001): 1–4. See also Eliot A. Cohen, "A Strange War," *National Interest* (Thanksgiving 2001): 3.
8. A full transcript of the news conference appeared in the *Washington Post,* October 12, 2001. 20.
9. Bob Woodward, *Bush at War* (New York: Simon & Schuster, 2002), 96.
10. Remarks to the New York Police Department Command and Control Center Performance, New York, February 6, 2002.
11. Quoted in the *Washington Post,* January 27, 2002, A13.
12. Quoted, respectively, by Judy Keen, "Bush Exhibits Political Skills on Global Stage," p. 2A/ *USA Today,* November 25, 2002, and Woodward, *Bush at War,* 341.
13. "He least likes me to say, 'This is complex,'" said Condoleezza Rice. Nicholas Lemann, "Without a Doubt," *New Yorker,* October 14–21, 2002, 164–80.
14. On this theme, see Christopher Layne, "The Unipolar Illusion: Why New Great Powers Will Rise," *International Security* 17, no. 4 (1993): 5–51.
15. *The National Security Strategy of the United States of America* (Washington, September 2002), including President Bush's speeches at the National Cathedral (September 14, 2001) and West Point, New York (June 1, 2002).
16. Isaiah Berlin, *Four Essays on Liberty* (New York: Oxford University Press, 1969), 52.
17. "Europe as Germany and France. ... I think that's old Europe." Secretary Donald Rumsfeld's briefing at the Foreign Press Center (January 21, 2003).

18. Martin Walker, "What Europeans Think of America," *World Policy Journal,* vol. xvii (Summer 2000).
19. Huntington is quoted by Nicholas Lemann, "The Next World Order," *New Yorker,* April 1, 2002, 46. Amitai Etzioni, *Political Unification Revisited: On Building Supranational Communities* (New York: Lexington Books, 2001), xxxi. Also, Simon Serfaty, "Europe Enlarged, America Detached?" *Current History* 102, no. 662 (March 2003): 99–105.
20. See Simon Serfaty, "American Reflections on Europe's Finality," in *The European Finality Debate and Its National Dimensions,* ed. Simon Serfaty (Washington: CSIS Press, 2003), 1–20.
21. Thomas L. Friedman, "They Hate Us! They Need Us," *New York Times,* June 15, 2001, 39.
22. Theodore White, *Fire in the Ashes: Europe in the Mid-Century* (New York: William Sloane Associates, 1953), 384.
23. Stefan Zweig, *The World of Yesterday* (London: University of Nebraska Press, 1964), xx.
24. Hannah Arendt, *The Origins of Totalitarianism* (San Diego: Harcourt, 1994), vii.

11

LIBERALISM AND POWER

by Peter Berkowitz

THE HUMAN RIGHTS ERA AND THE PERSISTENCE OF NATIONAL INTEREST

FROM ITS BEGINNING IN the early morning of March 20, 2003 with a cruise missle attack targeting Saddam Hussein to President Bush's declaration on May 1, 2003 of the end to major combat, the American-led coalition's achievements in Operation Iraqi Freedom proved, in a variety of ways, unprecedented. Never before had a military force moved so much armor and so many troops so far so fast, or bombed from the air with such precision, or surgically excised a totalitarian regime while largely sparing the civilian population and preserving the country's material and commercial infrastructure. The humanitarian achievement also proved unprecedented. For not only were civilian casualties and damage to nonmilitary targets minimized to a hitherto unmatched extent. Never before had a complex and massive military operation so effectively prepared for the delivery of food and water and other basics in order to relieve civilian suffering. But perhaps the most

remarkable achievement of Operation Iraqi Freedom was the unprecedented weaving of military might and humanitarian assistance.

By contrast, the international debate about the legal merits of the
use of military force to disarm Saddam Hussein that led up to
Operation Iraqi Freedom proved soberingly familiar. Among the permanent members of the UN Security Council—itself not a body whose
structure derives from any recognized norms of international law but
that survives as a rickety institutional relic of the post–World War II
political settlement—debate was derailed by the national self-interest
of several permanent members of the council parading as deference to
international law and international institutions. Of course reasonable
people and nations could quarrel with the Bush administration's diplomacy, and with its key contention that in a post–September 11 world,
Saddam's tyranny—with its (now very much in doubt) weapons of
mass destruction and (now confirmed) programs to develop weapons
of mass destruction, its harboring and funding of terrorists, and its
murderous brutality toward its own people—posed an intolerable
threat to U.S. national security interests and to global order. Yet the respectable if not decisive legal argument put forward by the United
States and Great Britain, rooted in a perfectly plausible reading of
Security Council resolution 1441 passed by unanimous vote in
November 2002 and of sixteen other Security Council resolutions over
the course of twelve years that preceded it, was met with adamant opposition and resolute obscurantism from France, Russia, and China.
They were not content to claim that their legal arguments were superior. Rather, with France at the forefront (and Germany cheering from
the sideline), they made a mockery of the truth by resolutely maintaining that the legal arguments advanced by Great Britain and the
United States were devoid of merit. And they insisted that any response to Saddam's defiance of the United Nations consistent with international law must take the form of more diplomacy, more
inspections, and more multilateralism. Yet in the interpretation of
Saddam's obligations, of U.S. prerogatives under international law,
and of the UN's role in dealing with the Iraq crisis, the impartiality of
these permanent members of the Security Council was severely com-
promised by their extensive commercial ties to Saddam's Iraq, their

resolute evasion of the Iraqi sanctions they had voted to impose, and what they perceived to be their national interest in reining in the United States by frustrating any and all of its political and military initiatives.

What the all-too-predictable post–September 11 international debate over Iraq, taken together with the U.S.-led coalition's unprecedented achievements in the waging of Operation Iraqi Freedom has demonstrated, in other words, is that the breathtaking advance of the humanitarian ethic has not yet, nor is it likely to, eliminate a sizeable role for national self-interest in international politics, even in the foreign policy of those—this certainly includes Europeans and Americans—whose moral and political orders in various ways powerfully affirm the humanitarian ethic. What is puzzling is why American and European perceptions of their national interest are diverging so dramatically.

Robert Kagan goes a long way toward solving the puzzle. Written in the shadow of September 11 and published in the months leading up to Operation Iraqi Freedom, his incisive analysis of strategic culture in the United States and Europe suggests that the trans-Atlantic allies are increasingly likely to disagree about the role of international law and international institutions in securing the conditions for global order. "It is time to stop pretending," Kagan provocatively declared at the start, "that Europeans and Americans share a common view of the world or even that they occupy the same world." Drawing on Thucydides, recent history, and common sense, Kagan made a compelling case that a nation's strategic culture is determined by its political situation. Militarily strong nations like the United States will naturally see the virtues in military strength and will naturally seek to exercise them to advance their interests, whereas militarily weak nations like those of Europe, making a virtue out of necessity, will attempt to vindicate their interests by championing the supremacy of international law and diplomacy. America enforces its will because it can. Europe falls back on the United Nations because it must.

Yet there is more to the puzzle than Kagan allows. Contrary to the provocation with which his book begins, Europe and America, in a decisive respect, occupy the same world and share a common view of it. Behind the "great and growing disparity of power," and the resultant divergence of short-term national interest and perspective is a remarkable area of agreement. It was not written in stone, for example, that the debate between the United States and Europe about Iraq would revolve around how best to secure human rights and promote democracy, rather than, say, whether human rights and democracy are universally valid and desirable. In fact, a nation's strategic culture is determined not only by its political situation but also by its moral and political principles, particularly those widely shared background ideas about what human beings are and what they deserve that give shape and direction to all spheres of a nation's life. To be sure, Kagan noted that the United States and Europe are offspring of the Enlightenment. But he does not adequately identify the moral and political tradition that links the United States and Europe.

The tradition in question is best called liberalism. One critical element within this tradition is the Enlightenment, which teaches that universal principles of reason govern moral and political life and that all human beings can be educated to live in accordance with them. But the Enlightenment ideal does not go to the heart of the matter, which is freedom, or more accurately, equality in freedom.

The liberal tradition rests on the moral premise of equality in freedom, or the natural freedom and equality of all. It is the tradition, among others, of Locke, Montesquieu, the fathers of the American Constitution, Kant, Tocqueville, Constant, and Mill. Like all great moral and political traditions, it is in part constituted by a debate over the practical implications of its fundamental premise. Conservative liberals, liberal liberals, and radical liberals are united by their commitment to equality in freedom; they are divided by opinions about what beliefs, practices, and associations best secure it. Some matters, such as the need for regular competitive elections, toleration, freedom of speech and press, and an independent judiciary are relatively settled. Others, such as the role of the government in the economy, remain quite contentious. The disagreement between the United States and Europe over strategic culture turns out to be a new and critical chapter in the continuing debate that constitutes the liberal tradition over the best means for securing individual freedom.

PHILOSOPHICAL ROOTS OF THE STRATEGIC DIVIDE

Liberalism is above all devoted to establishing a form of government that is able to secure conditions under which individuals can enjoy the personal freedom to live as they see fit. Securing political freedom gives rise to a number of enduring challenges. Three are of particular importance to understanding the divide that has opened up between the United States and Europe about the use of power in international affairs. The first challenge concerns freedom and rule: In what circumstances can the laws under which citizens live be reasonably seen as expressing and advancing, rather than as denying or curtailing, their freedom? The second challenge deals with equality and the passions: How does equality before the law and as a condition of social life affect citizens' common human striving for preeminence and power? The third challenge goes directly to the question of sovereignty and foreign affairs: What principles should guide a liberal state in its dealing with other states, some of which are bound to have adopted very different policies for safeguarding their citizens' freedom, and some of which reject the safeguarding of individual freedom as a goal of politics and even as a genuine human good? Taken together the answers to these questions suggest that in recent years European strategic culture has put an undue reliance on international law and institutions and that the cause of freedom is best served, as the United States has frequently argued throughout the past quarter century, by states that recognize, and are prepared to act on the recognition, that global order and liberty under law regularly require the exercise of military power in international affairs.

Freedom and Rule

A frequently remarked on ambiguity inheres in the liberal understanding of legitimate political authority. What kinds of laws do individuals who are by nature free and equal have an obligation to obey? The answer the liberal tradition gives is those laws, that individuals have chosen because they believe them to serve their interests or, in other words, to which they have consented. Individuals have an interest in consenting to give up some of the their natural freedom and in living under laws to which they, along with fellow citizens, have also consented because life under laws that bind others equally is perferable to an untrammeled freedom for oneself that exposes one to the untrammeled freedom of others. But individuals need not give their formal and public consent to every particular law enacted by the state. That would be utterly impractical. It is enough for people to consent to the basic political framework, the constitutional order, through which particular laws are enacted by representatives who remain accountable to the people. Having consented to the underlying system through which laws are made and implemented and enforced, and through which controversies that arise under the law are adjudicated, and having had a say in choosing officeholders through free and fair elections, one has in effect consented to obey even specific laws or rulings about the laws that one finds onerous or foolish. The diminution of freedom that one voluntarily and rationally chooses to incur in political society in exchange for the benefits of life under laws that bind others equally can be seen as an expression of one's freedom, a voluntary and rational choice.

But of what does the original act of consent consist? What deeds must be performed, what signs must be given, what conditions must be met in order to establish consent? After all, none of us were there when the Constitution was debated and ratified. We did not give our actual consent, nor have we been asked recently. And even if we were to be asked, many of us would be in a poor position to consent responsibly, owing to a weak grasp of the structure of government established by the Constitution and unfamiliarity with the alternatives. In what sense, then, can we be said to have consented?

In practice, responds the liberal tradition, we must be understood to have consented tacitly. We give tacit consent to the laws and basic political framework of a free society by choosing to stay and live under them rather than leave and live somewhere else. In accepting the laws' benefits, we agree to bear their burdens, including obedience to duly enacted laws that we regard as wrongheaded. To be sure, the doctrine of tacit consent is not in every way satisfactory. In the real world material and moral constraints—poverty, sickness, ignorance, prejudice, and familial and cultural ties—leave many individuals with no realistic alternative but to live out their lives in the country of their origin. Their consent is not freely given but, one might say, coerced by circumstance. However, the liberal tradition resists seeing every kind of coercion as incompatible with consent or making the state responsible for overcoming every form of coercion under which we labor. The paradigm form of coercion that it opposes is that of lawlessness or arbitrary laws. To the extent that the liberal state goes further by assuming responsibility for combating the inexhaustible variety of material and moral constraints on individual freedom—which it irresistibly does because the distinction between legal coercion and material and moral coercion is imperfect—it risks sanctioning the sorts of massive invasions of personal freedom liberalism is sworn to protect against.

Indeed, the liberal theory of consent threatens to turn into its very opposite when the idea of consent is severed from any concrete action undertaken by those who have allegedly given it. This happens when consent is no longer seen as an open and voluntary affirmation or, more tenuously, as implicit in our actions but as derived from our natures as free and equal beings. Such a conception disjoins consent from anything we self-consciously say or do or think. Instead it elaborates principles and practices that it would be rational for us to choose whether we and even if we have considered those choices and rejected them. It then declares some choices as in principle invalid on the grounds that no reasonable person could possibly choose them and announces that other rules and regulations are not only valid but also should be seen as binding because no reasonable person could possibly fail to choose them. Such a step is tempting and perhaps on rare occasion appropriate, because the very idea of consent carries with it the idea of rational, self-aware choice. It also is dangerous because the idea of consent also carries with it the notion of open and voluntary affirmation. Despite its danger, proponents commonly wield the doctrine of derived consent to nullify the agreements people actually reach and to establish people's obligation to uphold arrangements of which they have never heard or to which they strongly object.

Although the doctrine of derived consent has roots in liberal ideas about freedom and rule, in practice it is more likely to menace individual freedom than it is to serve it. Hints of the doctrine of derived consent can be seen in the teachings of Hobbes and Locke, according to whose theories the outline and main provisions of the social contract are objective and universal. Although he wrote as a friend of freedom, Rousseau made explicit some of its startlingly illiberal implications through the idea of the general will, which stirred many of the French revolutionaries to ruthless violence, particularly the imperative connected to the doctrine of the general will of forcing individuals to be free. Kant elaborated a sublime version of the doctrine of derived consent in his moral philosophy, contending that each person should regard himself or herself as a legislator for, but also a subject in, a universal kingdom of ends. The doctrine is savagely embodied in the Leninist idea of a dictatorship of the proletariat, in which party leaders rule despotically on the grounds that they alone know and are capable of advancing the people's true interests. In his famous lecture "Two Concepts of Liberty," Isaiah Berlin warned liberals against the illiberal temptation inhering in the doctrine of derived consent: it is one thing to say that people may be confused about their interest or are making poor choices; quite another to say that those who rule are capable of discerning the people's true interests; and yet another matter to argue that the people can be made more free through a government that, contrary to their expressed preferences, imposes on them through law their supposed true interests. The doctrine of derived consent lives on in muted terms in the writings of Jürgen Habermas and John Rawls and in the sprawling school of academic political theory known as deliberative democracy, which was inspired by adherents' common conviction about the power of reason to determine democratic policies independent of the actual opinions and votes of democratic majorities. It is subscribed to by large numbers of international human rights lawyers.[1]

The doctrine of derived consent lives on as well in European strategic culture. Indeed, it has become the mainstay of the European outlook. Although reliance on international law and international institutions as the primary means of dealing with other countries may suit the interests of militarily weak nations, as Kagan suggested, such reliance is justified through arguments and appeals that presuppose or celebrate a doctrine of derived consent.

Consider, for example, the case for investing the United Nations with greater authority to promulgate laws that bind all nations, for establishing an International Criminal Court, and for granting to the courts of sovereign states universal jurisdiction to try certain classes of crimes committed anywhere and by any parties. The growth of international law in its various manifestations, it is said, advances the cause of human rights by supporting the spread of freedom and equality around the globe. Yet such endeavors only make liberal sense if their legitimacy can be squared with consent. The only form of consent, however, that the spread of international law rooted in the decisions of the United Nations could be consistent with is derived consent. It is obviously not the product of actual consent because almost half of the nations represented at the United Nations lack democratic legitimacy. Its legitimacy could not flow from tacit consent either: individuals who object to the directions taken by the international order have no other planet to which they can move. So the United Nations, the International Criminal Court, and local European courts claiming universal jurisdiction must maintain that their actions and edicts reflect universal laws that all individuals would agree to if they were rationally considering their true interests. Indeed, Europe's arguments on behalf of international law reflect its liberal heritage, and such arguments at minimum prick the conscience and command the attention of the United States because of its own liberal heritage.

The well-known problems that arise domestically for the doctrine of derived consent are exacerbated in the international system where, because of the distance and levels of government separating the people from those who speak for them on the world stage, consent and accountability, already stretched in the modern nation-state, are greatly attenuated. What if delegates to the United Nations and justices on the International Criminal Court and local European judges claiming universal jurisdiction get the universal rational norms wrong? Or misapply them? What if the universal norms are invoked not on principled grounds but on grounds of self-interest? What if the self-interest is not enlightened but cynical? And what if the cynical appeal to self-interest does not reflect the sort of human lapse concerning which we must always be on guard but is rather a by-product of the spirit that liberalism fosters?

208 ＊ PETER BERKOWITZ

Equality and the Passions

In fact, the wayward passions that equality stirs up provide good cause to worry that nations imbued with the liberal belief in equality in freedom will be tempted to invoke universal principles on grounds ranging from the dubious to the disgraceful. The connection between high-minded liberal principle and the abuse of it to which wayward human passion is inclined is obscured by those who insist that liberalism is nothing more than a set of shared procedures for organizing moral and political life. Even the soundest principle requires care and courage in its application to concrete circumstances and shared procedures shape the sensibilities of those who are subject to them.

Liberalism, like every political regime, constitutes a way of life. It translates its guiding premises and principles into political institutions. These institutions reinforce the guiding premises and principles in citizens' hearts and minds; thus amplified, citizens import them into private life and culture. The reverberations of equality in freedom in all spheres of our lives foster many appealing qualities: curiosity, casualness in social relations, openness to new experiences and ideas, and a respect for human beings of diverse backgrounds. But not all the qualities that equality encourages are humanly attractive or good for a liberal state. Equality, for example, also encourages a certain arrogance, one-sidedness, and resentment.

Consider first the arrogance. Regimes based on the principle of equality embody an obvious claim to justice, as even the classical political philosophy of Plato and Aristotle, which is highly critical of democracy, reminds. It makes sense for all people to share in political power because we have common needs and desires, limitations, and vulnerabilities. From this, however, partisans of equality are inclined to reason that all people are equally well equipped to hold office and to judge the conduct of affairs of state. But such reasoning rests on the fallacy that because we are equal in one or some morally relevant respects we are equal in all respects.

The one-sidedness promoted by the rein of equality is related to the arrogance. It comes to the fore in a democracy that protects individual rights, or a liberal democracy. According to the classical liberal critique of equality, the critique elaborated by friends of democracy and equality such as Tocqueville and Mill and that is fully compatible with their devotion to the principle of equality in freedom, the problem is not only that majorities think they always know better; it is also that the experience of equality leads to the desire for more of it, and so majorities eventually cease to be satisfied with the characteristically liberal forms of equality, which is formal equality, or equality before the law and equality of opportunity. These forms of equality can coexist with many forms of inequality; in fact, they produce inequality as the competition under law between diverse individuals for society's scarce goods results in winners and losers. One way to combat the inequality that arises out of equality before the law and equality of opportunity is to guarantee equality of results. This approach calls on government to become the great equalizer, expanding its role from guarantor of rights to imposer of burdens and distributor of benefits. The benefits can eventually come to include such intangible goods as the sense of self-esteem.

The battle against inequality is partly a matter of justice. What sense does it make to speak of equality of opportunity when some people are so unfortunate —whether owing to the cruelty of fortune or to the malfeasance of others or their own folly—as to be bereft of a bootstrap with which to pull themselves up? But it involves injustice as well, because achieving the new forms of equality requires sacrificing other goods. When it treats citizens unequally in order to compensate for the myriad unfairnesses of life, the government jeopardizes the right of individuals to be treated equally before the law and to dispose of private property as one sees fit.

In addition to promoting the inclination to make exaggerated claims on behalf of equality and the desire to expand its domain, the experience of equality also fosters resentment of those who are stronger, more successful, and happier. This, as Nietzsche argued in his career-long polemic against equality, is where things get ugly. For the demand for equality is no longer driven by a desire to lift up the disadvantaged but rather to hold back and pin down the prosperous and the preeminent. When resentment takes hold, the appeal to individual rights can serve as a vehicle for the unconscious as well as the calculated and cynical bid for power. Wielding equality as an instrument of domination, resentment uses liberal rhetoric to secure an illiberal end.

Many of the wayward passions stirred up by equality are at work in Europe's ambition to portray international law and international institutions as the comprehensive means for securing global order. All nations of the world, by virtue of the sovereignty they exercise, are equal in an important sense. The liberal spirit intensifies among Europeans the sense of equality among nations, whereas the reality of American power and European weakness painfully reminds Europe of the sense in which they are unequal. So the Europeans make a priority out of increasing the realms in which they can regard themselves as equal. They arrogantly confuse equality among nations in respect of sovereignty for equality in all respects, including equality in regard to competence and accountability. They one-sidedly assume that more equality between states in international affairs is always to be preferred, denying in the process such other relevant attributes of states as population size, respect for human rights and the rule of law, and the power to defend justice by force. And resenting the power on the international stage exercised by a more powerful United States, a resentment that is fomented by the triumph of the norm of equality in the international arena, they can in moments of weakness cynically seize upon international law and international institutions and employ them as a shackle to bind the strong, regardless of the justice of the initiatives undertaken by the strong. Ironically, this weapon of the weak is especially effective against strong nations that share their basic commitment to the natural freedom and equality of all. It is especially effective, that is, against the United States, a state of unprecedented power imbued with an acute liberal conscience.

Sovereignty and Foreign Affairs

What kind of world do liberal states inhabit? So long as the world is not entirely composed of liberal states, the liberal tradition is largely in agreement with Hobbes's dark assessment that life outside the boundaries of an established state, and therefore between states, is "solitary, poor, nasty, brutish, and short." It is not that morality is nonexistent, or that reason is in abeyance, in the anarchic international arena, an arena that, from the point of view of standard liberal social contract theory, is akin to a state of nature. Rather, reason teaches that without a properly authorized, internationally recognized sovereign power, it would be unreasonable for a state to suppose that other states will regard themselves as bound by universal laws. To be properly authorized, a sovereign must be consented to by the people and must have the power to enforce laws, but there is no universal or international sovereign to which all of humanity, or all the nations of the world, could be said to have consented; certainly not the United Nations, which also lacks another indispensable attribute of sovereignty, the power to enforce its laws.

Kagan wrote as if on the question of the natural condition of states, Hobbes and Kant represent antipodes corresponding to the divergent orientations toward power adopted by America and Europe. Whereas Hobbes thought that the international order is irreducibly violent, and thus that only power can decide disputes among nations, Kant believed, suggested Kagan, that nations must conduct themselves in relation to other nations in accordance with universal moral laws. Kagan, however, is mistaken about what Kant believed. In fact, contrary to Kagan, Kant is, on the crucial point, in close agreement with Hobbes. To be sure, Kant laid out preconditions for a perpetual peace among nations and elaborated articles that define such peace. But he did not argue that a nation must act as if perpetual peace has been obtained when it has not. That would be folly. Absent a properly constituted world government, which in Kant's view requires the nations of the world to more or less become liberal democracies and for them to agree to be bound by a common authority, nations should understand that they are effectively in a state of war. Kant did argue that states have an obligation to bring about a condition in which reason can at last govern international affairs. But he did not suggest that that condition naturally obtains or that when it doesn't states must pretend that it does.

What does his mistake concerning Kant have to do with Kagan's larger argument about strategic culture? Kagan treats the difference of opinion between the United States and Europe about how world politics actually operates as an open question, as if it were a theoretical matter for which there are respectable alternative views. But this is not the case—certainly not within the liberal tradition. The supposed antipodes, Hobbes and Kant, are in agreement about the harshness of international politics, and the need for power to back right. Moreover, whether the international arena today displays the qualities that limit the reach of international law and international institutions and make the exercise of power necessary is an empirical question to which there is a correct answer. And it is not the answer that Europe tends to give. As Kagan implicitly acknowledged, "Those who favor security through international law and institutions will constantly downplay the world's irrationality and brutality." That is a polite way of saying the European position distorts reality to justify its foreign policy.

Moreover, Europeans are wrong to believe that they live, as Kagan put it, in a "post-modern paradise." Comfortable they may be, and they are insulated to a considerable extent from the illiberal and undemocratic comings and goings in much of the rest of the world. But because Europe includes only a fraction of the world's nations, the paradise cannot be Kantian, for real peace, according to Kant, requires liberal democracy everywhere. Nor is the European paradise postmodern, in the sense of having overcome the need for military power. Again, as Kagan himself pointed out, the European Union depends on the military might of the United States, not only for the defense of European borders but also for the policing of hot spots around the globe. And European peace and security could be shattered at any moment by rogue states or by terrorists wielding weapons of mass destruction. Europe may resent U.S. power, it may refuse to develop its own, and it may honestly believe that every use by the United States of power abroad threatens the universal validity of Europe's liberal utopian aspirations, but its resentment and refusal and honest belief do not change the fact that its peace and prosperity and freedom rely in myriad and critical ways on armed forces not its own.

BEYOND THE PSYCHOLOGY OF STRENGTH AND THE PSYCHOLOGY OF WEAKNESS

U.S. and European strategic culture not only reflect the universal political propensities that Kagan called the psychology of strength and the psychology of weakness. They reflect as well competing liberal interpretations of the place of law and power in international relations though not, as Kagan's analysis too often implied, equally valid interpretations, under varying geopolitical circumstances, of the liberal stance toward power. The European view also gives expression to characteristic liberal exaggerations, temptations, and self-deceptions.

The liberal provenance of European strategic culture should put the United States on guard against its own wayward tendencies. The mistakes exhibited by contemporary European strategic culture—the aggressive reliance on a doctrine of derived consent, the cynical use of norms of equality to enhance its own power and prestige and weaken that of its perceived rival, and a self-induced blindness to the political realities and military necessities of international affairs—certainly suit militarily weak nations committed to the natural freedom and equality of all. But they also appeal to many progressive liberals in the United States, as any brief survey of political science scholarship, writings by law professors on international law, or the pages of the New York Times will attest. So our situation is more dire than Kagan acknowledged. He not only downplayed the disreputable motives that readily seize upon the brand of liberal utopianism many Europeans espouse but also neglected the powerful attraction of that same liberal utopianism for many American intellectuals—despite, or as a reaction to, American strength.

As long as there are liberal states some will be strong and some will be weak and their differing capacities will incline them to adopt opposing views, or a common view with opposing emphases, about the role of law and power in international affairs. Their strategic culture, however, will be determined by their military might as well as by their liberalism, though not strictly determined. Indeed, as long as there are liberal states, there also will be partisan battles not only between strong ones and weak ones but also within liberal states, both the strong ones and the weak ones, over how consent and the rule of law should be understood internationally, over what the norm of equality calls for in regard to weighing the interests and voices of other nations, and over the circumstances that justify the use of military force. In international relations, as in domestic affairs, liberalism never calls for a simple choice between the path of law and the path of power. It always calls for a wise blending of them.

Note

1. I explore in greater depth the disadvantages of the doctrine of derived consent in "The Demagoguery of Democratic Theory," *Critical Review* 15, no. 1–2 (Winter–Spring 2003).

12

THE ATLANTICIST COMMUNITY

by Tod Lindberg

THERE IS NO QUESTION that the aftermath of September 11, 2001, has laid bare a divergence in view between the United States and Europe over the question of the place of power in international affairs. Insofar as countering terrorism and the proliferation of weapons of mass destruction has become a priority likely to dominate U.S. security policy for a generation or more, and insofar as the United States will likely seek recourse to military measures on occasion in this period, the divergence is likely to persist. Transatlantic relations may go through periods of relative warming in the years ahead, but they seem likely to be punctuated by occasions in which the differences reemerge starkly. We have, in all likelihood, doses of bitterness ahead of us every bit as unpleasant as the bitterness over the Iraq war.

In addition to disputes over specific matters ahead, the "background level" of affection felt on either side of the Atlantic toward the other is unlikely to return to pre-9/11 levels, let alone to reach again the heights of the spike in solidarity immediately following 9/11. It's also interesting to ask the question, What will it mean and what will it feel like to be pro-European in America or pro-American in Europe? Will these increasingly become sensibilities one keeps to oneself? Perhaps a solution for some will be to give voice to one's approval or sympathy only following a prologue sufficiently derisory to deflect criticism—for example, "Of course the Americans are trigger-happy and arrogant beyond belief, but in the case of this brutal dictator, good riddance"; or, "Of course the Europeans are pusillanimous and feckless, but they do have troops on the ground doing peacekeeping in Afghanistan and the Balkans."

But what I want to do here is take a large step back from all the disagreement and see if it does not, after all, take place within a frame of broader agreement about fundamental issues—more fundamental, even, than the question of the proper role of the use of force internationally, which is itself a mischaracterization of what was at stake in the dispute over Iraq, as we shall see.

To show how this is so, I would like to radicalize the discussion by proffering a thesis so contrarian in the current context that I should probably begin by asking readers' indulgence. It is this: There are no fundamental disagreements or differences between the United States and Europe. Existing differences are often more apparent than real. When real, the differences are in all consequential cases actually agreements to disagree. And in any case, the views of Americans and Europeans have been converging for some time and will continue to do so.

THE NORM OF PEACE

Let's begin with two questions: Will the United States ever go to war with Germany or France? Will France ever go to war with Germany?

At one level, the questions are absurd. Who asks such things? If we turn our attention to a consideration of where in the world war might break out, the last countries one would think would meet in combat would be the United States, France, and Germany. Insofar as war is serious business and should be approached accordingly, consideration of such scenarios as these seems to be at best a waste of time.

It is not. I do not, of course, mean to single out France and Germany. The questions under consideration here are really whether war is possible between European countries, or between the United States and any country or countries in Europe or a European collectivity, the European Union. The question is absurd because the answer is clearly "no." But the implications of a "no" answer are nothing less than profound.

As it happens, there is no point in human history prior to the end of the Second World War at which one could offer the same answer about any such group of countries. We need not belabor the point. What we are talking about is nothing other than the history of violent political conflict and organized warfare since the beginning of time. When tribes or peoples or states have had contact with one another, the results often have been violent, and even during periods of peace, it seems unlikely that the parties allowed themselves the luxury of thinking that another war was impossible—and that if any such forecasts emerged, serious-minded contemporaries regarded them as delusional, as indeed they proved to be when the next war came.

Perhaps in light of history, we should modify our "no" answer in such a fashion as to avoid the radical proposition that war is impossible. One could adopt a "never say never" approach to the question. At the same time, however, we probably want to avoid overcompensating by describing matters in such a fashion as to make a wholly implausible war seem more likely than we all know it to be. One might say this: *for the foreseeable future,* war in Europe or between the United States and Europe is impossible. Because the unforeseen is by definition unfore-seeable, we do not know what might change, and so we have an out in case the change turns out to be catastrophic: we hold open the possibil-ity of an *unforeseeable* war.

But there is a problem here. The qualification "for the foreseeable future" only seems to offer protection from the charge that the claim is radical. In fact, the claim about war's impossibility "for the foresee-able future" is itself radical. Historically, at no time have people ever reasonably believed that war is impossible for the foreseeable future. On the contrary, it seems fair to say that, historically, people have fore-seen war as a distinct possibility more or less constantly. Helmut Kohl did not regard another European war as an impossibility for the fore-seeable future when he took office in 1982 nor when the Berlin Wall came down in 1989 nor when the Soviet Union broke up in 1992. His efforts on behalf of European integration were a product of precisely the foreseeability of war to him and were meant to make such a war less likely by knitting Germany ever more tightly to its neighbors.[1]

No, I think we must face up to the times in which we live and make radical claims when it is reasonable to do so—when radical changes in the international environment have taken place. If current conditions persist, and there is no reason to think they won't or are in any way necessarily time-limited—for the foreseeable future, in other words—war in Europe or between the United States and Europe is impossible. The United States and Europe have no disputes between them that any country would think it desirable to try to settle by force.

TRANSNATIONAL COMMUNITY

By "the United States and Europe," I mean first of all the American government and governments in Europe, as well as the transnational European Union. But my contention is also broader: it is that the people of the United States and Europe constitute a single transnational ethical community, the Atlanticist community—first and foremost, because of their insistence on settling their disputes peacefully.[2]

It is, of course, possible to cite any number of surveys of popular attitudes in the United States and Europe on political and moral matters and on public policy preferences indicating that Americans and Europeans are in general not so far apart. Even on such issues as the death penalty, over which elites contend fiercely, public opinion in Europe is not very different from public opinion in the United States.[3] Such measures of public opinion are at one level revealing, and probably do reflect the sense of the Atlanticist community I am describing. But, of course, public opinion in Europe and the United States sometimes diverges sharply, as it did over Iraq. We must thus probe a little more deeply than the polls do to see what Americans and Europeans have in common.

At bottom, it is this: In no serious case do we think of each other as entirely "other"; that is, as outsiders who may constitute a willful threat—as potential enemies, in other words. Early in Carl Schmitt's *The Concept of the Political,* he proposed that "the political" is about a state's designation of friends and enemies.[4] Perhaps in keeping with his Nazi sympathies, he devoted the rest of his essay to a consideration of the enemy and paid no further attention to the question of the friend. The enemy is the exception, the one with whom all juridical relations have been destroyed or are absent and on whom one makes war. In Schmitt's world, "the political" seems incomplete when the state has no enemy.

Yet the category of friend is worth attention as well. I will leave aside the question of whether it is meaningful to say that states as such can be friends.[5] But people can be friendly across the boundaries of states. If the people who constitute the political decision makers in one state see themselves as friendly toward the people who constitute the political decision makers in another state, then they will shape the political decisions of their states, including questions of war and peace, accordingly.

The states under consideration here, namely, the United States and the European countries, are all democratic, which means that their leaders are accountable to the people in periodic elections. Their people are also liberal and bourgeois, which means that they have a strong preference for living in a community whose members settle disputes peacefully and in which, accordingly, disputes are rare and circumscribed. They understand themselves to live in such a community—and they understand that those of other nationality in the North Atlantic area, for example, live in such communities.[6]

There are, of course, "rights" that governments are sometimes called upon to enforce. But there is also right conduct, the unity of respect for right and duty toward others, that people are by and large in the habit of practicing among themselves. This sense of right conduct is not necessarily determined or bound by nationality. When people think of each other as having in common a sense of right conduct, they are in this sense members of an ethical community that is similarly unbound by nationality. Members of such a community need not know each other personally, any more than members of ethical communities at the national level must be personally acquainted for bonds of friendship to be in place. Members are, any given one to any given other, friendly strangers.[7] In the case of the Atlanticist community, the bourgeois and liberal life lived by the people throughout the community delineates right conduct.

Any given person is a member of a number of overlapping ethical communities, which are not all the same in terms of the obligations of right conduct they impose on members: the family; the marketplace where one earns one's living; what Hegel called the "corporation" but what we might find exemplified in a professional association, a political party, or, following Robert D. Putnam, a bowling team—an institution of common purpose in which members attain recognition as individuals insofar as they contribute to the common cause;[8] one's nation; and groups that extend beyond national borders (the Atlanticist community is one such, the Catholic Church another).

Now, if it happens that there are conflicts between the obligations imposed by one community and another—if, that is, the person at the center is unsure what "right conduct" is—then there is a problem. And, indeed, the transnational ethical community is the weakest link, precisely because it lacks the immediate ties of face-to-face human contact as well as the power of a state.

This weakness opens my argument to the charge that it simply presupposes no conflict between the nation and the transnational group, because in the event of such conflict, the transnational community would dissolve, thereby calling into question its existence altogether. But recall that there are no communities apart from the people who sustain them and that people not only conform themselves to right conduct but also by their actions set the norms of right conduct in the future. Far from presupposing an absence of conflict, I am offering a description of how it is that conflict does not arise: with regard to the political decisions made by governments, especially the ultimate political decisions à la Schmitt, decision makers conduct themselves in such a fashion as to avoid conflict.

For our purposes here, I find it unnecessary to try to specify what, precisely, constitutes the complete body of political decision makers of each state (what Alexandre Kojève called the "exclusive political group").[9] Is it the electorate as a whole, because the governments in question are democratic? Or is it their elected representatives? Or is it some subset of those representatives? Or is it some broader set designed to include unelected persons who nevertheless possess the quality known as "influence"? I need merely note the near unanimity of opinion on the question at hand, namely, transatlantic and European war and peace, across all these categories—and further that any serious deviationism (of which, one should note, there is next to no sign) would quickly be countered, indeed punished. No president or prime minister who valued his or her office would propose such a war, because a more likely outcome than war would be losing office.

INSTITUTIONS OF COMMUNITY

The preeminent state-to-state manifestation of the Atlanticist community is the North Atlantic Treaty Organization (NATO), a military alliance that binds members to treat an attack on one as an attack on all. The continuing relevance of NATO in the absence of an external threat, such as the Warsaw Pact once posed, is a subject that has been much discussed. But NATO is not just a defensive alliance. It is also, in effect, a permanent peace treaty among its own members.

One might ask how NATO differs from, for example, the Kellogg-Briand pact of 1928, in which the signatories permanently foreswore war, to no discernible effect. First, there was little or no sense of ethical community among the signatories to the Kellogg-Briand pact, a treaty between sovereign states that each one might or might not choose to abide by. Second, more than a treaty, NATO is an organization, an institution whose members join to find common purpose, to work together on security issues broadly construed. No decision can be taken over the objection of any member, so the organization by and large avoids the danger of working at cross-purposes with itself. NATO has thus been a means by which governments and peoples have broadened and deepened their ties. And although Greece and Turkey, to pick an example of two countries whose people have been fighting from time immemorial, did indeed extend their violent contentiousness into the period in which both were members of NATO, it seems reasonable to say that over time, NATO membership has helped them reduce tensions.

A few remarks about the European Union are in order as well, notwithstanding that European integration is very poorly understood in the United States and is not yet, in my view, much of a factor in sustaining a sense of Atlanticist community among Americans—on the contrary, some Americans view the European Union with deep suspicion. But European integration, as Jacques Delors, Helmut Kohl, and Alexandre Kojève among many others have envisioned, has been a huge force in the emergence of a transnational ethical community in Europe. Indeed, they are two sides of the same coin. One could say that from Brussels, a sense of "Europeanness" has been defined and built one idea at a time. This is not an identity that is meant to supplant national identity—in other words, "Europe" is not an ethical community that is intended to replace the French or German communities. The idea, rather, is an agreed-on overarching structure that is not in conflict with national governments.

The political element of this moves in two directions: representatives of national governments, meeting in Brussels, decide issue by issue what they can agree on among themselves, and national governments bring their own laws into conformity with the result of these decisions. This is to say that the various constraints operating on each national member dictate the ambitiousness of the overall European agenda at any given point. And in turn the negotiated result in Brussels reshapes the national members.[10] The agreed-on criteria for joining the euro, for example, constituted huge leverage for domestic reform in a number of would-be members, and the prospect of membership in the European Union has been a powerful catalyst for sound policy choices in Central and Eastern Europe.

One could say that the creation, extension, and deepening of Europe have correspondingly diminished the extent to which the nations of Europe practice politics as nations. Some have couched this negatively, in terms of giving up sovereignty, and this is in a certain sense undeniable. But another way of looking at it is that a large and growing number of once-political issues—including issues of the sort that might once have led to war—have now been settled. Further controversy about one's rights and obligations (right conduct, again) will be resolved juridically according to procedures that all parties have agreed to and whose outcome they have agreed to abide by. Note that what binds the parties is not the proceeding itself—in the sense that a domestic court has the full lawful power of the state at its disposal and indeed stands for the state. What binds the parties here, in the international context, is the idea that the proceedings are binding. This idea is at the core of the transnational ethical community under consideration here.

This exercise in social construction may be baffling to Americans (and to many Europeans), but it is striking how much of the European-American relationship already consists of relations of this kind. We are all trading nations, to pick the most obvious example. For trade to work, contracts have to be enforceable based solely on their terms and not on the identity of the contracting party or other extraneous matters. In a dispute with a Belgian in a Belgian court, an American must be treated like a Belgian; there can be no "Belgians win" rule, or the system breaks down. The more secure this relationship is, the more likely are Belgians and Americans to see each other not as American or Belgian but as any given member of a community in which people can trust each other in their business dealings. Likewise, there is a substantial and growing amount of transatlantic rule writing across a vast array of policy areas. Again, one may see this as a diminution of the political sphere or even a loss of sovereignty. But no one in either the United States or Europe, whatever their concerns about sovereignty or Iraq policy, seems to mind that the parties to a trade dispute will go to the World Trade Organization to seek a resolution rather than, for example, mining each other's harbors. Indeed, when certain hot-headed Americans (and to a lesser degree, Europeans) vented their feelings on Iraq in calls for boycotts and other sanctions, they quickly discovered how interconnected the United States and Europe actually are and how difficult—and costly—it would be to sever ties.

All of which suggests, I submit, that the Atlanticist community is here to stay. Perhaps for the foreseeable future? Well, of course. But it is also possible to say with some precision what would have to happen for war to break out between the United States and France or between France and Germany. In at least one of the countries, the "exclusive political group" would have to be replaced by a group with very different ideas about how Americans should get along with Europeans and how Europeans should get along with each other. Perhaps this could take the form of a coup d'état in one of the countries in question or the emergence of a mass political movement glorifying violent conquest. What happened in Weimar Germany is an illustration of the replacement of one exclusive political group—broadly liberal and the basis for the assessment of many Jews that Germany was a good home—with another of decidedly different view.

That the Nazi power grab took place not so long ago will perhaps make people anxious about how long the foreseeable future will last before a change of this entirely foreseeable character takes place, leading to catastrophe. I can offer no assurances in this regard; any such assurance would necessarily be subject to empirical validation. Unfortunately, although the proposition is falsifiable (by the outbreak of war), it is not provable by the continuation of peace. Nevertheless, the proposition that the conditions for war with Europe or within Europe will inevitably arise again is no less speculative just because there was a time, until recently, when it held.

But the Europe of today does not at all resemble the Weimar Republic. There is no end to the list of contrasts, but let two examples make the point. Some months before the introduction of the euro, I visited the Bundesbank in Germany. In the lobby was a display case with an exhibit of historical banknotes. The last one on display before the timeline noted the onset of the Nazi regime was a 10 trillion mark note. It's probably fair to take this as the Bundesbank's last word on what currency devaluation and hyperinflation can do to social and political stability—and therefore, a crystallization of the bank's own mission, since extended by the European Central Bank throughout the euro zone. Also, consider the reaction throughout Europe to the prospect of a genuinely right-wing party coming to power in Austria in 2000. It was overwhelmingly negative, including sanctions against Austria at the European Union. A judicious observer would have to note that the Freedom Party in Austria in the 1990s is not the same as the Nazi Party in Germany in the 1930s. The former was objectionable beyond redemption not for its proposed agenda but merely for saying inexcusable things about what the Nazis were actually doing or preparing to do in the 1930s. Similarly, when voters in France in 2002 found to their horror that owing to inattention in the first round of presidential balloting, they had given themselves a second-round choice between the incumbent Jacques Chirac and the right-winger Jean-Marie Le Pen, they set aside ambivalence about Chirac and turned out overwhelmingly to repudiate Le Pen.

The general point is that any attempt to unmoor national government policy from the Atlanticist ethical community in order to recreate politics in a Schmittian sense is something the community, including governments still acting in conformity with the community's ethos, will determinedly resist. This resistance would come first from the exclusive political group currently in charge in the country at issue. These groups are large and extraordinarily stable and have vast resources at their command. In a sense one could say that the resistance to the emergence of a violent political alternative to the status quo is ongoing, through such means as the education of children to value peace and the exclusion from respectable forums of public debate ideas that are contrary to the spirit of the Atlanticist community. The resistance would, of course, continue beyond national boundaries, as other community members made clear how high a price a would-be violator of the community's norms would have to pay.

Others may disagree, but I think the likelihood of success of such an effort is somewhere between minuscule and nil. Nevertheless, in the last contingency, if I am wrong, and a new exclusive political group bent on violence against its neighbors does in fact manage to seize power somewhere, what then? Well, I think the answer is that it would be met with the resistance of the united community, including war. That seems far more likely than a usurper's discovery of such deep fissures in the supposed community that it is easily able to recruit allies to the cause of war and conquest. The case of the former Yugoslavia is illustrative here. Europe and the United States eventually united in support of military action aimed at stopping the violence-bent but isolated exclusive political group around Slobodan Milosevic, first in Bosnia-Herzegovina and later in Kosovo.

If a future Milosevic emerges in the heart of Europe—and bear in mind that for the purpose of our discussion, Milosevic's Yugoslavia of the 1990s was located on the doorstep of Europe, not within it—I submit that the ensuing war, the one that would refute my broad claim here, would have a character that in fact reinforces this claim. The war would be fought between someone bent on breaking current transnational norms and the much larger number of countries determined to enforce them. The aim of the war for the latter would not be, for example, ratification of the general proposition that war is once again an accepted and routinely acceptable state practice among the nations in question. The purpose of the war, from the point of view of the remaining community, would be to end war and restore the community—which would entail the restoration in the offending nation of an exclusive political group willing to rejoin it.

From where we are now, it would be a matter of great difficulty to make our way back to the nineteenth century. I am aware of no plausible account of how we might do that, and generalizations about war being the way of the world and organized violence being an essential element of the human condition are no substitutes. Human nature is revealed in the here and now; an account of human nature that disregards its current manifestation is inadequate.

WHAT "WE" DO

So now we have a proper context for the recent disagreement between the United States and Europe over the utility of force. There is, in fact, unanimous agreement that we will not use force against each other. The question, then, becomes under what circumstances will "we" use it elsewhere. James M. Goldgeier and Michael McFaul usefully described the world situation in terms of a core of modern, developed states including the United States and Europe and a periphery of states that are underdeveloped, often misgoverned, and sometimes failing.[11] The core is indeed a zone of peace—whether its source is liberal in the sense of the democratic peace, or Kantian, or the product of the transnational community I have been trying to describe. The periphery is a zone of often-violent conflict that at times threatens to impinge on the tranquility of the core. (Goldgeier and McFaul made this argument many years before 9/11.) Because of its global security responsibilities, the United States has one foot in the core and one foot in the periphery, a position that is likely to persist.

But to the extent that the core is not merely an aggregation of states but also the organizing principle of their aggregation—namely, a transnational ethical community—it is not quite right to say that only the United States has a foot in both worlds. The footprint in the periphery is that of the community as a whole as well as that of particular state members.

We have already established, for example, that NATO can operate "out of area." The Kosovo campaign was the first such exercise (though arguably designed in part to establish that the Balkans were not to be excluded from the designation "European"). In 2003 the European Union took full charge of the peacekeeping force in Macedonia, and in fact European military units are deployed all over the world as peacekeepers. The United States fully supports these missions. NATO invoked Article 5 within days of the 9/11 attacks, and though the United States insisted on waging by itself the war that toppled the Taliban, in 2003 NATO took charge of the military peacekeeping presence in Afghanistan (which in fact entailed not infrequent combat with rump Taliban elements). Notwithstanding the contentiousness over Iraq, NATO agreed to provide assistance in (really, to administer) the occupation sector for which Poland was assigned responsibility. Moreover, intelligence cooperation in the ongoing war on terrorism, much of which involves murky activity in the periphery by numerous agencies of the core, has by all accounts been very good.

These are all things we are doing together; we agree on them. The agreement at the governmental level is, once again, in my view a product of something more than traditional, Westphalian, state-to-state diplomacy. Here, one begins to see the Atlanticist community pushing outward from its own geographic territory—not only addressing security threats such as terrorist-harboring states or potentially destabilizing refugee flows but also acting out of a shared sense of what constitutes progress and of the desirability of pursuing it: political, social, economic.

Some things, of course, we pursue separately but in an atmosphere of mutual support. Europeans rightly pride themselves on the amount of foreign aid their governments provide around the world. Sometimes, though, separate pursuits do not at first seem to be characterized by mutual support. Nongovernmental organizations active internationally, many of which have their origins in or receive major support from Europe, often speak out in opposition to the United

States. But once again, the distinction between disagreement and the agreement to disagree is easy to miss. In almost all cases, these organizations seek to influence the actions of the United States and other governments; "opposition," such as it is, is very tightly circumscribed. Nongovernmental organizations did not descend on Baghdad in support of the Baathist regime. For an example of an international nongovernmental organization that means business in opposition to the United States, one should look to al-Qaeda, not *Médecins sans Frontières* or the coalition promoting a ban on land mines.[12]

If we are often together in agreeing to use military power abroad, and we are often supportive of one another when we choose not to act in concert, and if we sometimes express disagreement that is circumscribed in such a fashion as to allow it fairly to be characterized as agreement to disagree, then I think we should face up to the fact that we are still "we," even when the subject is as contentious as Iraq—or, to pick another conspicuous example, how much support Palestinians deserve in their quest for statehood.

An ethical community is characterized not by unanimity of opinion but rather by a shared sense among members of right conduct toward one another. In the case of the Atlanticist community, this formal definition has as its content a liberal, bourgeois respect for freedom and equality. The ongoing contentiousness of democratic politics at the national level is an indication of the sometimes bitter disagreement that remains and of the constraints all parties accept with regard to disagreement. We will argue, but we will settle matters peacefully—by such means as having elections, taking our controversies to disinterested third parties, and drawing straws. Those who obtain power avoid the temptation to treat it as absolute—to infringe on the agreed right conduct of others.

What, then, to make of the disgust—not to mince words—that the American position on Iraq evoked in some quarters in Europe? Was this not a sign of a fundamental division? Well, no, it was not a sign of fundamental division. The precise character of this response is instructive. Disgust is what you feel when you are trying and failing to draw a distinction between yourself and another. Disgust asks, How could you?— when, of course, I could not, and you are enough like me that I would expect you to agree with me. Absolute Otherness, in the form of an enemy, is not disgusting; it evokes a different response, perhaps fear and flight, or a will to kill. Absolute Otherness conjures a vision of annihilate or be annihilated—absolute negation. Disgust actually presupposes a sense of commonality or community. European disgust for Americans (and vice versa) is oddly hopeful: one has failed to measure up, but one could and should.

Europeans sometimes say that they resent Americans' vision of America as a model of universal applicability and desirability. Is this vision not the height of arrogance? Others might prefer to follow a different model, a path of their own. By what right (apart from sheer coercive power) would Americans deprive them of that right? Yet it is striking that those making these assertions have not, as a general rule, ordered their own lives in a fashion that even the most ardent exporter of "the American way" would find the least deviant from it. In this respect, the American way could perhaps more accurately be characterized as the Atlanticist way. Americans are arrogant not for their belief in their way but for their belief that the way is exclusively theirs, an American way. Europeans likewise hew to this way—they would not and do not choose to live any other way. Once again, there is no disagreement within the Atlanticist community about the internal arrangements of the community. The dispute that remains concerns the applicability of the norms of the community outside its territory.

And here, Europeans and Americans voice support for universal human rights, freedom, the dignity of the person, equality, and so on. In other words, the content of the Atlanticist community is in principle applicable everywhere. So the difference is not over ends but over how to arrive at them. There is agreement that a world in which human rights were universally respected would be a better world, not only for those who currently believe in and uphold human rights where they can, starting with their own countries, but also for people who do not currently enjoy such respect and even for those who do not currently agree that human rights deserve respect. There is no consequential disagreement between Europeans and Americans on the normative question of the desirability of such a world.

Gilles Andréani has argued persuasively that there is altogether too much loose talk about American empire these days.[13] The term is neither a descriptive nor a useful or desirable policy prescription. It is misleading in another sense as well. Those who deploy it, often Europeans against the United States, misconstrue their own role in this supposed empire: if there is any such thing as the empire, Europeans are not to be numbered among its colonial subjects. Rather, they are highly influential citizens. They have a great deal of say in the conduct of its business, not only at home—within the territory of the Atlanticist community—but also abroad, elsewhere in the world. They are not, to be sure, the ruling party, but they are a well-organized, effective, influential, and—I might add—loyal opposition.

In this sense, the description offered by the neo-Marxist theorists Antonio Negri and Michael Hardt in their book *Empire* is far closer to the mark than any reflagging of Pax Britannica. The advanced capitalist system with its state subunits is Empire.[14] But this, too, can be misleading, insofar as it encourages people to try to export political concepts that have their utility chiefly in relation to states. There is, precisely, no political unit of which all the residents of Empire are citizens properly so-called; nor is there an emperor of Empire. Rather, there is the transnational community I have been trying to describe and the way the ideas and sentiments swirling within it play out among all the actors coconstituted by members of the community, such as states, however powerful such actors may be in their own right.

Europeans should be careful not to underestimate their influence on the United States. In some cases, accounts of a supposed lack of influence seem to serve an ulterior purpose: if one has no influence, obviously, one cannot be held in any way accountable for outcomes. Yet examples of influence are so abundant that the failure to take note of them seems almost willful, whether by Europeans trying to maintain an artificial distance or by Americans who insist that the United States is powerful enough to do what it pleases regardless of what others think or say.

Two examples, taken not from the fuzzier worlds of commerce or cultural "soft power" but from the front lines of power politics, should demonstrate the point. First, it was largely European pressure that elevated the Israeli-Palestinian peace road map to the top of the Bush administration agenda following the end of the Iraq war. Throughout the first two years of his administration, Bush seemed content to leave the matter to the parties and to avoid high-profile American engagement as broker or arm twister. Whether this was a product of indifference, a pro-Israel conviction that U.S. inaction served Israeli interests, pessimism about the prospects for success, fear of angering domestic political constituencies, or something else or some combination, the Bush administration did very little—until pressure from Europe mounted significantly in 2002–03, especially in relation to the coming Iraq war. Bush did not arrive spontaneously at his position in favor of a Palestinian state. The road map is every bit as much a European document as an American one, and the peace process as a whole is now the jointly owned policy of the United States and Europe.

Second, the Iraq debate has had a huge influence on the United States. To put it as bluntly as possible, in the aftermath of the war, I don't think anyone in the United States who takes national security policy seriously wants to go through anything like the diplomatic train wreck leading up to it any time soon. It was exhausting and unpleasant. True, the Europeans who opposed the war were not able to stop the United States. But they would be wrong to count their efforts a failure. They were able to make it difficult for the United States to go to war— difficult far beyond what the overwhelming military power of the United States would perhaps lead one to expect. To the extent that there was concern that the United States (or perhaps the Bush administration) was about to embark on a program of willy-nilly regime change, that concern ought to have been allayed. To see this, imagine, if you will, that Europe as a whole had gone along with the Bush administration wholeheartedly on the question of Iraq. Would that have made the likelihood of subsequent U.S.-led military interventions greater or lesser? It seems to me that in depriving the United States of a substantial measure of recognition of the legitimacy of its actions, European opponents of the war have at a minimum driven up the psychic cost of going to war for Americans. The United States has the power to do so again and may yet do so, taking its own authority (and a "coalition of the willing") as legitimation enough. But something more in the way of legitimacy has been shown to be available by virtue of its absence in the case of Iraq. And U.S. policy makers understand perfectly well that the doctrine of "preemption" or "prevention" spelled out in the Bush *National Security Strategy of the United States* in 2002 is not a new norm for U.S. action but rather a doctrine that applies only to limit cases.

In sum, it may be the case that the only thing that can really constrain power on the scale the United States possesses is agreement among Americans to be constrained. But Europeans need to understand that they have been and can continue to be quite persuasive in this regard.

CONVERGENCE

The question of European views versus American views inevitably invites objections based on nuance and complexity, if not indeed hairsplitting: what European means; whether New Europe is more American than European; what to do in the case of Americans holding European views—to say nothing of the status of Canadians, those New World Europeans. One can, however, get past all the difficulty here by speaking of the Atlanticist community as it should be spoken of, namely, as a whole. Europe and America are the two poles of opinion within it; their geographical status is consequential but not decisive.

Were this ethical community a polity (and it is not), the respective views of Europe and America would likely each be dominant in one of the two leading political parties. In multiparty democratic states, it is the dynamic interaction of political parties (and not simply the views of one or another, whichever happens to be in power) that shapes the law, which in turn is widely accepted (though some, viewing the process or the outcome or both, may find themselves feeling disgusted). As things stand in the Atlanticist community, what we have is the interaction and at times confrontation of the European and the American poles shaping community norms, including norms for how the community deals with nonmembers. The confrontation is ongoing, but it is not static, a manifestation of merely a permanent tension. It produces results along the way. It is constructive, and the standards of right conduct it constructs, though not law, are rich and durable—and serve as a backdrop against which confrontation moves to a new stage.

Over time, the workings of this interaction, I submit, have produced convergence and will continue to do so. The scope of confrontation has narrowed and continues to narrow. That the confrontation is often bitter is no indication of the substance of the matters at issue. The fact is that we are arguing over things we never would have argued over before, because there were then so many more important matters to argue over—matters that have now been settled, such as whether we will resolve our disputes peacefully and whether we will bother to try to find a common approach to matters external to our community.

The death penalty often is mentioned as an issue that fundamentally divides the United States and Europe. So it does. But not so long ago, the death penalty was all but universal. It was also probably generally regarded as nobody else's business—a matter for states to settle for themselves, in good Westphalian fashion. More recently, among European elites, a norm of opposition emerged, leading eventually to the abolition of the death penalty throughout western Europe. The European Union enforces this sentiment by insisting that member states be rid of the death penalty—and of course this means that aspiring members must do away with it to be admitted. Europeans countries not only have gotten rid of the death penalty; Europeans have grown quite accustomed to looking beyond their own national borders in passing judgment on this subject. They have found the United States wanting, and they have said so in no uncertain terms.

But meanwhile, support for the death penalty in the United States has been declining. Domestic American criticism has mounted sharply. Some states have imposed moratoria on executions. Concern about racial disparities in implementation is widespread, and African Americans, who used to support capital punishment by a substantial majority, have in the past decade switched to substantial majority opposition.[15] I find it difficult to construe this as evidence of a widening gap. What appears in a snapshot as a gap is actually a moment in a process that is unfolding, one that consists of a reversal of established opinion over time. European opinion has led it. American opinion seems to be following it (albeit at a rate that is unsatisfactory to Europeans). Whether this movement leads in time to the abolition of the death penalty in the United States, I do not know. But it gives every

234 ✶ TOD LINDBERG

appearance of motion in one direction only. Note that the United States is not making the case that Europeans should reinstate the death penalty, that American states without the death penalty do not seem much inclined to consider adopting it, or that anyone is advocating the broadening of existing death penalty legislation in order to increase the number of executions.

One could add any number of similar examples in which a division manifesting itself at the present moment looks rather different construed over time. This is especially true as the European pole of the debate moves on into the terra incognita of a post-Westphalian exercise in social construction and international or transnational rule making. Note that I am not claiming that where Europe goes, the United States will follow. Rather, it is the constant interaction and confrontation of the poles that produce the community's standards of right conduct at any given moment. A rule for the community proposed by its European pole or its American pole, even if it is fully accepted by governments associated with one pole or the other, remains empty as a community rule until it is accepted as a rule and followed as a rule by all community members. Such norms are not a social contract to which people and nations nominally agree they should adhere. They are norms only because people and governments actually do adhere to them.

I have confined my analysis here to what I have called the Atlanticist community. That is because it is quite the largest, most robustly developed transnational ethical community in the world today. But it is hardly far-fetched to speak of a broader liberal, bourgeois community of which the Atlanticist community is a part. There is nothing I have said here that does not apply fully to Australia, for example, and in a sense, one might as well change the name of the community to allow for the inclusion of the people of all states whose exclusive political groups conduct affairs according to the peaceable norms of the community. "Atlanticist" is a reflection of its historical roots; it is not a limiting characteristic. It is possible that with regard to NATO, the less interesting part is "North Atlantic," the more interesting being the "Treaty Organization." And perhaps the European Union is, over time, more interesting as the "Union" than as "European."

What, then, are the limits?[16] I do not know, but I propose that the way to find out is for those of us who enjoy living a perpetual peace among ourselves, as friends and friendly strangers, to work to augment our numbers. But then, if we failed to do that, we would not be ourselves.

Notes

1. See Jeffrey Gedmin, "Helmut Kohl, Giant," *Policy Review* 96 (August–September 1999).
2. See Michael Mandelbaum, *The Ideas That Conquered the World: Peace, Democracy, and Free Markets in the Twenty-first Century* (New York: PublicAffairs, 2002).
3. Joshua Micah Marshall, "Death in Venice: Europe's Death-Penalty Elitism," *New Republic*, July 31, 2000.
4. Carl Schmitt, *The Concept of the Political* (Chicago: University of Chicago Press, 1996), 26–27, 35–37.
5. Wendt makes this case. Alexander Wendt, *Social Theory of International Politics* (Cambridge: Cambridge University Press, 1999), 298–99.
6. See the discussion of "Collective identity and structural change" in Wendt, 336–43.
7. Kant refers to "hospitality" as the limit of "Cosmopolitan Right": "In this context *hospitality* means the right of a stranger not to be treated with hostility when he arrives on someone else's territory." "Perpetual Peace: A Philosophical Sketch," in *Kant: Political Writings*, 2nd enlarged ed., ed. H. S. Reiss (Cambridge: Cambridge University Press, 1991), 105. My formulation here is meant to go farther.
8. See Paul Franco, *Hegel's Philosophy of Freedom* (New Haven, Conn.: Yale University Press, 1999), 275–76. Also, Robert R. Williams, *Hegel's Ethics of Recognition* (Berkeley: University of California Press, 1997), 255–56.
9. Alexandre Kojève, *Outline of a Phenomenology of Right* (Lanham, Md.: Rowman & Littlefield, 2000), 89-90, 134-35.
10. See J. H. H. Weiler, "Federalism without Constitutionalism: Europe's *Sonderweg*," in *The Federal Vision: Legitimacy and Levels of Governance in the United States and the European Union*, ed. Kalypso Nicolaidis and Robert Howse (Oxford: Oxford University Press), 54–70, especially p. 68.
11. James M. Goldgeier and Michael McFaul, "A Tale of Two Worlds: Core and Periphery in the Post–Cold War Era," *International Organization* (Spring 1992).
12. Tod Lindberg, "How to Fight a Superpower," *Weekly Standard,* December 31, 2001.
13. See Gilles Andréani, "Loose Talk of American Empire," in *Beyond Paradise and Power: Europe, America, and the Future of a Troubled Partnership,* ed. Tod Lindberg (New York: Routledge, 2004 [this volume]).
14. Michael Hardt and Antonio Negri, *Empire* (Cambridge: Harvard University Press, 2000), 160–203.
15. Pew Research Center for the People and the Press, "Religion and Politics: Contention and Consensus," July 24, 2003, http://people-press.org/reports/print.php3?PageID=728.
16. Kant wrote, "The peoples of the earth have thus entered in varying degrees into a universal community." I would amend that to say "people" rather than "peoples" and would take special note of "in varying degrees." Kant foresaw a universal community, but it is actualized only partially, not fully. *Kant: Political Writings,* 107.

ACKNOWLEDGMENTS

The Hoover Institution, Stanford University, not only is the publisher of *Policy Review*, the journal I edit, and generous in its support for my research, but it also has made this volume possible by providing support for the authors assembled here. I owe a special debt of gratitude to John Raisian, Hoover's director, for all of the above and much more.

Thanks as well to other Hoover colleagues who were helpful with this project: Richard Sousa, Stephen Langlois, Deborah Ventura, Celeste Szeto, and in Hoover's Washington office, Audrey Slayton and, above all, Kelly Dillon, who has been with me through thin and thick.

My agents, Glen Hartley and Lynn Chu of Writers' Representatives, Inc., found this book its home at Routledge. They also represent Robert Kagan, and I am grateful for the time they were willing to invest on my behalf in the continuation of a project that Bob began in *Policy Review* with his essay "Power and Weakness" and continued in *Of Paradise and Power*. Thanks also to Katy Sprinkel in the Writers' Representatives office.

My editor at Routledge, Robert Tempio, had the knack for quickly arriving at the right answers to questions that had long been vexing me. He is proof that just because you know something about editing a journal, which I think I do, it doesn't mean you know all you need to know about editing a book, which I know I don't. I think it is fair to call Rob an editor's editor, in more than one sense. My further thanks to Mimi Williams, Project Editor, for her efforts on behalf of this volume.

My thanks especially to the contributors assembled here. Estimable as each is in his or her own right, gathered under one roof, the whole is greater than the sum of the parts.

Thanks to my wife Tina and daughters Abby and Molly for putting up with my travels and everything else.

This book is dedicated to the memory of Robert S. and Dorothy Lindberg, my parents.

CONTRIBUTORS

Gilles Andréani is head of policy planning in the French Foreign Ministry. The views he expresses are his own.

Anne Applebaum is a columnist for the *Washington Post* and the author of *Gulag: A History*, for which she won a Pulitzer Prize.

Peter Berkowitz is associate professor of law at George Mason University and a research fellow at the Hoover Institution, Stanford University. He is the author of *Virtue and the Making of Modern Liberalism* and *Nietzsche: The Ethics of an Immoralist*.

Ivo H. Daalder is a senior fellow at the Brookings Institution and coauthor of *America Unbound: The Bush Revolution in Foreign Policy*. An earlier version of his essay appeared in *Survival*.

Steven Erlanger is cultural news editor of the *New York Times,* where he has been Central Europe and, subsequently, Berlin bureau chief and chief diplomatic correspondent.

Francis Fukuyama is Bernard L. Schwartz professor of international political economy at the Paul H. Nitze School of Advanced International Studies of Johns Hopkins University. He is the author of *The End of History and the Last Man* and *Our Post-Human Future,* among other books. This essay is based in part on the John Bonython Lecture delivered in Melbourne, Australia, in August 2002.

Timothy Garton Ash is director of the European Studies Center at St. Antony's College, Oxford University, and a senior fellow at the Hoover Institution, Stanford University. He is the author of *Free World: America, Europe, and the Surprising Future of the West,* among other books. A slightly different version of his essay appeared in the *New York Review of Books.*

Wolfgang Ischinger is Germany's ambassador to the United States. The views he expresses are his own.

Tod Lindberg is a research fellow at the Hoover Institution of Stanford University, and editor of *Policy Review.*

Walter Russell Mead is a senior fellow at the Council on Foreign Relations and author of *Special Providence: American Foreign Policy and How It Changed the World* and *Power, Terror, Peace, and War: America's Grand Strategy in a World at Risk,* among other books.

Kalypso Nicolaidis is university lecturer in international relations at Oxford University and coeditor of *The Federal Vision: Legitimacy and Levels of Government in the US and the EU.*

Simon Serfaty is professor and eminent scholar in U.S. foreign policy at Old Dominion University and director of European studies and holder of the Zbigniew Brzezinski chair of geopolitical studies at the Center for Strategic and International Studies. He is the author of *Taking Europe Seriously, Stay the Course, Memories of Europe's Future,* and *La tentation impériale.*

INDEX